bruce goff

bruce goff

ARCHITECTURE OF DISCIPLINE IN FREEDOM

Arn Henderson

UNIVERSITY OF OKLAHOMA PRESS : NORMAN

Also by Arn Henderson

Document for an Anonymous Indian (Norman, Okla., 1974)

The Surgeon General's Collection: [Poems] (Norman, Okla., 1976)

(coauthor) *Architecture in Oklahoma: Landmark and Vernacular* (Norman, Okla., 1978)

(coeditor) *The Point Riders Great Plains Poetry Anthology* (Norman, Okla., 1982)

This book is published with the generous assistance of the Cottonwood Arts Foundation, Norman, Oklahoma, and of the College of Architecture at the University of Oklahoma.

Library of Congress Cataloging-in-Publication Data
Name: Henderson, Arn, author.
Title: Bruce Goff : architecture of discipline in freedom / Arn Henderson.
Description: Norman : University of Oklahoma Press, 2017. | Includes bibliographical references and index.
Identifiers: LCCN 2016038236 | ISBN 978-0-8061-5610-1 (hardcover : alk. paper)
Subjects: LCSH: Goff, Bruce, 1904–1982—Criticism and interpretation. | Architecture—United States—History—20th century.
Classification: LCC NA737.G56 H46 2017 | DDC 720.92—dc23LC record available at https://lccn.loc.gov/2016038236

The paper in this book meets the guidelines for permanence and durability of the Committee on Production Guidelines for Book Longevity of the Council on Library Resources, Inc. ∞

1 2 3 4 5 6 7 8 9 10

For Eric and the memory of Beatriz and Alex

The artist must have a wide vocabulary
of digested and assimilated experiences inherited and acquired.
He must have an unlimited capacity
and range for feeling,
an insatiable curiosity and boundless enthusiasm.
He must live through all his senses really
to experience life and art
and to live and work as one as a part of something.

BRUCE GOFF

contents

Acknowledgments *xi*

Prelude *3*

1

Foundations *9*

2

First Designs *37*

3

A Language of Conceptualization *51*

4

Teaching Organic Architecture *89*

5

Professional Practice at OU *129*

6

A Continuing Presence *179*

Coda *269*

Notes *273*

Bibliography *281*

Index *287*

Acknowledgments

As a student in the School of Architecture at the University of Oklahoma from 1956 to 1961, I was introduced to the architectural expression of the illustrious Bruce Goff by Jack Golden, an advanced student who was my Basic Design studio teacher. The following year Herb Greene, an earlier former student who prepared the stunning presentation drawings of several Goff projects, accepted a teaching position at OU. From both I learned about the architecture of Goff.

My research on Bruce Goff was initiated with a grant from the Graham Foundation for Advanced Studies in the Fine Arts, which provided funds to travel to all of Goff's buildings. Although there are more of his buildings in Oklahoma than in any other state, their locations range from Minnesota to Texas and from California to Florida. During the fieldwork phase I had the opportunity to photograph the buildings, talk to the clients or current owners, and visit other architects who had worked with Goff on specific projects. Many of them were OU alumni who had studied with Goff in the early 1950s. The process of site visits was later extended through a grant from the State Office of

Historic Preservation for preparation of nominations of selected Goff-designed Oklahoma buildings for inclusion in the National Register of Historic Places. Both of these grants, and the OU Research Council, provided funds for several visits to the Art Institute of Chicago, the principal archive of Goff's drawings, paintings, books, photographs, and correspondence. The OU College of Architecture also provided sabbatical leave support and expenses incurred in printing photographs. I am grateful for the support of all of these institutions.

I have a most personal gratitude to those individuals who offered their knowledge, advice, and criticism. Herb Greene, my mentor during my student years, read early drafts of several chapters and provided sustained encouragement. Robert Bowlby, an OU alumnus who worked with Goff during the early office years in Bartlesville, Oklahoma, read one of my longer chapters and provided detailed commentary. Both Greene and Bowlby offered the hospitality of their homes for extended visits and many hours of discussion about Goff. Bowlby also provided excellent photographs of several of Goff's buildings. My visits with Auburn University professor Robert Faust, an OU alumnus who supervised construction of two Goff houses in Mississippi, and Ed Hansen, a classmate who apprenticed with Goff in the Bartlesville office, were enriching and informative experiences. Other OU alumni from the early 1950s I visited and interviewed offered observations into Goff's architectural expression that were important in shaping my work. I appreciate the interviews with Rex Slack and Robert Overstreet, both of whom had worked with Goff. Similarly, the multiple interviews with Blaine Imel, an OU alumnus of that era, were revealing. James Gresham provided new information through his student work and a comparative paper on Ludwig Mies van der Rohe and Goff. Moreover, his astute and intelligent suggestions upon reading the manuscript were greatly appreciated. And the extended telephone interviews with John Hurtig on architectural education were important. Hurtig and eight other architecture students at Kansas State University transferred to the University of Oklahoma after seeing an exhibit of OU student work in the early 1950s.

For their generous sharing of experience, I thank Bart Prince, Harvey Ferraro, and Nelson Brackin, all of whom worked with Goff. I had multiple opportunities to interact with Prince when he was at OU as a distinguished Bruce Goff Professor of Creative Architecture. We shared a seminar and he revealed many insights on Goff's values and ideals. A chance meeting with Harvey Ferraro at a conference on vernacular architecture was fortuitous. We talked about Goff and shortly thereafter he read an early draft of a key chapter of my manuscript. Nelson Brackin, who was a student of Professor Faust, worked with Goff during his years in Tyler, Texas. He valued Goff's commitment to teaching, as a dimension of apprenticeship, through assignment of Architecture 273 projects with examples of recorded music.

Mary Woolever, architectural archivist of the Ryerson and Burnham Libraries at the Art Institute of Chicago, graciously assisted my quest in search of both photographs and the correspondence of Goff. I thank David Levy, OU professor emeritus of history, for his assistance in clarification of data in Goff's personnel file. Tracy Chapman, OU architecture librarian, identified pertinent documents in the Witt Collection. I am indebted to my former colleague, the late Dr. Thomas Selland, director of the OU College of Architecture Design and Research Center, for providing research assistants to prepare ink-line drawings of selected Goff buildings. I am particularly grateful to Irene Fatsea, one of my graduate students, for her splendid drawings of the Joe Price House.

I thank Frank Parman, my classmate in Basic Design, thoughtful observer of Goff's architecture and friend over the ensuing decades, for his sustained encouragement. His Cottonwood Arts Foundation and Dr. Charles Graham, dean of the OU College of Architecture, provided financial support for publication. I thank Lauren Barnes for the many times she provided assistance with her computer skills. I thank editor Kent Calder for his encouragement and patience. I am indebted to Stacey J. Caskey, supervisor of printing, mailing, and document services at OU, for her development of the many revisions of captions of illustrations. I am also indebted to Emily Schuster and Bonnie

Lovell for their editorial reviews. A particular expression of gratitude is due the late Jerri Hodges Bonebrake, who was Goff's secretary and lifelong friend, for her generous sharing of both knowledge and her collection of documents. A special note of gratitude is extended to David G. De Long for his major publications on Goff (1977 and 1988), which were invaluable in my research. His detailed chronology of the life of Goff and the evolutionary development of his architectural expression represents a seminal definition.

I also have a moral obligation to acknowledge the many clients or current owners of Goff-designed buildings that I visited. When I knocked on their doors they all were delighted to know of my research interest. I am especially grateful to Joe Price for the many times I spent at his house in Bartlesville, Oklahoma. I was fortunate to oversee the rehabilitation of the house after he donated it to the University of Oklahoma. During a period of about two years I made more than twenty site visits and came to appreciate the design all the more. I would find something new with every visit.

As a gesture of appreciation for my undergraduate education at the University of Oklahoma, I thank my teachers. Although I was not a student during Goff's tenure at OU, my major professors—Jack Golden, Herb Greene, Shizuo Oka, and Arthur Kohara—were. They all generously shared their knowledge and experience. Finally, I have a most personal debt to my late wife, Beatriz. Her intelligence, linguistic skills, and observations were invaluable in both the editing process and the necessity of expanded explication of intentions and methodology.

bruce goff

If we are to have a beautiful
result we must find beauty
in the problem itself.

BRUCE GOFF

PRELUDE

On June 8, 1904, the day Bruce Alonzo Goff was born, Frank Lloyd Wright celebrated his thirty-seventh birthday. During the first year of Goff's life, forty-two-year-old Claude Debussy composed his masterpiece *La Mer*. With distinct but complementary philosophies of expression, both the architect Wright and the composer Debussy followed an interwoven path of originality on which Goff would also embark. Throughout Goff's career as an architect and teacher, the works of Wright and Debussy would provide a sustained theoretical influence and source of inspiration.

To understand the vast diversity of Bruce Goff's designs, one must acknowledge several interrelated issues. As my research evolved, several common factors helped me to understand such wide variation in his work: distinctive originality in his buildings due to the use of specific, identifiable elements; ideals derived from many sources that determined those manifestations of originality; and rationalism and continuity in design conceptualization. These factors initiated my intellectual odyssey to understand the meaning of organic expression, and, especially, of Goff's interpretation.

Readings on Frank Lloyd Wright, Claude Debussy, Gertrude Stein, Louis Sullivan, and Ralph Waldo Emerson offered a means of comparing Goff's spoken ideals with what he shared in his writings, interviews, and recorded university lectures. Through this research, I discovered multiple underlying values in Goff's quest for original and diverse architecture: first, a belief that the client and building site were major determinants of design; second, the application of other arts, especially classical music, as a source of inspiration; and third, the importance of "discipline in freedom" in developing design solutions.

Goff relied on a process of inductive reasoning for design concepts, a process I mirrored in my own research methods. His process of formulation was the antithesis of the deductive reasoning of his contemporary Mies van der Rohe, the apostle of the popular International Style. The premise for Mies's expression, with its limited forms and materials, defined a "style" with predictable results: one building would look like another. Goff, though, began with a wide range of premises, which led to the conclusion that one building would not, and should not, look like another.

Born in the tiny prairie town of Alton, Kansas, to Maud Rose Furbeck Goff and Corliss Archer Goff, Bruce and his family lived in several Oklahoma towns as well as Denver, Colorado, while his father sought work as a jeweler. His formative architectural years, though, began in Tulsa, Oklahoma, when at the age of twelve he became a summer apprentice at the prominent firm of Rush, Endacott & Rush. In retrospect it is likely that Bruce Goff's visions, in both professional practice and teaching, drew upon the self-reliant ethos of the American West, which nurtured development of his individualism and the ennobling courage to act on his ideals and convictions. In particular, Oklahoma became a place where he developed many of his ideas—and created many of his masterful architectural works.

I traveled throughout the United States to see all of Goff's extant buildings, but not all of his works are discussed here. During this period of building observation and interviews, I recognized a pattern of specific characteristics in Goff's buildings that suggested a presence of distinct values at work; these characteristics, and their frequency, provided the criteria for selecting buildings for analysis and interpretation here. I aggregated this pattern of characteristics into several major premises of design central to Goff's architecture. The intent of this methodology was to investigate Goff's ideological convictions as a continual presence in the process of creation. Thus the discussion in this text, which is intended to be both informative and interpretive, is limited to fewer than forty buildings, with a focus on the best of Goff's built work to demonstrate his values. Several unbuilt projects of outstanding design are also included as they are revealing of his aspirations.

The first two chapters of the book delve into Goff's early philosophical influences, which began with the luminaries previously mentioned, but went on to include the work of numerous other composers and architects, painters, and illustrators as Goff's philosophy and practice developed. From this multiplicity of influences, Goff developed the original design aesthetics that became a hallmark of his work. The third chapter discusses in detail the concept of organic architecture and the various ideals that informed Goff's practice. These included "discipline in freedom," a concept revealed to Goff in Debussy's musical arrangements. My discussion of organic architecture's origins, and its influence on and interpretation by Goff, is inspired by a colleague's comment that he "didn't know what organic architecture was, but I know it when I see it—all curves and cantilevers." In Goff's view, creative and original design was an act of negotiating the nexus of intuition and logic—and of finding solutions specific to both site and client.

The middle section of the book (chapters 4 and 5) details the reciprocal influences of teaching, and learning, at the University of Oklahoma. Goff's years teaching at OU, and as chairman of the School of Architecture from September 1947 to December 1955, defined a duality of diversity and continuity. His development of a new course in the curriculum for the fourth-year studio, Architecture 273, was pivotal in the intellectual translation of his ideals. The course content consisted of a series of short projects on specific concepts of architectural design without regard to building type or functional relationships. The objective was to provide an opportunity for students to explore their individual interpretations on the meaning of design concepts such as modulation, asymmetrical balance, rhythm, and mass. In his lectures Goff drew upon analogies from music and played selections to illustrate how composers might utilize similar ideas in composition. Goff's 273 studio emphasized a direct connection to the relevance music might have on architecture. Goff often said he learned more about architecture from music than he did from other architects. For purposes of understanding Goff's values, the content of this studio is particularly revealing. In retrospect the 273 studio was one of the most innovative pedagogical experiences in the history of American architectural education.

During his years at OU, Goff continued his professional practice, which stimulated student creativity and offered unique opportunities for students to participate in the construction of a design. Even as innovative courses such as his 273 course drew accolades (and criticism) from architecture schools across the nation, Goff drew inspiration from the creativity of the classroom environment. His OU years defined a peak in his career, when Goff made some of his most creative and best designs as an architect. Their remarkable diversity reflects his wide-ranging teaching philosophy, even as their continuities tie together this high point in his oeuvre to his earlier and later designs.

The last chapter of the book discusses Goff's philosophy and career after his 1955 departure from OU, spanning almost three decades to the last years of his career in the late 1970s and early 1980s. Remaining in Middle America for the rest of his life, Goff moved his office three times, establishing himself in Bartlesville, Oklahoma; Kansas City, Missouri; and Tyler, Texas. Each town marked the use of generalized concepts dominant in the later phases of his career, even as his best work introduced original interpretations that invariably reflected the aspirations of the client and attributes of the site. A brief coda summarizes the end of Goff's life, and his legacy in architecture.

Goff's buildings are unique in twentieth-century American architectural history. The sense of diversity with characteristic differences between one building and another is quite pronounced. Yet there are also unifying strands of continuity that reflect his values and convictions. His ideals are clearly manifest in his design language of conceptualization and demonstrate a keen sense of discipline amid the colorful expressions of a well-developed imagination.

I try to forget music because
it obscures my perception of
what I do not know or shall
know tomorrow. Why cling to
something one knows too well?

CLAUDE DEBUSSY

I learned more about
architecture from music than
I did from other architects.

BRUCE GOFF

1

FOUNDATIONS

At the age of twelve, Bruce Goff began his extraordinary odyssey of learning the art and science of architecture.[1] His first task was one of tracing the classical orders, but as his skills in drawing developed he soon tired of copying the work of others and began to design houses for hypothetical clients. His discovery of an office copy of the 1908 issue of *Architectural Record* with an illustrated article of Frank Lloyd Wright's "In the Cause of Architecture" had a great impact on him. He wrote an admiring letter to Wright, who responded with a cordial note and a giant portfolio published by Wasmuth in Berlin, the now-famous 1910 *Ausgeführte Bauten und Entwürfe von Frank Lloyd Wright* of drawings.[2] This was the beginning of a lifelong friendship.

Another early discovery shaped Goff's life and career when, in his adolescence, he discovered the music of Claude Debussy. The music of Debussy, with its freedom and quality of mystery, initiated a sustained source of inspiration for Goff with his realization that the overlapping tonal patterns and harmonic relationships with unresolved dissonance had a unique quality of originality.

Articles and books about Debussy further influenced Goff's emerging philosophy of aesthetic ideals, and Debussy's music inspired Goff's architectural vocabulary with the ideas of "composition" and "discipline in freedom" becoming central to his practice.

FRANK LLOYD WRIGHT AND LOUIS SULLIVAN

Frank Lloyd Wright sought to develop architecture that expressed American democratic ideals. Rejecting historicism—architecture that drew its inspiration from historical recreations—Wright stated in his manifesto in *Architectural Record* that there "should be as many kinds of houses as there are kinds of people and as many differentiations as there are different individuals."[3] This declaration ultimately became central to Goff's values, as did his axiom of integration of all elements into an organic whole.

Left, Frank Lloyd Wright, 1926. Library of Congress, LC-USZ62-36384.

Right, Claude Debussy. Portrait by Jacques-Émile Blanche, ca. 1907. Library of Congress, LC-USZ62-97414.

However, Goff's early stylistic dependence on Wright waned with the 1914 second installment of "In the Cause of Architecture," in which Wright expressed disdain of imitators who had little understanding of his underlying design principles.[4] Even though his theoretical ties to Wright continued, Goff sought alternative sources for inspiration. In 1920, he wrote to Louis Sullivan, who responded with a friendly note of encouragement for Goff's enthusiasm, "which is quite splendid in one so young, and to extend the hope that you never outgrow it."[5] Sullivan, the principal mentor of Wright, also adamantly rejected the resurgence of classicism in American architecture and sought to create forms that were true to their purpose. His conceptualization of architecture embraced an integration of form, function, and structure with imaginative ornament derived from nature. Goff was particularly attracted to Sullivan's small banks with designs of ornament that combined elements of symmetry and asymmetry.[6]

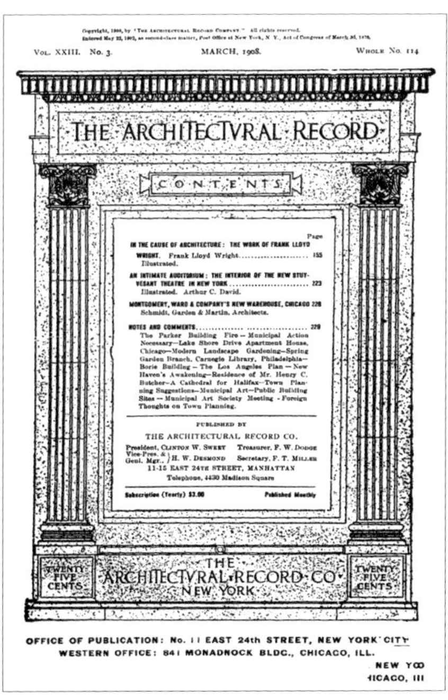

Copyright, 1908, by "The Architectural Record Company." All rights reserved.
Entered May 22, 1902, as second-class matter, Post Office at New York, N. Y., Act of Congress of March 3d, 1879.

Vol. XXIII. No. 3. MARCH, 1908. Whole No. 114

THE ARCHITECTVRAL RECORD

CONTENTS

	Page
IN THE CAUSE OF ARCHITECTURE: THE WORK OF FRANK LLOYD WRIGHT. Frank Lloyd Wright. Illustrated.	155
AN INTIMATE AUDITORIUM: THE INTERIOR OF THE NEW STUYVESANT THEATRE IN NEW YORK. Illustrated. Arthur C. David.	223
MONTGOMERY, WARD & COMPANY'S NEW WAREHOUSE, CHICAGO. Schmidt, Garden & Martin, Architects.	228
NOTES AND COMMENTS. The Parker Building Fire—Municipal Action Necessary—Lake Shore Drive Apartment House, Chicago—Modern Landscape Gardening—Spring Garden Branch, Carnegie Library, Philadelphia—Borie Building—The Los Angeles Plan—New Haven's Awakening—Residence of Mr. Henry C. Butcher—A Cathedral for Halifax—Town Planning Suggestions—Municipal Art—Public Building Sites—Municipal Art Society Meeting—Foreign Thoughts on Town Planning.	229

PUBLISHED BY
THE ARCHITECTURAL RECORD CO.
President, Clinton W. Sweet Treasurer, F. W. Dodge
Vice-Pres. & Genl. Mgr., H. W. Desmond Secretary, F. T. Miller
11-15 EAST 24TH STREET, MANHATTAN
Telephone, 4430 Madison Square

Subscription (Yearly) $3.00 Published Monthly

TWENTY FIVE CENTS THE ARCHITECTVRAL RECORD CO NEW YORK TWENTY FIVE CENTS

OFFICE OF PUBLICATION: No. 11 EAST 24th STREET, NEW YORK CITY
WESTERN OFFICE: 541 MONADNOCK BLDG., CHICAGO, ILL.

Left, Table of contents featuring the first essay in Frank Lloyd Wright's "In the Cause of Architecture" series for *The Architectural Record,* March 1908.

Right, Architect Louis Sullivan, ca. 1895.

Drawing from contemporary concepts of change as revealed in scientific theories of evolution, both architects developed philosophies of their craft imbued with an implicit belief in progress. In his book *The Autobiography of an Idea*, Sullivan acknowledged the influence of both Charles Darwin and Herbert Spencer.[7] Sullivan applied the Darwinian doctrine of natural selection to architecture with a conviction that not only was functional organization of a building the key to change but that architectural styles of the past were outmoded and hence unfit to survive. Furthermore, the idea of progress toward heterogeneity, revealed in the writings of Spencer, appealed to both architects. Spencer's theory stressed change as the most characteristic feature of all living matter and that such change was inevitable. Spencer maintained that discord would result from an organism's failure to adapt to environmental conditions. From this doctrine it was a rational extrapolation for Sullivan and Wright to suggest that only poor architecture would result when a building was not responsive to the specific aspects of an environment. Spencer also developed the idea that society itself was a social organism.[8] It was this glorification of science, together with the general philosophic and artistic movement of Romanticism, which provided the intellectual framework for the ideals of Sullivan and Wright. For them organic expression included both a Romantic approach to architecture, with form organized in harmony with nature for emotional purposes, and a functionalist approach, derived from a scientific view, of form organized to accommodate the function.

In the writings of both architects there are general themes that expand this doctrine: architecture is concerned with the process of change; architecture must address the specific conditions of an environment; and the creation of architecture is a supreme act of individuality. The concept of change in architecture, reflecting a naturalistic and evolutionary thesis, was constantly reiterated by Sullivan and Wright due to their shared tendency to glorify the present and disregard the past. Sullivan, who rebelled at his classical training at the École des Beaux-Arts in Paris, castigated the French architectural educational system as continuing "to cram their confiding pupils full of trashy notions concerning the classic and utterly ignore their own land and people."[9] Architecture, Sullivan believed, must reflect contemporary American society. It was an idea of continuous progress and is implicit in his comment that "the past is dead, and has been buried by a past that is dead."[10] The same theme of evolution was echoed by Wright when he said that "we cannot have an organic architecture unless we achieve an organic society."[11] For Wright, architecture must express society, and must therefore change over time.

Evolutionary change in Wright's expression is complex, as the distinctive periods of his long career are characterized by a marked difference in the appearance of buildings from one period to another. The initial houses in the Chicago suburb of Oak Park have no resemblance to either the later concrete block houses or the Usonian houses. Yet a continuity of design principles over an extended period of time, informed by his continual search for a "comprehensive order that might encompass both *composition* and *construction*," relates his buildings together.[12] In his early Prairie period, the ensemble of form, space, and construction was determined with the use of a modular grid in floor plans of axial symmetry. Major living spaces, anchored by a central fireplace, were expanded with modulated geometric proportional units of smaller secondary spaces to define cruciform or pinwheel plan configurations. Spatially these configurations created a dynamic fusion of balance of interdependent volumes with an interplay of horizontality, relating to the earth, and verticality, belonging to the realm of sky.[13]

In the middle years of his career Wright designed several houses with walls of patterned concrete block. Archeological publications of Maya architecture by the Division of Historical Research of the Carnegie Institution of Washington, beginning in the early 1920s, may have inspired his vision of an expression rich in texture and pattern, much like a tapestry. These "textile block" houses, too, relied upon a modular planning grid that reflected the size and shape of the building materials. The modest Usonian houses of the 1930s, constructed

Taliesin West, Frank Lloyd Wright Boulevard, Scottsdale, Arizona. Photograph in the Carol M. Highsmith Archive, Library of Congress, Prints and Photographs Division, LC-DIG-highsm-13141.

of brick and horizontal wood siding, also were determined by a planning grid even though they were asymmetrical in configuration, often with an L-shaped plan.[14]

The notion of architectural design addressing the specific issues of an environment is another theme in the literature of Sullivan and Wright. Organic expression as a reflection of theories of evolution is revealed in Sullivan's often-quoted axiom of "form follows function." Derived from both Darwin and Spencer, the meaning of Sullivan's statement is that architecture must develop its visual expression from the specific attributes of function, client, and site. The conditions of the specific problem—physical, social, environmental—should therefore determine the design. Sullivan expanded this concept with the statement that the architect "must cause a building to grow naturally, logically, and practically out of its conditions."[15] That Wright responded to variations of site, climate, and purpose is clearly illustrated with his combination studio–living quarters at Taliesin West, which is characterized by a sense of expansiveness and reflects the colors of the Arizona desert landscape. Wright's ideal was that a building should seem to grow organically out of its own particular environment.

Another theme revealed in the extensive writings of Sullivan and Wright on their philosophy is that the creation of architecture was a supreme act of individuality. This concept represents an amalgam of several ideas that includes theories of evolution, a general tendency of Romanticism to glorify the individual, and a belief in the importance of democracy. Evolutionary theories led to a concept of equating a building to a living organism wherein both the individual parts and the work as a whole result from a set of specific conditions. And since the conditions of any one building will differ from others, and will hardly ever recur in exactly the same form, architecture then becomes a unique event. In the view of Sullivan and Wright this sense of uniqueness should therefore be expressed.[16] This belief provided the rationale for personal and individual interpretation of organic design. Glorification of the individual arose from the Romantic notion that a human is a creature of feelings, intuition, and imagination, which were natural and appropriate impulses. Therefore, works of art that arose from this view might display great variation of appearance. The sense of freedom of self-expression that is implied in this view was the essence of American democracy.

Goff embraced the ideals of organic expression and was inspired by both the writings and buildings of Louis Sullivan and especially Frank Lloyd Wright. In a latter section of his 1932 prose poem "About Absolute Art," he pays homage to Wright with the passage:

One has shown the way for architecture organic with life
organic with materials
organic with Nature
organic with human-divinity
Frank Lloyd Wright
He has shown us how architecture may be absolute[17]

The notion that an architect's solution must arise from the specific issues of an environment is another major theme in the writings of Sullivan and Wright. Goff, too, believed that great architecture must evolve out of the specific architectural problem to be solved, especially in the relationship of a building to its site and the needs of a client. Paraphrasing Sullivan, Goff wrote,

> "The solution is within the problem," so if we are to have a beautiful result we must find beauty in the problem itself. We must recognize its potential in all of the requirements, in the nature of the site, materials, structure, etc., and through all of our aesthetic interpretations and solutions. Thus there can be no remembering of other solutions nor following of styles. Each thing we do will have its own style.[18]

And,

> Each time we do a building, it should be the first and the last. We must "begin again and again" if we are to solve our problems because all problems are different from each other, even if they may seem similar.[19]

By disregarding tradition and experiencing only the present, the design of a building became an intense and personal act of creativity. Both architects were contemptuous of classical and Renaissance ideals and declared a belief in the creative artist as unique. This notion is an essential element of the Romantic doctrine of individuality—of the artist as "an intuitive mystic seer" who values intuition and imagination.[20] Sullivan embraced, and extended, this fundamental axiom of organic expression when he wrote, "And why is he [the architect] a genius? Because he is a child of Nature"[21] and "to create is an absolutely natural process."[22]

Goff, in the same way, shared their view of the architect as a creative spirit when he wrote,

> Organic solutions can be arrived at along many paths: there is never just one solution. The creative artist works intuitively and instinctively with

> the one he feels best with: it is a matter of choice from among many possible solutions. Our most spontaneous choice is usually best because it is more direct.[23]

And,

> Beauty bursts forth when it must because the Artist feels the drive within himself to produce it and no amount of discouragement can stop him. It does so through necessity because each of us has the human right to participate in this universal creative renewal. The craving for Beauty has existed in all mankind in all times and continues to do so. He is fated to continue his search for it so long as he exists and his finding it for himself has made his existence more worthwhile.
>
> This Fatal Force drives the Artist to seek Beauty in unexpected places and he can find it in anything if he can only understand it. . . . This force is a secret, the mystery of which he is ever endeavoring to discover.[24]

CLAUDE DEBUSSY, FRENCH SYMBOLISM, AND GERTRUDE STEIN

Goff's 1932 prose poem is also significant in that it alludes to another individual who shaped his aesthetic ideals: Claude Debussy.[25] The composer magnified many of the ideas of Sullivan and Wright. In the music of Debussy, the sense of impermanence and the indefinite quality to the compositions inspired Goff to draw parallels between music and architecture. Goff's recognition of the use of unresolved harmonic passages that eliminated a formal beginning and ending would later be assimilated into his ideas about architectural composition.

Goff's attachment to Debussy began when he was in high school. A pianist friend, Ernest Brooks, introduced him to the music of Beethoven, Bach, Chopin, and other classical composers. Goff was not impressed by what he heard. Brooks later played Goff a recording of Maurice Ravel's *The Fountain*, although he personally was bewildered as it "didn't obey the rules of composition he had learned." But Goff was fascinated and proclaimed that he had "heard music for the first time." His curiosity led to a search for more information about Ravel. A magazine article in the library mentioned that Ravel was "the inferior of Debussy," which expanded Goff's quest for knowledge. Goff bought several records of Debussy, including his *Prelude to the Afternoon of a Faun*. Although comprehending the piece eluded him at first, he appreciated it the more he listened. Years later Goff commented, "I have heard it hundreds of times. It is still very mysterious, and very wonderful to me. . . . I have learned that I should never accept anything at face value or by snap judgments."[26]

Page of *Prélude à l'après-midi d'un faune*, composed by Claude Debussy. Printed by E. Fromont, Paris, ca. 1895.

Goff's interest in Debussy relates his ideals indirectly to the Symbolist movement, as Debussy found inspiration through the French poets associated with that movement. As a counterpart of Romanticism, a "second flood of the same tide," Symbolist poets and artists placed great importance on emotions and sensations of the individual, retaining an emphasis on subjectivity.[27] The inclination was to evoke or synthesize, rather than describe, with an ideal of intentional ambiguity. The major poets—Charles Baudelaire, Paul Verlaine, Arthur Rimbaud, and Stephane Mallarmé—all sought to communicate feelings through a complex association of ideas represented by "metaphors detached from their subjects."[28] The premise of their art was based on the notion that every feeling or sensation one has at any moment of consciousness is different from every other and such feelings are unique to each individual. The poet must therefore seek to find a personal language that will express his feelings and his alone. The language must convey feelings through the use of symbols and images so as to *suggest* rather than describe. The poet Mallarmé defined Symbolism thusly: "To name an object is to do away with the three-quarters of the enjoyment of the poem which is derived from the satisfaction of guessing little by little: to suggest it, to evoke it—that is what charms the imagination."[29]

The Romantic demolition of arbitrary rules for the attainment of beauty led the Symbolists to an acceptance of the subconscious as a source of inspiration. All the formulas of art were discarded, to be replaced with a standard the artist finds within one's self.[30] Intellectualism was thus viewed as a distraction from attending to feelings. Words, by the suggestive quality of their syllables, created an atmosphere of color and sound to allow inclusion of unfamiliar images, however volatile or intangible, to create a sense of mystery. It was the creation of a startling new poetry evoking "hidden links of distant and divergent things."[31] The Symbolists developed a literature in which "the visible world is no longer a reality, and the unseen world no longer a dream."[32]

The word "mystery" was prominent in the vocabulary of the Symbolists, almost to a point of being a slogan in their discussions of aesthetic creations. The central experience for all of them was the sense of mystery that might arise from introspection and intuition for the attainment of emotional content in their work.[33] Relying on the unconscious, dreams, daydreams, and fantasies, the Symbolists' goal was to achieve a heightened awareness and exhilaration that might infuse their work with imagination as they broke down the stylistic barriers between prose and poetry, coupled with an insistence on the "musicality" of poetry. But there was also an imperative of organization of visions according to their own wide-awake aesthetic standards. The importance of structure and deliberate composition in their creative process was possible only through consciousness.[34]

Debussy's rejection of the past, like the Symbolists', parallels the ideals of both Sullivan and Wright with their imperative of obligation to invent new forms. Upon composing *Prelude to the Afternoon of a Faun*—derived from an eponymous poem by Mallarmé and conceived of as a transliteration of mood and emotions—Debussy commented, "It was only logical that I should run the risk of displeasing people who are so devoted to one musical method that they are faithfully blind to its wrinkles or cosmetics."[35] Goff, too, was well aware of abandoning the security of the familiar to take risks that a design might survive the erosion of criticism. "We have to believe in what we are doing," Goff said, "that our efforts are worth achieving, worth striving for."[36] It was the challenge of having the courage of one's convictions.

The invention of "new forms" was the overture to another theme Goff also found in the philosophy of Debussy: the imperative of evolutionary change and growth. Debussy's commitment to his art, and willingness to take risks, was revealed when he said, "The struggle to surpass others has never been really great if disassociated from the noble ideal of surpassing oneself, though this involved the sacrifice of one's cherished personality."[37] For Goff the "sacrifice" was the realization that each composition has a life of its own and has no obligation to another composition one has previously created. There must be a "forgetting" of what one has done in the past so that one may allow each new work to develop its own order. Goff admired Debussy for not composing music without a creative impulse:

> The works that have real meaning and authority are the ones that spring from this inner necessity, the works that have to be created. The artist is more or less a medium through which they materialize. With Debussy's work we find each composition had its own sense of order. . . . It is truly an organic approach to art; this principle of not doing anything without an idea is most important to all artists.[38]

Goff found validation for the dimension of feeling and human emotion in architecture through Debussy's music. It was rich with feeling, and the source, Goff believed, was the magnetism of nature. Debussy wrote,

> Who will discover the secret of musical composition? The sound of the sea, the curve of the horizon, the wind in the leaves, the cry of the bird, register complex impressions within us. Then suddenly, without any deliberate consent on our part, one of these memories issues forth to express itself in the language of music. It bears its own harmony within it. By no effort of ours can we achieve anything more truthful or accurate. In this way only does a soul discover its most beautiful ideas.[39]

Goff believed Debussy was one of the great artists of all time because of his tremendous range of feeling through transformation of tonal harmony to suggest a sense of ambiguity and mystery. This perception of mystery in the music of Debussy gave rise to Goff's aesthetic ideals—architecture, too, must be imbued with this sense of mystery.

Goff's discovery of the writings of Gertrude Stein, who was also influenced by the Symbolist poets, was significant, for her thoughts not only corresponded with the ideals of both Wright and Debussy, with their insistence on change, but also stimulated a search for expressions of space in a "continuous present." Goff came across the idea of a "continuous present" in his reading of Stein's 1926 essay "Composition as Explanation." She said:

> There is singularly nothing that makes a difference . . . in the beginning and in the middle and in ending except that each generation has something different at which they are all looking. . . .
>
> Everything is the same except composition and as the composition is different and always going to be different everything is not the same. So then I as a contemporary creating the composition in the beginning was groping toward a continuous present, a using everything a beginning again and again.[40]

For Goff the concept of a "continuous present" seems to have had two meanings: one concerned with actual buildings, and the other reflecting an intangible reality of creation. In the former Goff postulated a building that did not have a traditional beginning, middle, or end. Such a building, like Debussy's composition *La Mer,* would be impossible to comprehend immediately. It would be an interspatial composition of multiple parts, each forming and contributing to a unified composition. In 1948 Goff cited Wright's Taliesin West as "a design in the continuous present . . . a much more complex organism. It is one of the most advanced compositions ever built."[41]

The other interpretation of the continuous present seems to be related to Goff's ideas on creativity and the mystery of sources and future meaning:

> Any genuine work of art is necessarily original. It is the first and last, of its kind, in the order of its existence. It had not been copied from anything and

Gertrude Stein in her Paris studio, 1930.
Library of Congress, LC-DIG-ppmsca-30616.

> is produced for the first time with freshness and authority. We soon tire of novelty if it lacks depth and meaning. A truly original work has these qualities and many more; it is the result of a natural growth of ordered ideas; there is no beginning, for no one knows, even its creator the many sources that nurtured it, and no one can know its ultimate effect, so it has no ending. It has emerged in the ever-continuous-present as a unique and valuable contribution to all men by man's own creative spirit; if it has value it will be timely and timeless, and it will also be both personal and impersonal with its creator.[42]

Goff's statement conveys multiple underlying themes of originality, growth, and of the absence of a beginning or ending, all of which reflect his interpretation of both Debussy and Stein. It also echoes Wright's optimism and belief in continuous change when he said, "The law of organic change is the only thing that mankind can know as beneficial or as actual; we can only know that all things are in process of flowing into some continuous state of becoming."[43] That Goff had very clear ideas of the visual opportunities for diversity and the unexpected in design that evolutionary change might offer is apparent in another statement:

> Change is part of a scheme of time thought of as the continuous present, and no matter how excellent or well-established things may seem to be, creative artists are always restless and forever seeking new expressions. If they are innovators and extend the horizon of their art, they are usually branded as revolutionaries or radicals by their contemporaries, who fail to realize that what seems to be revolution may only be evolution made apparent. Change brings with it the unexpected and it is this quality of surprise which engages our attention in a work of art; but since we cannot continue to be surprised by the same thing, the quality of mystery becomes necessary to sustain our interest. Mystery, however, defies analysis; no matter how well we come to know a work possessing it, such a work, like Nature, never gives up its secrets.[44]

GERMAN EXPRESSIONISM AND NATURALISM

In its early phase, the German Expressionism movement also drew inspiration from the French Symbolists. The social and economic conditions associated with World War I had produced a radical reaction to an authoritarian regime that stimulated the association of German artistry with political and moral change. Artists and intellectuals in Germany called for an age of spiritualism with the rhetoric of the sublime providing the stimulus between human emotion and the transcending objective of rationality. Although the transformation of society was never carefully defined, Expressionists took the ancient form of the crystal as their symbol of perfection in an idealized, utopian world.[45] In the 1919 play *Transfiguration*, Ernst Toller wrote: "The youth of all nations stride ablaze into the shrine of glowing crystal. Violently I behold radiant visions. No more misery, no war, no hate."[46] Expressionism, for a brief time in history, affected theater, film, literature, art, graphic design, and architecture. The avant-garde architects of Germany responded with architectural visions for a utopian society as one of sublime, transparent glass temples filled with light and color.

In his *Flowers of Evil*, Baudelaire sought to capture "the savagery that lurks in the midst of civilization" by equating moral judgments with new aesthetic directions.[47] In his essay "The Painter of Modern Life," Baudelaire defined modern experience as "the transitory, the fleeting . . . the half of art whose other half is the eternal and the immutable."[48] The "other half" for German artists was the Romantic ideal of the sublime. Artists found themselves operating in the "no-man's-land between intuition and reason." Kurt Hiller, one of the theorists of German Expressionism, argued the source of rationality was in experience rather than in knowledge and the essence of experience was comprehended mystically. Expressionist art was thus guided by emotion rather than reason.[49]

Goff was greatly affected by the Expressionists and rejoiced in their images,

Illustration by Carlos Schwabe for the cover of Charles Baudelaire's *Les Fleurs du Mal*, 1900.

though he apparently had limited interest in their philosophy. Both Goff and his students were influenced by the geometry of the Expressionists, which emphasized crystalline shapes as well as spirals.[50] He also was stimulated by Surrealism and particularly attracted to the works of the German artist Max Ernst with his paintings of eroded forms, the Chilean surrealist Roberto Matta and his paintings resembling intergalactic space, the Argentine painter Leonor Fini with themes of woman as sorceress, and the Viennese Ernst Fuchs, founder of the Phantastische Schule, and his art of grotesque and erotic mythic, biblical and apocalyptic themes.[51] He liked the art of the Viennese painter-printmaker Friedensreich Hundertwasser and his images of brightly colored, ornamental streetscapes and landscapes often embracing gigantic and iconic humanoid faces. Goff acknowledged the architect's talent with the design of an apartment block in Vienna with the façade resembling his graphic work. Goff was also familiar with the works of other architects of that era and spoke to students of designs and drawings by Hans and Wassili Luckhardt, Fritz Poelzig, Hans Scharoun, Bruno and Max Taut, Peter Behrens, Otto Bartning, Walter Gropius, and others.[52]

Goff was also attracted to the work of the Austrian Secession, also known as the Vienna Secession.[53] Founded in 1897 by artists including Gustav Klimt, Koloman Moser, Joseph Maria Olbrich, and others, the movement shared Wright's departure from Beaux-Arts historicism and embraced the era's iconoclasm. The tortured expressionistic portraits and drawings of Egon Schiele and especially his precursor Gustav Klimt, drew Goff in with their decorative and suggestively erotic subject matter. He had two Klimt paintings among his own personal collection of art. Goff also admired the architecture of Josef Hoffmann and his design of the Palais Stoclet in Brussels, which became one of his favorite buildings. He knew of Hoffmann possibly as early as 1920 through purchase of a portfolio of painting reproductions by Klimt. The portfolio, and the box containing it, were both designed by Hoffmann.[54]

Goff was also familiar with the work of Claude F. Bragdon (1866–1946) who, like Sullivan and Wright, embraced many of the ideals of the Arts and Crafts movement with its emphasis on the integration of architecture and applied arts. As architect, illustrator, and stage and costume designer, Bragdon created designs that were notable for their harmonious color schemes. Bragdon's writings on the geometric basis of ornament appealed to Goff.[55] Moreover, Goff's interest in music, and his emerging awareness of its affinity with architecture, would have been piqued by Bragdon when he wrote, "There is nothing unreasonable in attempting to apply the known facts of musical harmony and rhythm to . . . architecture . . . presented here as 'frozen music'—ponderable form governed by musical law."[56]

Possessing an innate sense of curiosity, Goff also learned about avant-garde art, literature, and music from reading the periodicals *Dial* and *Broom*. Another influence was the Russian-born fashion designer Erté (Romain de Tirtoff), whose work appeared on the covers of *Harper's Bazaar*. Goff was attracted to his exuberant use of colors and geometric shapes. Erté believed that clothes should be designed to reflect the personality of the client rather than the designer. This belief reinforced Goff's conviction that buildings too should be designed to reflect the personality, needs, and desires of a specific client. Thus, since all clients were different, the architect should strive for a variety of solutions.[57]

Philosophy (final state), by Gustav Klimt, 1907.

MUSIC

Later in life, Goff said he "learned more about architecture from music than I have from architects, in spite of the debt I owe Mr. Wright."[58] By 1968 Goff wrote that he had "over 5,000 recordings of native and modern music."[59] This love of music, begun with Debussy, expanded throughout his lifetime.

Goff did not share Wright's admiration of Beethoven but instead was attracted to French and Russian composers.[60] In addition to Debussy, Goff favored French composers Maurice Ravel, Darius Milhaud, Olivier Messiaen, and Erik Satie. His interest also extended from the Russian composer

Modest Mussorgsky and his contemporary Nikolai Rimsky-Korsakov to twentieth-century composers Béla Bartók, Pierre Boulez, Pierre Henri, Arthur Honegger, Sergei Prokofiev, Arnold Schoenberg, Roger Sessions, Karlheinz Stockhausen, Igor Stravinsky, Edgar Varèse, and Heitor Villa-Lobos. He cared nothing at all for earlier European music, especially that of "the three B's" (Bach, Beethoven and Brahms), and he characterized the works of Mozart as "musical wallpaper."[61]

Along with his interest in these composers of the nineteenth and twentieth centuries, Goff was fascinated by traditional Sub-Saharan African music and its complex rhythmic patterns. This music is traditionally composed with simultaneous repetition on percussion instruments, augmented by singers who might whisper, hum, grunt, or imitate animal sounds. He was also attracted to Asian music, such as the liquidlike gamelan compositions of Java and the Gagaku court music of Japan, whose vocal palette included harsh gutturals, falsettos, and soft low grunts. He liked the music of India, with the blurred, sliding sounds of the sitar and its ragas of free improvisation placed between alternating passages of fast and slow ornamental themes that contrasted with a droning, unchanging background. He was fond of the music of Duke Ellington and admired American composer Harry Partch's music made with unique homemade instruments. Years later both were invited as guest lecturers when Goff became director of the School of Architecture at the University of Oklahoma. Goff was also attracted to the electronic music of Edgar Varèse and met him in New York in 1952. Goff later wrote, "I got to know Varèse quite well and found him one of the greatest people I have yet met."[62]

During his years in Tulsa, Goff briefly experimented in music composition with a favored method of hand-cutting holes in the paper rolls for a player piano. Sidney K. Robinson has observed the direct correlation between the acoustic pattern and the visual pattern of the player piano rolls, which suggests the interchangeability of sight and sound.[63] Goff's technique of composition was analogous to the composer Heitor Villa-Lobos tracing the outline of a Brazilian mountain range on graph paper to transfer the undulations into the rise and ebb of a melodic line. Collectively the sight/sound continuum of both Goff and Villa-Lobos echoes the Symbolist poet Arthur Rimbaud assigning colors to vowels in one of his poems. Although Goff did not continue to compose music, he became an acute and discriminating listener and drew parallels between architecture and music throughout his life.

ART

Goff's cognizance of the arts as potential sources of inspiration for design may have been further stimulated by Wright's admiration of Japanese art. Goff, like Wright, began collecting prints and books on Japanese art at an early date, and his later discovery of the Edo period painter Itō Jakuchū became a continuing source of stimulation. In his many bird paintings, Jakuchū posed majestic, ornamental cocks contrasting with abstracted plants as a fusion of realism with organic expressionism. Prominent illustrators, including Aubrey Beardsley, Maxfield Parrish, Harry Clarke, Kay Nielsen, and Arthur Rackham, also received Goff's attention.[64] His circle of friends included a diverse group of young musicians, painters, sculptors, and writers who broadened his intellectual interests toward both painting and music.

It is ironic that Goff would refer to himself as an architect and composer early in his career, yet he seldom mentioned he was a painter even though he painted throughout his adult life. Nor did he even refer to his paintings as such, but rather as "compositions." It was a term he later used in his discussions of architecture, art, and music as noun, adverb, and adjective. Similar to his wide array of musical inspirations, Goff drew from Japanese art, Art Nouveau, the Symbolist movement, and Surrealism, and in their totality his paintings reflect a sense of imagination and modes of feeling. He assimilated the ideals of those art movements from specific artists who interested him and went on to produce an original and authentic body of work.

Goff frequently said his compositions were simply spontaneous abstractions

Rooster and Hen with Hydrangeas, by Itō Jakuchū, eighteenth century.

for moments of relaxation. They were often completed in one or two days. Yet the process of painting, as improvisation, created issues of design that he might never have encountered otherwise. Painting thus also served as a stimulus for his imagination and craftsmanship. Some of the paintings suggest a reference to his architectural values, especially with the inclusion of elements of rhythm and pattern as dominant motifs. A generalized theme reveals an immersion in the organic vitality of nature but with forms unknown to man that evoke a landscape of mystery as a romantic secular search for the supernatural in nature's manifestations. His paintings are a clear echo of Debussy: "I have made mysterious Nature my religion."[65]

Goff's fascination with Japanese art is particularly prominent in some of his paintings. One painting (at right), a masterpiece of contrasting forms with "space not intended to be seen," reflects a concept deeply imbedded in Japanese landscape painting. In the painting, a black square, pushed to a corner, is at one level of perception an element that is empty. It is analogous to the puppeteers of the Bunraku theater as an unseen force, moving about dressed in black as they animated their puppets. Yet the black square is also pulled toward the flowering organic growth inscribed by the arc below, as a process of transformation is imminent. There is a sense of tension between the black void of nothingness and the organic growth, suggesting a symbolic polarity.

Goff especially admired the woodblock prints of the "floating world" of *ukiyo-e*, with their overlapping and interlocking forms, bold colors, and vibrant patterns. He collected portraits by Kitagawa Utamaro and Tōshūsai Sharaku, the landscapes of Katsushika Hokusai and Utagawa Hiroshige, and later, the prints of modern Japanese artists Hasui Kawase, Akihiko Yoshida, and Kasamatsu Shirō. Goff also liked the early work of Maruyama Ōkyo, in which the brushwork ranged from delicate, light strokes to broad, sweeping shaded strokes to suggest forms. He was inspired by the art of Ogata Kōrin, especially his painting *White and Red Plum Trees* and its abstract river of swirling Klimt-like volutes of gold slicing through the middle of the composition and contrasting with the realistic flowering plum trees on either side.

Painting by Goff featuring "space not intended to be seen." Photographs of this and others of Goff's paintings, 1939 to 1953, are from a portfolio in the College of Architecture Library, University of Oklahoma.

Facing page, Painting by Goff featuring abstract bird, 1939–53, from portfolio. College of Architecture Library, University of Oklahoma.

His favorite, though, was always Itō Jakuchū.

Another of Goff's paintings (at right) has an undertone of eroticism that correlates with the decadence and sexuality of the Symbolist movement. The dominant element of the painting is a large abstract bird with outstretched wings, its neck thrusting upward and open mouth positioned over the bright light of the sun. A stylized pattern of spermatozoa swims downward on the neck of the creature. A spiraling pattern of frail, linear sticks energizes the composition, dividing at the end to hold some precious, mysterious object. Emanating from the orb of light, the delicate sticks merge with a curving tubular form converging under a wing of the bird. Is it a painting of a bird of prey, or of an androgynous hybrid?

In one of Goff's more surrealistic paintings (see page 33) there is a subtle and hidden decomposing image. The principal element is a series of stacked, vertical arced forms that diminish in size with an array of jellyfish-like tentacles as a crown. The arced forms, with their strong contrast and pattern of circular openings, convey a mysterious, totemic presence. To the left, an assemblage of transparent/translucent forms in a loose, melting configuration terminates in a decaying humanoid face with distinct eyes and teeth. It is a theme of transformation, of the death of a corrupt present and rebirth of an ideal world.

Goff's paintings often embrace the substance and energy of the natural world. Another of his paintings (see page 32) suggests the presence of some unknown creature of a mysterious species belonging neither to earth, sky, or water.

Another painting has a dominant hard-edge black mast with a ragged fringe emerging on one side with an array of small geometric blocks on the other side (see page 34). The verticality of the composition is amplified by an overlapping random pattern of vertical lines.

Later in life, Goff would create a painting of his interpretation of Debussy's *La Mer* as a pictorial representation of feelings arising from the music. He also did paintings of the twenty-five stanzas of Rimbaud's famous poem "The Drunken Boat."

Painting by Goff, 1939–53, from portfolio. College of Architecture Library, University of Oklahoma.

Painting by Goff suggesting death of a corrupt present and rebirth, 1939–53, from portfolio. College of Architecture Library, University of Oklahoma.

Painting by Goff, 1939–53, from portfolio. College of Architecture Library, University of Oklahoma.

Goff at work on a painting.
Photograph by Robert Bowlby.

From his early years as an intern to the heights of his professional practice, Bruce Goff drew inspiration from a plethora of sources. Wright and Debussy formed the core of his inspiration at an early age, and their work would reverberate throughout his career. When paired with a vast range of influences across time, location, and artistic mediums, and the brilliant creativity of Goff's mind, they built the foundations of his trademark originality in architecture, teaching, and art.

You design according to the nature of the thing: one with site, one with nature, one with the materials from which the building is built—and ask why concerning everything in it and get a good answer from the building itself.

FRANK LLOYD WRIGHT

Mystery in art starts at the precise moment when our intellect fails to help us.

BRUCE GOFF

2

FIRST DESIGNS

As he embraced artistic influences from further and further afield, Goff continued his architectural work at the firm of Rush, Endacott & Rush in Tulsa as a part-time employee. His first building designs reflect the multiple avenues of art from which he drew inspiration. But they also reflect another burgeoning philosophy: the idea that each architectural design was a solution specific to the client as well as the physical site upon which it would be built. Though at times economic necessity would limit his expressions, Goff was able to grow and sustain his philosophy of originality as well as his dedication to his clients' wants and needs.

⚠

The first of Goff's designs was completed in 1919, when he was fifteen years old. The design had been a hypothetical building that a visitor to the architecture firm had seen and recommended to B. L. Graves of Los Angeles for a summer house.[1] The design had a pronounced Wrightian affinity with its broad overhanging roof, terraces, clusters of windows at the corners, and a hearth with three fireplaces that were served by a central chimney, along with a kitchenette, at the center of the symmetrical square plan. Alcoves, projecting from the exterior walls onto the terraces, defined storage and sleeping spaces, with fold-down beds built into three of the alcoves. The fourth alcove, opposite the kitchenette, contained the bathroom. With the beds folded up during the day, the alcoves could be used for various social activities; at night privacy was provided by closing a curtain attached to a beam overhead. This concept of spatial and functional flexibility in Goff's early work is significant, as it was to evolve into a type developed further in later projects.

The Graves House was followed by a house design for Wallace McGregor in Tulsa. Constructed in 1920, the flat-roof building had boxed eaves, parapets, and a second story toward the rear of the house. It was a composition of layered forms of white stucco, with Prairie School–style fenestration rising in height from front to back. Even the steps of the sidewalk leading to the front porch with its massive piers are framed by small, free-standing stucco boxes rising from the earth to define the path of entry. The placement of smaller forms in front of progressively larger forms as a variation in scale was a design concept Goff learned early in his career.

Upon graduation from Tulsa Central High School in 1922, Goff joined the architectural firm in a full-time capacity and increasingly assumed design responsibilities.[2] Tulsa had entered a period of accelerated growth after statehood in 1907, a primary factor contributing to opportunities for Goff. The population of Tulsa increased from 7,298 in 1907 to 18,182 in 1910, then rose to 72,075 in 1920, reaching 141,256 in 1930.[3] The population increase was due to the discovery of oil in Tulsa and the surrounding areas, the biggest oil strike in the world at the time. The revenues from the oil industry made Tulsa a wealthy city, matched with civic and commercial building that reflected the achievements of the oil barons. Between 1922 and 1933 Goff acquired broad experience through work on projects that varied in scope and complexity. Designs

Wallace McGregor House, Tulsa, Oklahoma, 1920. Photograph by Brenda R. Spenser. Oklahoma Historical Society, Oklahoma State Historic Preservation Office, National Register of Historic Places file.

included an office building, church, residences, small commercial buildings, warehouses, and alterations to existing buildings.

The seven-story Tulsa Building, designed in 1925, Goff's first realization of a large building, shows his assimilation of other sources of influence. A steel structure clad in limestone, the Tulsa Building has vertical piers with multiple reveals overlapping the spandrels, which are terminated at the cornice with ornament, recalling Eliel Saarinen's 1922 second-place-winning entry to the *Chicago Tribune*'s skyscraper design competition.[4] In the summer of 1927, during construction of the Tulsa Building, Goff met the sculptor Alphonso Iannelli, who was collaborating with Barry Byrne on the design of the nearby

Christ the King Catholic Church. Goff knew of Iannelli's work with Wright on Midway Gardens in Chicago and later said he was the "first person of importance from the outside" that he had met.[5] Iannelli told Goff about a recent two-month tour with Byrne of new European architecture in Germany, Holland, and France.[6] It was a fortuitous meeting for Goff. He and Iannelli corresponded with each other, and Iannelli would send him publications of the work of leading architects. Later that year Goff traveled to Chicago, where Iannelli took him to see the buildings of Sullivan and Wright firsthand and introduced him to Byrne. Goff admired Byrne for his integrity. Although Byrne had apprenticed with Wright, he sought to distance himself from Wright's influence in development of his own expression.

Goff's finest achievement in architecture during the years in Tulsa was the 1926 design for the Boston Avenue Methodist-Episcopal Church. The building is defined by three major components: a semicircular auditorium seating 1,800 worshipers, a rectangular block of education and office space, and a tower positioned asymmetrically. Major entrances on the north and south sides of the building provide access to both the auditorium and a social lobby. A secondary entrance on the east side has a porte cochere to shelter those arriving by automobile. The tower, rising above the north entrance, reached a height of more than 250 feet with a prayer room on the top floor. With an exterior cladding of cut Bedford limestone and buff-colored terra-cotta spandrels, the building is replete with vertical elements terminated with angled, geometric finials. The glass in both the sanctuary and tower has a pleated form, which sustains the vocabulary of the ornamental finials.

The design of the church was in collaboration with Adah Robinson, Goff's former high school art teacher.[7] The sculptor Robert Garrison, also a former student of Robinson, participated in the design as well. Garrison designed the stylized sculptures that appear over the major entrances; the sculptures depict historical figures associated with the Methodist Church. The north entrance is defined by sculptured portraits of the Wesley family, the founding members of Methodism.

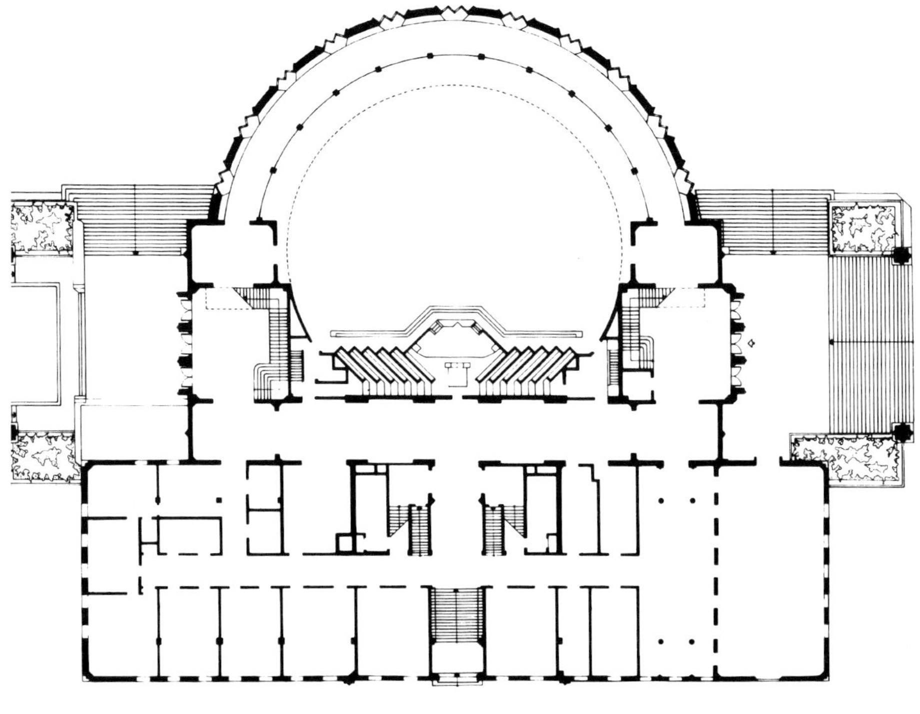

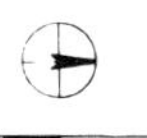

Boston Avenue Methodist-Episcopal Church. Plan drawing, University of Oklahoma (OU) College of Architecture, Design and Research Center. Courtesy College of Architecture, University of Oklahoma.

The south entry features a circuit rider as the central figure flanked by sculptures of the first bishop and the first superintendent.

Robinson conceptualized the motifs of the seven-pointed star, the praying hands at the cornice of the building, and the stained-glass windows in the sanctuary with incorporation of two native Oklahoma flowers, the tritoma and coreopsis.[8]

Although Goff alluded to the building as being "Neo-Gothic," there are several precedents for the design of the church. The plan organization was derived, according to Goff, from a Louis Sullivan church design of 1910 for Cedar Rapids, Iowa, with a semicircular sanctuary abutting a rectangular block.[9] However, the relationship of specific components of the Tulsa church was determined by the site. South Boston Avenue, a major street of access to downtown Tulsa, bends at an oblique angle at the intersection of East 13th Street. Goff positioned the auditorium at the point of directional change of

Facing page, Boston Avenue Methodist-Episcopal Church, north façade, 1301 S. Boston Ave., Tulsa, Oklahoma, 1926. Bruce Goff and Rush, Endacott & Rush, architects, with collaboration of Adah Robinson.

Boston Avenue Methodist-Episcopal Church, sculpture on south entry. Ryerson & Burnham Archives, Art Institute of Chicago.

Boston Avenue. The soaring tower, over the north entrance facing 13th Street, was aligned with that section of Boston Avenue extending from downtown to create a prominent visual termination. The tower recalls the transformation of the popular Gothic skyscrapers of the 1920s which, through a process of simplification, were stripped down to the essential vertical elements. There are also subtle references to Byrne's Christ the King Church, under construction while Goff was designing the Methodist church. Byrne's church included a rhythm of elongated hexagonal frames for stained-glass windows on the sides of the sanctuary. The geometric shape of those windows may have been the source of the monumental frames defining the major entrances of the Boston Avenue church. The prominent lantern at the top of the tower, constructed of copper and glass fins in a stepped, crystalline configuration also suggests German Expressionism as yet another source.

In his 1930 book, *The New World Architecture*, Sheldon Cheney praised the church for its sculptural and ornamental presence. He admired the visualization of functional organization revealed by the differences in expression of the major components, with the tower acting as a balancing fulcrum. The interior social lobby, which extends through the building, demarks the duality of preaching and education as a subliminal gesture towards humanization.[10] The Boston Avenue Methodist Church is regarded as one of the great churches of America for its distinctive expression and is now designated as a National Historic Landmark.

The church was Goff's most important accomplishment in Tulsa but one that caused him intense personal distress. During the construction process Adah Robinson publicly proclaimed she was the designer of the church in its entirety. Mrs. C. C. Cole, whose husband was the church building-committee chairman, suggested seeking advice from Robinson, a member of the congregation, as the committee was not satisfied with design proposals from several architects. Robinson offered to design the church if allowed to collaborate with Goff, and consequently with the firm of Rush, Endacott & Rush. The committee agreed, and a contract was prepared specifying the architect's cooperation with her "in all matters pertaining to the artistic features of the project."[11] Goff claimed he did not participate in meetings with the committee as Robinson was afraid his youthful appearance might diminish the committee's confidence in their collaboration. Even Goff's initial sketch, which was signed by him, was presented to the committee solely by Robinson. She alone acted as intermediary and, under these circumstances, evidently claimed the design as her own. Although she contributed to the conceptual design of some of the decorative details, her claim as sole designer of the church is not credible.

The Page Warehouse (1927) was Goff's next major Tulsa project.[12] It was an innovative design of two interwoven patterns creating a rhythmic exterior for the boxlike form. One pattern was established by exposing concrete columns with angled shear brackets and the projecting edge of a flat slab. Coated with cream-colored stucco, these components of typical warehouse construction clearly expressed the structural system as a major element of architecture. The other pattern, which was dominant, explored the potential of a segmented wall. Goff created a vertical rhythm of stepped bands of buff-colored brick, which projected beyond the face of the structural frame. Each of these bands was inset with a narrow, steel-sash window, deep in shadow, extending from floor to ceiling. The interplay of the two patterns suggests an awareness of the architectural aesthetics then emerging in Europe. The deliberate articulation of column and slab reverberated with the structural determinism of avant-garde French architects, and the rhythmic brickwork recalled buildings of the Amsterdam School. Despite its prosaic utilitarian function, the design of the Page Warehouse revealed Goff's commitment to creative expression. His transformation of a "storage box" into a distinctive building in the urban landscape was a remarkable testament to his design convictions. The Page Warehouse was demolished in the 1970s for construction of an expressway.

Another major project, the 1928 Riverside Studio, was designed as both living quarters and a studio for music teacher Patti Adams Shriner. The design recalls precepts of emerging European architecture with its white stucco exterior walls and flat-roofed rectilinear forms. With an irregular plan of projecting wings combined with roofs of varying heights, Goff used the steep site to great advantage. The result was a composition of cubic forms cascading down a hill to a symmetrical entry façade enlivened with contrasting geometric motifs. The massing of forms toward the top of the hill, defining the living area for Ms. Shriner, is one of informality with an asymmetrical arrangement of spaces.

Page Furniture Depository and Warehouse, Tulsa, Oklahoma, 1927. Bruce Goff, architect. Historic Architecture and Landscape Image Collection, Ryerson & Burnham Archives, Art Institute of Chicago, Digital File #29033.

The two-story entrance hall was the building's prominent feature, offering an ideal opportunity to visualize relationships between architecture and music. The pattern of stepped rectangular windows alternating with black glass tile drew inspiration from musical scales. The large circular window in the foyer, overlooking the Arkansas River, had an abstract geometric pattern etched in the glass that was derived from musical scores Goff composed while he was working on the design.[13]

A fountain at the entry was designed by Iannelli to further link the Riverside Studio's reference to music. Water dripped over an abstract marble sculpture into cascading chromium cups of varying size, creating musiclike tones as water splashed into the pool below.[14] The rich colors, patterns, and rhythms of the abstract wall murals by Olinka Hrdy (1902–1987) on the interior further amplified the space's musical associations. The mural in the foyer depicted the "Symphony of the Arts," which included painting, architecture, music, and dance.

Eight other panels in the Recital Hall represented various genres of music. Measuring sixteen feet tall by five feet in width, the murals were folded to extend onto the ceiling.[15]

Riverside Studio, built in Tulsa, Oklahoma, 1928. Photograph by Luca Guido.

Goff's conviction of the importance of providing meaning for a client was achieved through collaboration with a sculptor and painter in a search for an original expression. And Goff had clear ideas of his objective: it was an opportunity to express the intimate relationship of music and architecture.

Goff built little in the closing years of the 1920s, although he further explored the use of angled geometries in hypothetical projects as well as commissions that remained unbuilt. One of the most inspired of those designs was the fraternity house for Phi Beta Delta (1930) on the University of Oklahoma campus.[16] The cruciform plan of bilateral symmetry had an axis centered on an angled irregular form on the façade that functioned as a chapter room and study hall. This two-story faceted component, with a cladding of diamond-shaped panels of polished aluminum, also had diamond-shaped corner windows. Individual rooms were positioned on a cross-axis behind the congregate space and each room was canted outward with a repetition of the

Above, Riverside Studio, entry. Photograph by author.

Facing page, Study for Tulsa Riverside Studio Murals: Symphony of the Arts, by Olinka Hrdy. Watercolor, 1928–29, 23¾ x 10½ in. Fred Jones Jr. Museum of Art, the University of Oklahoma, Norman; Gift of the artist, 1966.

corner window motif. Compositionally, the visual effect was one of a regular rhythm of forms at a smaller scale contrasting with the larger form on the façade. The pattern-rich design is significant for its expression of individual components as elements of a larger composition, a theme that often appears in Goff's later work.

The concept of angularity expanded the possibilities for the exploration of innovative architectural forms that Goff advocated in "A Declaration of Independence," published in 1930.[17] His insight into the potential of complex geometries suggests a maturity that would hold forth the promise of professional development. But Tulsa, like the rest of America, was soon caught in the throes of the Depression. Although Goff was licensed as an architect in 1929, there was little work.[18] He became a partner in the firm but it soon dissolved, and so Goff attempted to practice on his own for two years. During this time he maintained correspondence with Iannelli, who encouraged him to come to Chicago so they might collaborate on projects. He also had an offer from Wright to join him at Taliesin as a senior assistant but declined, believing he might lose his own identity. In 1934 Goff relocated to Chicago with the hope of expanding Iannelli's industrial design firm to include architectural services. They worked together on two projects but the results were disappointing to Goff and he soon tired of designing industrial products. The following year, with Iannelli's recommendation, he accepted a part-time teaching position at the Chicago Academy of Fine Arts. In 1936 Goff took a position as chief designer of the Vitrolite division of the Libbey-Owens-Ford Glass Company. In this capacity he was responsible for both the design of alterations to existing buildings and a hypothetical design for a tall building to promote the use of Vitrolite, a structural pigmented glass product whose use in architecture proliferated during the first quarter of the twentieth century. Although Goff learned about a variety of glass products, and his experience there probably intensified his interest in reflective materials, he soon felt his ideas were being compromised and so he left in mid-1937 to return to part-time teaching and independent practice in Chicago. Still, he had limited opportunities to build. By the end of 1938 he had constructed only a few houses in the Chicago area, and none of them reflected the intensely creative individuality of his later work.

At age thirty-four, Bruce Goff had more than twenty years of experience in architecture. He had entered the profession in a propitious location, at a time of economic prosperity. Tulsa's boomtown days led architects to ample commissions, which provided Goff an opportunity to learn through the process of building at an established firm. Like Frank Lloyd Wright, he was self-taught and, like Wright, he recognized architecture as a supremely individual act of

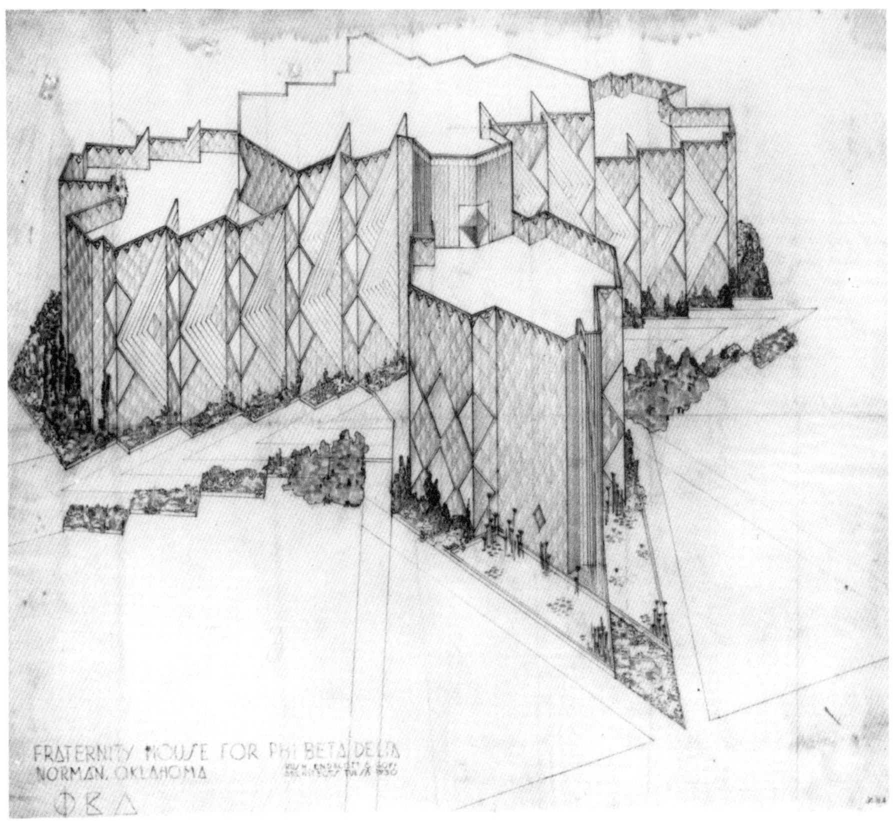

Phi Beta Delta fraternity house at OU, project. Bruce Goff Archive, Ryerson & Burnham Archives, Art Institute of Chicago.

creativity. That he assimilated many influences is evident from three major buildings in Tulsa—the Boston Avenue Methodist Church, the Page Warehouse, and Riverside Studio. The differences between the three buildings affirm a fundamental premise Goff embraced early in his career: each structure requires its own solution.

The human spirit is free to blossom in structure as organic as plants and trees . . . buildings, too, are children of Earth and Sun.

FRANK LLOYD WRIGHT

The arts energize each other and they draw continuous sustenance from the world that surrounds the human creator.

DAVID MICHAEL HERTZ

3

A LANGUAGE OF CONCEPTUALIZATION

In a discussion of architectural symbolism, historian Robert Harbison observed that Bruce Goff apparently started over with each new commission since his various works differed so much in appearance. Harbison added, "Perhaps this variety is a code which could be cracked, and one would see the same principle dependably repeated."[1] But there is no Rosetta stone that might be decoded to discover a common "principle" of conceptualization. Goff's designs derive not from a single ideal but from manifestations of multiple values. There are, however, several generalized *premises* that define Goff's design ideals. These premises include an individualistic interpretation of organic architecture, recognizing the necessity of "discipline in freedom" in the act of composing, a search for geometry as a determinant, a thematic orchestration of form and surface, and the inclusion of symbolic expressions of nature. Collectively these values characterize a language of conceptualization. They exemplify his aspirations for each design to assert its own originality.

ORGANIC ARCHITECTURE

The 1932 poem by Bruce Goff, referred to in the previous chapter, titled "About Absolute Art," defines his ideals and provides a direct extension of the philosophy shared by Louis Sullivan and Frank Lloyd Wright. In its prelude, Goff wrote:

We no longer need imitate Nature to show our love for it
Rather should we assimilate its essence into ourselves
Then what we do will be tribute to it
  organic with it
  harmonious

It is time to recognize our natural human-divinity
  to shape from and with this
  organically
  our lives
  our work
It is time to be free
  naturally natural
  create absolute art[2]

Drawing upon Sullivan and Wright's established philosophy, Goff's interpretation placed the individual front and center as the engine of change in organic expression.

In his Princeton lectures of 1931, Wright illuminated the concept of organic expression by implying that ultimate reality is a single unifying organism within nature itself. Wright then defined "organic" as applying "to living structure—a structure or concept wherein features or parts are so organized in form and substance as to be, applied to purpose, *integral.* Everything that lives is therefore organic."[3] In his poem, written the following year, Goff drew parallels with Wright's philosophic analogy of a building as a living integral structure.

Goff believed it was through assimilation of the "essence" of nature that architecture, harmoniously organized, corresponds to the organic principles of the natural world. He further proclaimed that one's life and one's work were inextricably intertwined, just as nature and art were fundamentally one. Moreover, his premise of "human-divinity," shaped organically, was the path to freedom for the creation of "absolute" architecture.

Yet Goff's praise of Wright's philosophic interpretation of "organic architecture" does little to illuminate the meaning of the term. The origins of organic expression can be traced through Ralph Waldo Emerson, Walt Whitman, and Charles Darwin to the German Romantic philosophers. The concept of "organism," and hence organic expression, developed in the nineteenth century from the fusion of Romanticism and functionalism. In the former, humankind—as a creature of emotions and intuition—could achieve meaningful existence only by living in harmony with nature. In the latter, nature was viewed as an evolutionary organism developing according to its own laws. Philosophically, the Romantic view was a pantheistic interpretation of the universe in which God, as well as man and all his works, were subordinated as part of nature. The functionalist encompassed a scientific view that embraced nature and all expressions of humankind, including art forms, as an organism with a life of its own, characterized by change, growth, and development.

Although the Romantic movement was well established at the onset of the nineteenth century, it gained momentum with the transcendental idealism of German Romantic philosophers. Immanuel Kant was a major contributor to the doctrine of organic expression and influenced both other philosophers and Emerson. Kant was among the first to equate beauty in art to nature with an implied concept of the organism and the notion of continuous development. Similarly, Johann Wolfgang von Goethe contributed to the organic conception of nature and art. Opposed to the artificiality of French rationalism early in his career, Goethe came to regard naturalness and simplicity as the prime virtue of all art. Admired by both Emerson and Wright, Goethe believed that a knowledge of organic nature was necessary for an artist to develop. He maintained that art mediates between nature and freedom, since it is produced by the artist according to nature's operating principles. Johann Gottfried von Herder, often quoted by Wright, was both a student of Kant and friend of Goethe, and was an important source for the doctrine of organic expression in art with his theories on the development of human civilization. In his view, the cultural evolution of humankind was part of the evolution of nature rather than a manifestation of man's rational free will. Herder challenged the notion of a uniform standard of beauty acceptable to all people at all times. Art, to Herder, was the product of a specific context of time and place.

Similarly, Friedrich Wilhelm Joseph von Schelling conceived nature and humanity as a single, unified organism and defined beauty in art as an expression of a spirit of nature. Even though the artist may never fully understand his own work, Schelling believed the ultimate purpose of art was beauty. He was among the first to suggest that art would be diminished by any form forced upon it that was not true to its purpose. It is no wonder then that both Sullivan and Wright despised the resurgence of classicism in American architecture. It was Friedrich von Schlegel, though, who first applied the word "romantic" to characterize *modern* art. For Schlegel held the view that to achieve a sense of vitality, art should seek an enlargement of its boundaries and a progression toward a remote ideal rather than return to a simpler and primitive state of nature. Moreover, Schlegel articulated the notion that a condition of organic expression in art was that it must reflect the spirit of a region or even a nation. It was a forward-looking philosophy, one that acknowledged cultural differences but also adhered to progress and hence optimism.[4] It resembled closely the views of Sullivan and Wright, especially with their insistence that the essence of the American spirit was to be found in their own region, the Midwest.

Inspired by the German Romantic philosophers, American thinker Ralph Waldo Emerson extended the concept of organic expression. Emerson attacked the use of revival styles in architecture in *The American Scholar* with the statement, "If the American artist will study with hope and love the precise thing to be done by him, considering the climate, the soil, the length of the day, the wants of the people, the habit and form of the government, he will create a house in which all there will find themselves fitted."[5] Emerson was also influenced by his friend Horatio Greenough, who articulated the idea of organic expression and a functionalist doctrine of subordination of the parts to the whole. In a letter to Emerson he said, "Here is my theory of structure: A scientific arrangement of spaces and forms to functions and to site; an emphasis of features proportioned to the *gradiated* importance in function; color and ornament to be decided and arranged and varied by strictly organic laws."[6]

The ideas of both Emerson and Greenough and the importance they placed on adaptation to environmental circumstances shaped the ideas of Sullivan and Wright, who insisted that American architecture must express the people's characteristic democratic spirit. Yet it was Walt Whitman, who glorified nature, science, democracy, and the common man, who most inspired Sullivan and Wright. Whitman felt that his own poetry, and the larger concept of organic expression, reflected both a specific time and environment. Organic expression, Whitman believed, could only have occurred in democratic America in the latter half of the nineteenth century. Whitman's functionalist posture was clearly related to Wright's acceptance of evolution with his view that art emerges from circumstances and anything that "distorts honest shapes . . . is a nuisance and revolt."[7] For both Sullivan and Wright these ideas became the foundation for their own philosophy of life and art.

The concept of change with an implicit belief in progress, as revealed in scientific theories of evolution, served to strengthen the doctrine of organic expression. In his book *The Autobiography of an Idea,* Sullivan acknowledged the influence of both Charles Darwin and Herbert Spencer.[8] Sullivan applied the Darwinian doctrine of natural selection to architecture with a conviction that not only was functional organization of a building the key to change but that architectural styles of the past were outmoded, and hence unfit to survive. Furthermore, the idea of progress towards heterogeneity, revealed in the writings of Spencer, appealed to both architects. Spencer's theory stressed change as the most characteristic feature of all living matter and posited that such change was inevitable. He maintained that discord would result from an organism's nonadaptation to environmental conditions. From this doctrine it was a rational extrapolation for Sullivan and Wright to suggest that only poor architecture would result when a building was not responsive to the specific aspects of an environment. Spencer also developed the idea that society itself was a social organism.[9]

This glorification of science, together with the general philosophic and artistic movement of Romanticism, provided the intellectual framework for Sullivan and Wright's ideals of organic architecture. For them organic expression included both a Romantic approach to architecture, with form organized in harmony with nature for emotional purposes, and a functionalist approach, derived from a scientific view, of form organized to accommodate the function. Goff, in turn, would merge this theme with other influences to form the core of his unique interpretation of the meaning of organic architecture.

DISCIPLINE IN FREEDOM

Claude Debussy reflected the ideals of the Symbolist poets when he said, "Discipline must be sought in freedom, and not within the formulas of an outworn philosophy only fit for the feeble-minded. Give ear to no man's counsel; but listen to the wind which tells in passing the history of the world."[10] Goff would later deem Debussy's *La Mer* "interspatial," saying that "[it] has so much freedom that people didn't think it had discipline when they first heard it . . . actually it has the finest order of discipline. The construction is there, but it is not obvious. It is finer, freer and more complex than the old masters."[11]

For Goff, like Debussy, discipline came not from outworn formulas of the past—or the overused formulas of the present—but from recognition of the order in a given composition and understanding the reason for its being.[12] In

Goff's view, it was imperative to acknowledge the developmental order in the moment of the present. A conceptual idea had a life of its own and must be nurtured. The importance of this premise is apparent in his writings, his teaching, and his buildings.

For Goff, discipline did not mean punishment or self-denial. It meant simply a sense of order and a sense of belonging together.[13] It was a *feeling* "of continuity, of grammar, or language, or means, so that you feel that is part of the same composition," and not part of the order of another composition.[14] Feelings were of primary importance to Goff as a driving force:

> [I had] a strong intuition so I stumbled on to a few things. . . . I know from my own experience that I can save lots of time, lots of lost motion, lots of unfortunate mistakes . . . the more I know about design . . . the more scientifically I can regard design as the ways and means of doing something the more it saves me from resorting to trial and error as a result of just intuition.[15]

Goff believed the ability to understand the order inherent in the composition would lead to a richness of expression and great variety in a design.[16] He argued that the "architect should be free to operate with any color; any texture and he shouldn't have to apologize for doing a certain design, or have to justify himself. It is a matter of having a great many ideas . . . to use them to make a whole design that is still part of the Continuous Present."[17] Goff thought that any rules could be broken but "you have to use discipline, there is no such thing as doing a work of art without discipline and order."

Goff's perception of the duality of imagination and reality, both as a conviction and a stimulus in conceptualization, reverberates with a line from Wallace Stevens's famous 1922 poem "The Emperor of Ice Cream": "Let be be the finale of seem."[18] Although the phrase sounds like a Zen koan, the meaning is that whatever exists or takes place is the concluding reality of what it is. Stevens's lyrical poem, as a fusion of imaginative, differentiated "word play" and reality, presupposes the importance of understanding and acknowledgement of the conceptual idea underlying the composition and the necessity of disciplined development. It reflected Goff's belief that the "reader"—whether of architecture or poetry—brings their own experience, intelligence, and feelings into the interpretation. The premise, for both Goff and Stevens, was pregnant with purpose and value for the realization of originality.

GEOMETRY AS SPATIAL DETERMINANT

Goff advocated an exploration of different geometric shapes and forms in architecture early in his career and explored variations of angular geometry in both hypothetical designs and unbuilt projects during the Depression years. This led to a belief in the importance of "new" geometry, beginning in the 1940s. The impulse for new, and different, geometries served both his quest for originality in design and a means of separation from precursors.

Goff's conceptual ideas, visualized by geometric configuration, are revealed in the floor plan as the primary ordering device of functional and spatial organization. In his buildings there are three general typologies of formal configurations giving definition to the shape and arrangement of floor plans: centroidal, rectilinear, and composite geometry. Centroidal floor plans refer to those designs with the dominance of a major space visualized by a primary geometric form. In this typology, Goff used a variety of geometries for the primary form. These range from the most common geometries of triangle, square, and circle to the more complex polygonal forms such as hexagon, octagon, and dodecahedron. In centroidal designs the primary geometry is visualized on both the exterior and interior by pitching the roof to the locus of the symmetrical form with the converging interior volume defining a vertical axis with a skylight at the apex.

Some of Goff's houses in the centroidal typology are defined by a symmetrical geometric form in its totality with the congregate space at the center surrounded by ancillary spaces at the perimeter. Others also locate the living room at the center of a symmetrical space within a larger asymmetrical composition. In either configuration it would seem there is a subtle suggestion of correspondence between the visions of Goff and the values of Debussy and the Symbolist poets. Both turned inward into their subjective world of the imagination. A life of the mind, posited by Goff in an inward-looking space of beauty and repose, reflected some of his deepest feelings toward an ideal place.

Rectilinear plan geometry, with all the components parallel and perpendicular to one another in an orthogonal relationship, is a configuration that characterizes most of Goff's early buildings and some of his post–World War II work. Buildings in this typology range from simple rectangular plans to L-shaped and irregular linear plans. The plan organization of the Paul Colmorgan House (1939) in the suburb of Glenview, Illinois, is rectilinear but with multiple interior levels and a staircase that projects into a natural woodland.[19] It is the sequence of these spaces merging with the sculptural form on the exterior that is distinctive. The stair landing defines an alcove with an extending flower box that is cantilevered over a lily pool below. The alcove walls are glass with views into the woodland yet are shielded from the street by a pattern of two-inch-diameter saplings fastened to the exterior sill to form a visual screen. The principal exterior materials are muted red Chicago common brick with weeping mortar joints and stained rough-sawn spruce siding. The relationship of the house to the earth is dramatized by the shed roof sloping toward the woodland and terminated with two scuppers positioned over the stair alcove landing as a focal point of both the exterior form and interior vertical circulation. The scuppers, eight feet in length, also feature built-in light fixtures on the underside. The house is an extraordinary expression of harmony with the natural world, surrounded by trees, wildflowers, and water. And when it rains the scuppers are transformed into waterfalls.

The typology of composite geometry represents the widest range of plan variations and often combines angular or curved geometry with linear elements.

Following spread

Left, Paul Colmorgan House, Glenview, Illinois, 1939. Isometric drawing, OU College of Architecture, Design and Research Center. Courtesy College of Architecture, University of Oklahoma.

Right, Colmorgan House, exterior. Photograph by author.

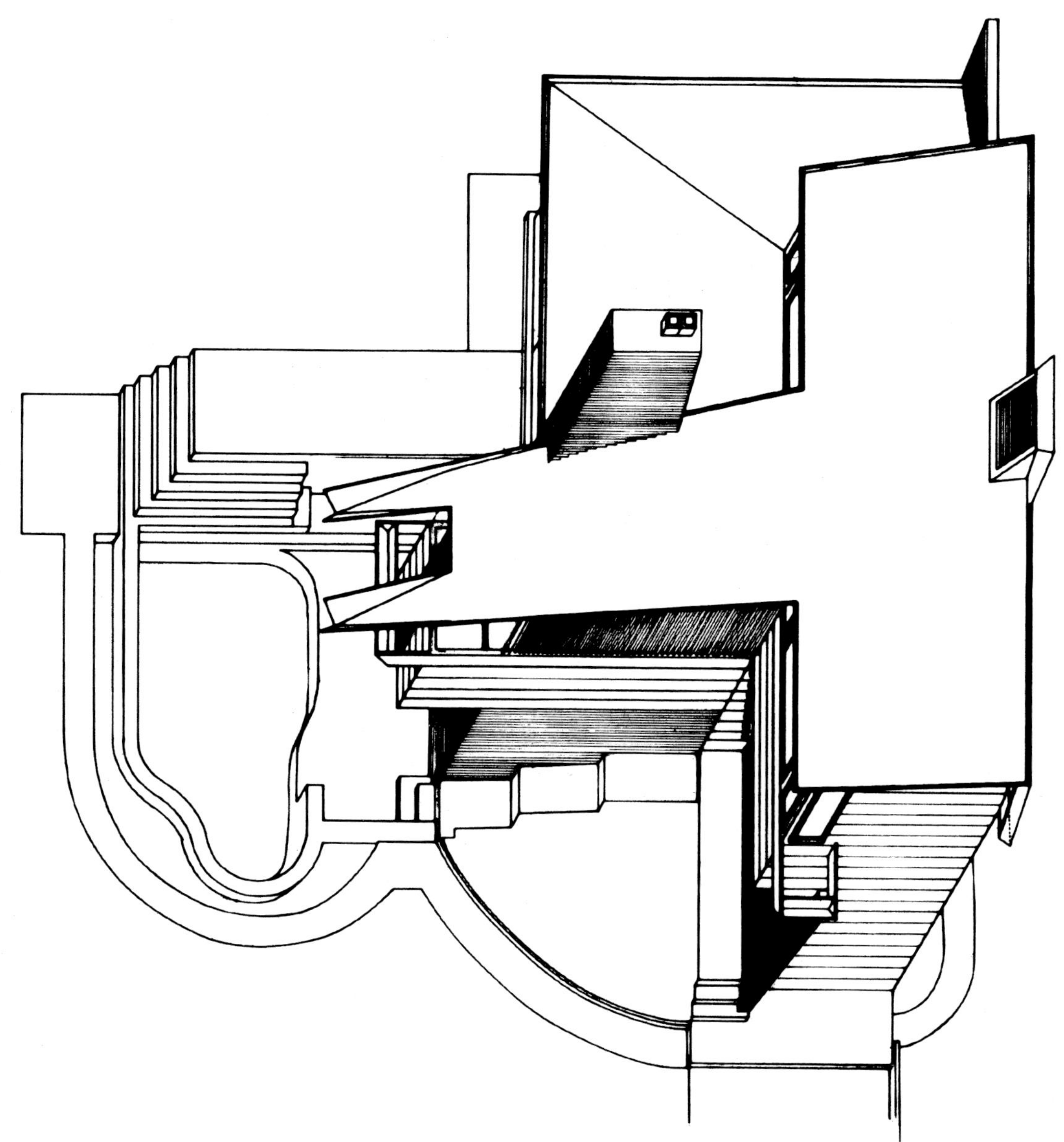

Some of the plans in this group are symmetrical, while others are asymmetrical compositions of complexity. The Irma Bartman House, or "Triaero" as Goff called it, of Fern Creek, Kentucky (1941), was commissioned as a weekend retreat.[20] Goff created a remarkable design of minimal space with an equilateral triangular plan and clipped corners to designate exterior reflecting pools and the entry. The delicate cantilevered trellises, supported by angled struts at the corners, extend the flat roof as a tailored visual element to effectively amplify the shape of the plan. The kitchen, bath, and fireplace, defined as an angular core, are centrally located with living space and sleeping areas on two sides of the core. Although the concept of free and continuous circulation was compromised by the inclusion of a garage on the third side, it is an impressive composition thematically developed of articulated forms and pattern. The enclosed space is one of hexagonal geometry of unequal sides with glass walls overlooking the pools and a continuous clerestory on the longer sides of the hexagon. Extending from two sides are angular closets separated from the overhanging roof by the clerestory. Goff articulated the form of the closets by defining their projection in both plan and elevation at a sixty-degree angle to maintain a geometric unity with the equilateral plan. On the exterior the closets are covered with a striated pattern of redwood battens and copper strips. The same material defined the ceiling inside the house and the striated pattern is repeated thematically on the floor with alternating light and dark boards.

The Bartman House is particularly significant not only for Goff's assimilation of crystalline geometry but also as a design foreshadowing an extended language of conceptualization. It is a design of a triangular theme that is transformed into a hexagonal space. The flat roof with trellis extensions is another differentiated form magnifying the illusion of a delicate, floating element that both contrasts and blends in pattern with the opaque forms below. The Bartman design marked the beginning of a period of distinctive artistry with thematic compositional development.

During the years from 1955 to 1960, Goff completed three houses based on radial designs, six houses combining rectilinear and angular geometry, and two houses with a hybrid, curved geometry that are almost zoomorphic in character. Even within the fabric of designs based on a composite geometry there were many variations of plan conceptualization. Many of Goff's designs suggest an oscillation between hard-edged geometric shapes and forms that are more fluid. Yet with the variety of possible conceptualizations, particularly evident in both centroidal and composite designs, it is problematic to determine why he might choose one form of geometry over others or a compositional configuration of symmetry versus asymmetry.

One of the major characteristics of Goff's houses is an open plan, which allowed an extension of interior vistas with only a suggestion of boundaries. Beginning with the Unseth House (1940), Goff used an accordion wood screen as a device to alternately open spaces for views and ease of circulation or close spaces for privacy. In other designs the screens might form different configurations, but the use of accordion-folding partitions to extend or enclose space was the same. In contrast to the complex articulation of forms in the Colmorgan House, the Unseth House is triangular, with extensions in two corners defining a garage on the front and porch on the back. The geometry of the plan is further emphasized by the diagonal positioning of the siding and the rhythm of angular fixed-glass windows and independent operable shutters for ventilation. Goff incorporated a brick fireplace on an exterior wall with a large triangular skylight that turns down the wall to define high fixed-glass windows mirroring the shape above. The effect is one of a folded glass prism, penetrated by a tall masonry form. Conceptually the design of this component recalls Wright's corner windows, but the relationships are dramatically altered. The continuity in geometry with this ensemble is sustained by the angled pattern of wood on the ceiling, interior walls, and exterior surfaces. The Unseth House was an important accomplishment for Goff as it was the first building constructed with a "new" geometry predicated on congruence between the triangulated floor plan and exterior form.

Following spread

Left, Irma Bartman Weekend House, Fern Creek, Kentucky. Plan drawing, OU College of Architecture, Design and Research Center. Courtesy College of Architecture, University of Oklahoma.

Right, Bartman residence, Fern Creek, Kentucky, 1940–42. Bruce Goff, architect; photograph by Jimmy Wallace. Bruce Goff Archive, Ryerson & Burnham Archives, Art Institute of Chicago.

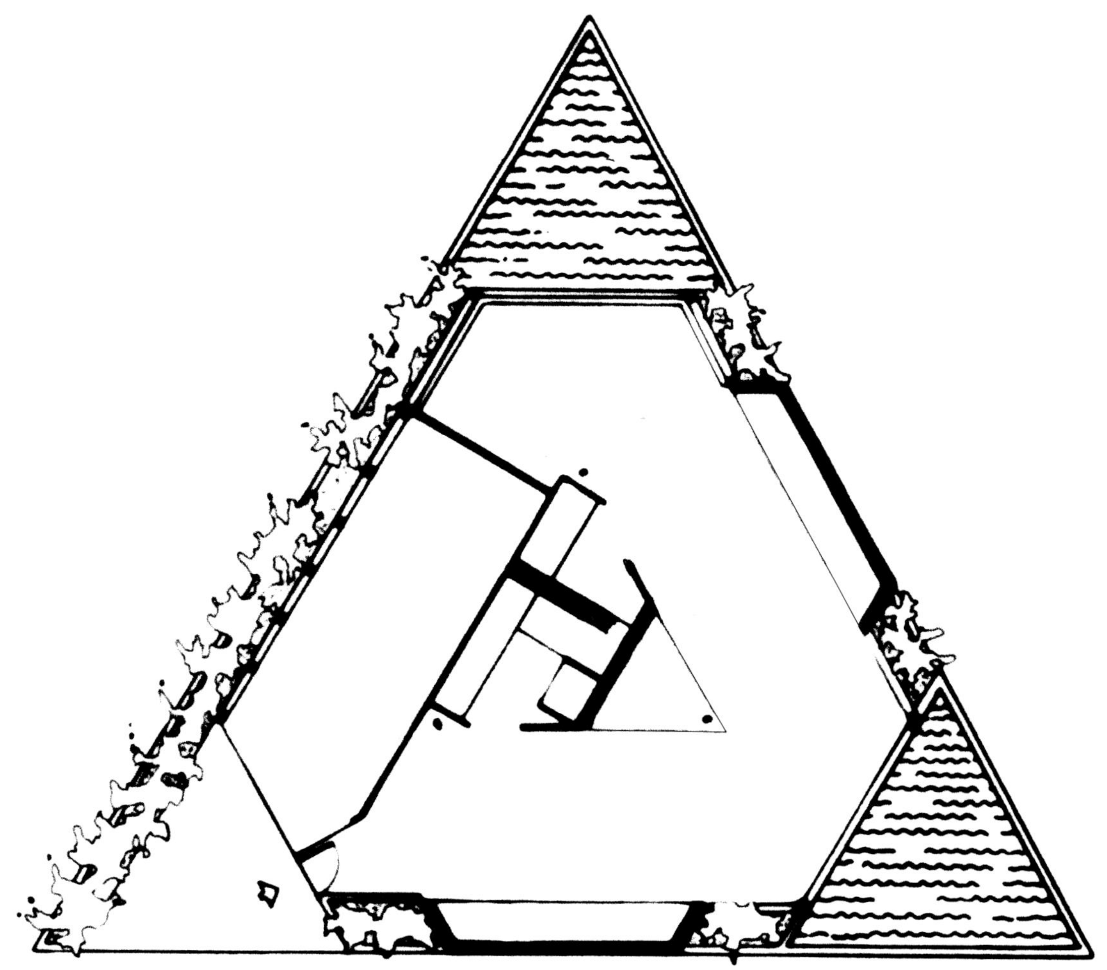

Goff frequently developed a configuration of spatial and functional definition arranged as a split-level design. This strategy defined major spaces at three different levels—at grade or the entry level, up a half level, and down a half level. The trilevel relationship offered the opportunity for modulation by cantilevering the upper level both to evoke a sense of lightness to that form and to provide shade for high windows at the lower level. It also served as a convenient zoning device and allowed varied compositions at the intersection of these volumes.

Nearly all of his residential work illustrates a concern for hierarchical modulation by differentiating ceiling heights according to function. Goff recognized the importance of intimate protected spaces for individual activities and acknowledged this dimension of human needs by variation of the enclosing ceiling plane. But he was also concerned with visual relationships and continuity between form and space. A major way of achieving this continuity was by defining the plane of the ceiling and the plane of the roof as one. There are few

Below, Helen Unseth House, Park Ridge, Illinois, 1940. Plan drawing, OU College of Architecture, Design and Research Center. Courtesy College of Architecture, University of Oklahoma.

Facing page, Unseth House, detail of façade. Photograph by author.

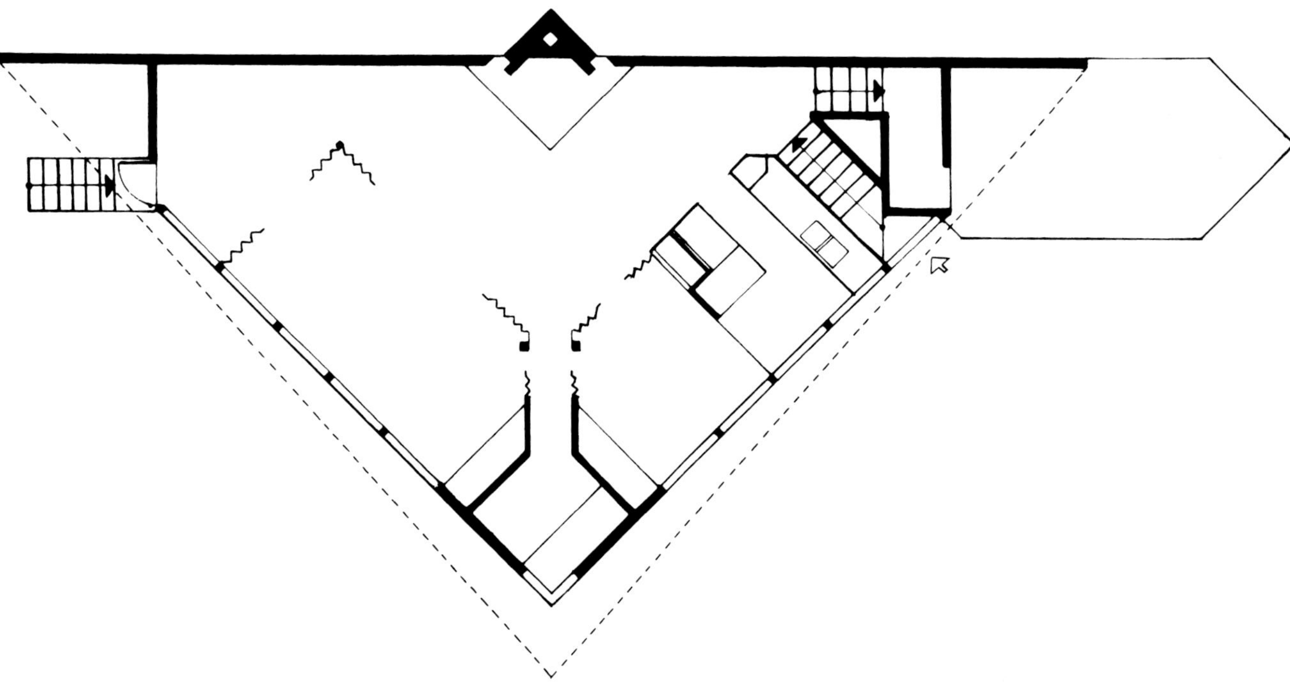

Left, Unseth House, detail of angular skylight, interior. Photograph by author.

Right, Unseth House, detail of angular skylight, exterior. Photograph by author.

attic spaces in his buildings, and the correspondence between roof and ceiling is the same irrespective of plan geometry. There is nearly always a predictable relationship between exterior form and interior volume. This concept can be seen in the second design of the Garvey House (1954), with all the activities contained under a single low-pitched conical roof. The private functions are positioned around the perimeter to define a central living space that might also accommodate musical performances. This open, pavilionlike structure is quite logical in its relationship of function to spatial definition. The outer ring of everyday living space, smaller and intimate, is sheltered by the lower ceiling while congregate activities at the center are defined by a larger volume.

A visualization of structure in some of his buildings, as an extension of geometric configuration, is another manifestation of Goff's ideals of conceptualization. In the 1947 Ford House the fusion of curved metal ribs, angled skylight struts, and horizontal bands of the chimney cap terminating the vertical axis is a pattern-rich expression of structure as a defining element. The Wilson House (1950) is another example of structural innovation. Constructed of exposed surplus boiler tubes, the structural frame defined both the corners and the top and bottom of each module. The logic and precision of the design, with its repetitive modules combined with a dominant expression of structure, placed the Wilson House at the very center of architectural concerns of the

1950s. It is ironic that Goff, viewed by some of his contemporaries as wildly romantic, embraced a primary axiom of structural expression defining the International Style to produce a building of striking originality.

Goff's use of structural wood decking supported by laminated wood beams became the primary method of spanning distances beyond what was possible with conventional framing. It was an attractive material to Goff because it reduced the number of necessary components.[21] The structural decking could serve both as a substrate for the roofing membrane and as a ceiling surface that could be stained or left natural. The structural system provided the opportunity to create large open spaces; it was relatively inexpensive and had a cantilever capability with a thin fascia. Goff's interest in unique structural solutions, particularly designs with a cable-supported roof, did not diminish. Goff had a fascination with the potential expression of a building element that might be suspended in space. Although only a few of these were built, a notable exception was the 1982 Japanese Pavilion of the Los Angeles County Art Museum completed several years after his death. The expression of a network of structure—columns, curved beams, and cables rising into the sky above—mitigated the bulk of the walls below. It was a major building and the crowning visualization of form and structure of his career.

ORCHESTRATION OF FORM AND SURFACE

A compelling aspect of Goff's architecture is the composition of forms that are thematically articulated components. His buildings present an array of ideas with great variety from one design to another, yet there are several underpinning concepts that often determine the expression of form and surface. Variations of these concepts offered many possibilities, and the permutations expanded with selection of building materials. These concepts include the definition of the roof as a dominant element of design; modulation of form by extension of the service or private functions beyond the perimeter wall plane;

visual dichotomies through contrast to establish a differentiation of components; and the incorporation of rhythmic elements expressed on the façade or major elevations. This array of conceptual ideals illustrates the many possibilities in creation of diverse solutions.

The concept of dramatizing the roof with deep cantilevers was one Goff used often. Although he developed many variations of form, the notion of a dominant roof was derived from both Wright's Prairie houses and Goff's admiration of Japanese architecture. An extended roof, as a metaphor of protection, might also give a quality of lightness to a composition with a form that would appear to hover in space. As an extension of dramatizing the roof, he also would often cantilever beams, pinnacles, or scuppers to sustain the illusion of lightness.

Another way Goff generated visual interest was through contrasting components. This sense of visual differentiation has a remarkable parallel to the later work of Debussy, with its series of autonomous musical ideas defining his compositions. Similarly, much of Japanese painting is often visualized in fragments rich in contrast. Goff's expression suggests a transposition of ideas, derived from both music and art, in creating compositions of contrasting elements. Frequently his expression was one of light, frail elements played against solid, anchoring masses. This sense of duality would be further amplified by different attributes in materials, such as color, texture, and pattern. Goff also generated interest through repetition of rhythmic elements. This characteristic of a dominant rhythm found a variety of expressions with a wide range of scale hierarchies. In the 1947 Ledbetter House the angled sawtooth pattern of fixed glass on the façade establishes a primary rhythm while the glass ashtrays from Woolworth's set in wood mullions generate a secondary rhythm. It is a concept of two simultaneous rhythms, much like counterpoint in music. The scale of the two rhythms is quite different, yet they are in harmony with one another as the materials of both are glass.

The diversity of form in Goff's architecture corresponds to his selection of building materials to achieve a varied expression. Visual relationships were of

H. E. Ledbetter House, Norman, Oklahoma, 1947, exterior photograph. Ryerson & Burnham Archives, Courtesy of Art Institute of Chicago.

paramount concern, but he also was pragmatic and would substitute materials when it was necessary to reduce costs even when a project was under construction.[22] There are some houses built primarily of only one material, but many of them feature two, and occasionally more, materials in addition to glass. The principal building materials are most often rather conventional, and, with the exception of a preference for masonry, Goff did not seem to favor any single material or combinations of materials. He would often create textural dichotomies—smooth versus rough, natural versus manmade—to achieve a rich tactile expression.

At the zenith of his career Goff was sometimes ridiculed, primarily by other architects, for the use of common household objects in the expression of his architecture. There are several factors that influenced his receptivity toward novel juxtapositions. His fascination with the originality of Debussy's music, the collage compositions of the surrealist painters, and the found-object sculptures of Marcel Duchamp and Man Ray undoubtedly nurtured his receptivity to creative applications of "found objects" in his architecture. These experiences of discovery would have been amplified by his knowledge of the aesthetic theories of the Symbolist poets with their emphasis on mystery. By the time Goff came to the University of Oklahoma in 1947 he had clear ideas about the role of surprise and mystery in architecture. In an article in a 1948 issue of *Architectural Forum* he said: "People who aren't afraid, don't mind being surprised . . . and they don't mind mysteries which can't be deciphered."[23]

There was a specific experience in his life, though, that was important in the development of his ideas in the use of building materials. As a chief petty officer in the Seabees during World War II, Goff designed several facilities for military personnel and, of necessity, had to be inventive because of the scarcity of building materials. These circumstances created the realization of design possibilities that ultimately were integrated in the development of his aesthetic values. His wartime experiences simply expanded the opportunity for creative expression. When he remodeled the officers club at Dutch Harbor in the Aleutian Islands he sandblasted surplus fir plywood, "which brought out the grain in relief . . . to give it more distinction."[24]

During his last year in the Navy, Goff designed and constructed numerous additions and improvements to Camp Parks, near San Francisco. In the Star Bar of Camp Parks, Goff created screening elements of surplus plywood cut with circular openings to subdivide the space. White string, stretched to form warped planes, created an illusion of enclosure overhead, and a cone-shaped wire construction contained balloons animated by a fan below. Plywood, stained with shoe polish, was cut into small tiles for the floor covering.[25] He also designed and built the Camp Parks Chapel, utilizing Quonset hut construction to create a linear vaulted space 200 feet long with massive salmon-colored brick pylons and tinted glass in the arched ends with a reflecting pool at the entry.[26] Matchett Herring Coe of Beaumont, Texas, designed the underwater sculpture in the pool and the cross set in the brick pylon at the entry. The cross was reversible for Catholic or Protestant services and could be replaced with a tablet of Moses for Jewish services.[27] Upon completion, the building won the praise of both Alfonso Iannelli and Erich Mendelsohn. It was soon published in *Architectural Forum* and thereafter appeared in several anthologies on modern architecture. After the war, the church was relocated to the nearby town of San Lorenzo.

Goff also designed a prominent sign for Camp Parks with red letters attached to a thirty-three-foot, six-inch-tall yellow tower. The word "Camp" cantilevered from the top with "Parks" attached to the vertical tower. The first letter of the sign (C) and the last letter (S, which morphed into a hexagon) used Goff's own unique stylized font. As Camp Parks expanded, the sign was relocated from an obscure corner of the facility, where it sat for many years. It was rehabilitated and placed at the main gate with the expectation it would be listed on the National Register of Historic Places.

Some of the buildings constructed in the years following World War II are particularly innovative in Goff's palette of materials. With the passage of time, though, his inclusion of common objects as elements of design began to decline, and to some extent his interest in using unorthodox materials in unique ways also diminished. Development of mirror tile, with its property of reflectivity, served Goff's interest for ornament and murals in designs of subsequent years. His experiences as head of the design department of the glass manufacturer Libbey-Owens-Ford in Chicago and Toledo, Ohio, during the 1930s introduced Goff to a variety of glass products and applications that undoubtedly nurtured his interest in reflective materials. He was also attracted to a striated, translucent glass, manufactured as "Flutex," for use in locations where both natural light and privacy were desired.[28] His experience as chief designer probably influenced his preference for the use of polished plate glass. The optical clarity and distortion-free reflections of plate glass assured an intensified contrast with surrounding opaque materials, especially materials rich in pattern or texture.[29]

The Price Studio of 1956, with subsequent additions in 1966 and 1974, provides examples of the inclusion of ornament as an element of architecture. The design was the largest of Goff's houses built and one of his most significant

Camp Parks entrance sign. Courtesy of Lisa Cipolla, Garrison Cultural Resources Program Manager, USAG Fort Hunter Liggett. Sign rehabilitation by Joseph Scott Murphey, architect. Photographs by Murphey, 2014.

Following spread

Left, Camp Parks Chapel. Plan drawing, OU College of Architecture, Design and Research Center. Courtesy College of Architecture, University of Oklahoma.

Right, Camp Parks Chapel, façade. Photograph by author.

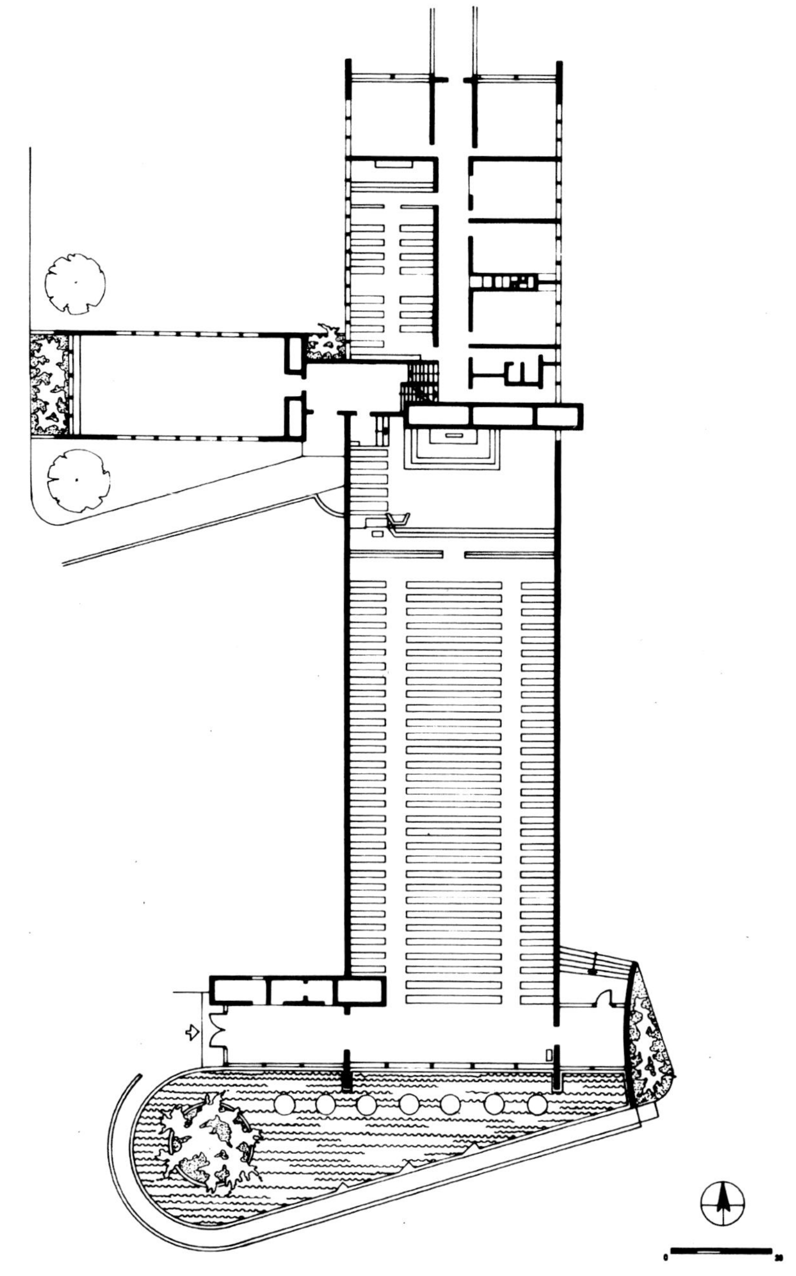

Above, Joe Price House bath. Photograph by George W. Lewis.

Facing page, Ornament on glass in Price House tower, third-floor retreat. Photograph by author.

works. It was also important in another way: since it was built in phases, the house showed great variety in the evolution of Goff's use of materials as ornament over a twenty-year time period. In the original studio Goff designed oversized doors with a large panel of plate glass that provided a surface for an abstract collage with a variety of transparent, translucent, and opaque materials. Goff, in this instance, embraced design principles of both Sullivan and Wright with their insistence that ornament must be an integral part of architecture.

In the 1966 museum addition, built to accommodate Joe Price's growing collection of Japanese art, Goff included a Japanese bath in the basement with an overhead glass aquarium to visually connect the spaces. The walls of the bath had an abstract geometric tile mural that continued on both the floor and ceiling with a color hierarchy of reflective gold and platinum tiles with linear elements of several shades of green with accents of light blue, red, orange, violet, and yellow hues. Goff challenged conventional definitions of walls, floors, and ceiling as discrete elements and created a space where only the force of gravity gives reference. Though bounded by finite dimensions, the extension of the mural walls onto both floor and ceiling gave new meaning to a concept of ornament as a defining component of architecture. It was a quantum leap in design through the creation of a three-dimensional ornament that was a habitable space.

The tower addition of the Price House in 1974, with the use of reflective materials, further reveals Goff's evolution in ornament. In the third floor retreat for Price, sections of opaque walls were covered with a triangular motif of violet-colored mirrors and the ceiling had a rhythm of angled, mirrored Plexiglas panels. The glass walls at the ends of the diamond-shaped plan of the retreat were defined by flamboyant curvilinear murals of colored glass, plastic, sequins, beads, rhinestones, and artificial insemination tubes from his turkey-farmer client in Minnesota. On the back of one of his photographs of the interior Goff made the notation "Kaleidoscope Room."

SYMBOLIC EXPRESSIONS OF NATURE

Expressions of earth, air, fire, and water in Goff's architecture suggest an awareness of the philosophy of Naturalism. The concept of that philosophy originated in the writings of early Greek philosophers in their attempts to explain the phenomena of natural events through empirical investigation. Multiple and differing precedents of expression have been drawn from Naturalism in the world of artistic endeavors. In the literature of the Roman Empire, the poet Horace used images of water—in its forms of both repose and devastation—to shape his lyrical *Odes*.[30] His poetry had a great influence on European poets of the seventeenth and eighteenth centuries. In modern times a counterpart of Naturalism was depicted in Emile Zola's pessimistic novel *The Land*.[31] It was a depressing, deterministic view of the environment as a force shaping human behavior. Yet Frank Lloyd Wright viewed the environment optimistically with his 1920s Hollyhock House defining a continuum of fireplace with a skylight above and a basin of water below. It was a compressed composition of praise for the beauty of nature.

The presence of idealized references to the natural world in Goff's buildings is pervasive, and his commitment to visualization of nature was sustained as a value through the imaginative interpretation of features commonly found in many houses. Provision for natural light from a source above, a place for a fire, the tranquil effect of pools of water, and an expression of elements embedded into the earth, or plane of the floor, were all prominent in Goff's conceptual language. He utilized these features to satisfy basic human needs but also to magnify symbolically our relationship of dependency upon the natural world.[32] These features are expressed as autonomous elements in most of the houses, but in a few centroidal designs, several of them are arrayed on a vertical axis as a source of intense visual stimulation.

The Ledbetter, Ford, Bavinger, Price, and Duncan Houses, with stone or coal rising from the earth, are clear expressions of the world of nature, and stone or coal's inclusion on the interior amplifies this association. Spatially, Goff's best work is rich with references to nature combined with the integration of built-in furniture. In "Notes on Architecture," written in 1957, Goff illuminated his ideas on furniture and suggested there should be no such thing except in buildings already constructed.

> Instead, sleeping, eating, working, storage and other functions should be accommodated or provided for with arrangements integral and part of the entire architectural scheme . . . if the architect has really worked out his scheme organically, he must have by necessity considered what is usually called "furnishing" as fundamental to his scheme, rather than something put in afterwards.[33]

His concept of furnishings integrated with the architectural expression was best realized with the design of the Bavinger House. Here, "rooms" are defined as a series of bowls suspended within the larger, spiraling space. This arrangement of "floating" bowls established a dominant rhythm that, like the enclosing spiraling space, ascends upward while reaching toward a ribbon skylight at the perimeter, resembling the flower of an exotic plant in bloom.

With the Bavinger design Goff challenged and redefined traditional notions of interior space and furnishings and, as such, gave new meaning to Frank Lloyd Wright's axiom of integration of all elements into an organic whole. Nothing can be taken away, nor can anything be added, without compromising the composition. The integration of these elements is so tightly woven that even the presence of a simple plastic chair in front of Gene Bavinger's studio easel seemed curiously out of place.

One of the prominent characteristics of Goff's design language is a reliance on clerestories, skylights, and high windows to introduce natural light into interior spaces and dramatize the presence of the sky above. They would allow the changing position of the sun throughout the day to alter the appearance of interior spaces. By using skylights and clerestories, an interior space might be very bright at one time of the day or quite subdued at another time. They not only provided for modulation of an interior space by natural light but also were a way to reveal a selected feature or focal point.

The use of high windows and clerestories has other architectural implications. Visually it was a way of separating one form from another. Most often it is a roof that is separated from a wall with glass, and by cantilevering the roof over a transparent void, Goff created the illusion that the roof is a detached autonomous plane. His tendency to introduce natural light from above limits views to the exterior. Yet there is a relationship between the plan geometry and the degree of restriction. In houses with centroidal plan geometry, direct views to the exterior are often restricted while those with composite and rectilinear plan geometry tend to be more accommodating to the surrounding views. There are probably several reasons why Goff would limit views to the exterior. Many of his houses were built on standard-sized lots in rather ordinary suburban neighborhoods. Goff believed the close relationship with neighboring houses would compromise privacy if large expanses of glass were used. Goff was also committed philosophically to expressions of nature in a composition, and he would be selective in the landscape features included, or meant to be seen, and those excluded. Through the use of high windows, clerestories, and skylights one could see clouds floating in the sky, the passage of sun and moon, and the tops of trees.

The source of this concept of idealization is probably derived from his interest in Japanese art. In Japanese scroll and screen paintings, elements of the natural world are often depicted abstractly to reveal the essence of a mountain, tree, or flower. Much is omitted, but by selective focus there is the potential for an intensified aesthetic experience and an invitation to speculate on meaning. Japanese art is often imbued with a quality of mystery, which encourages introspection. Similarly, Japanese gardens invite speculation. At the edge of the Zen garden of *Ryoan-ji* in Kyoto, thousands of people from all over the world have sat quietly gazing at a few rugged stones in a bed of carefully raked gravel. It is a composition of extraordinary restraint with a profound sense of mystery. Goff too was acutely aware of the value of mystery in architecture, which is manifest in selected features of his buildings. In the Price Studio, Goff brought natural light into the prismatic volume with a large axial clerestory with an angular hood. The ceiling of the planes defining the hood was covered with small goose feathers individually glued to the surface to slope in the same direction.[34] Suspended planes of translucent plastic strips gently oscillated from air currents within the house. Looking upward to the light one saw delicate white feathers metaphorically transformed into floating white clouds and the oscillating plastic strips into a mysterious sheet of cascading rain. It was a garden of the sky rather than a garden of the earth.

Many houses by Goff feature fireplaces as an element of the living environment. Although a common feature in American domestic architecture, the fireplace in Goff's imagination offered the opportunity to create an artifact signifying an elemental force of the natural world. And the fireplace might provide a rich aesthetic experience as a monumental expression or one of great delicacy. Unlike Wright, who would locate the fireplace as a centralized interior element, Goff was flexible in its placement. In some houses it is located on the exterior wall of the space served, and in other houses it has an interior location as a centralized component. There is no discernable pattern in placement as relates to the plan geometry, except in centroidal designs the fireplace is often at the center of the prismatic volume.

Goff's buildings often feature reflecting pools as an important component of the design on either interior or exterior spaces and occasionally in both locations. Goff may have been inspired by Bruno Taut's 1914 Glass Pavilion at the Cologne, Germany, Werkbund Exhibition with its interior water feature. The glass dome of Taut's pavilion, commissioned by the German glass industry, incorporated a suspended disc inset with a design of colored glass as a mechanical kaleidoscope. The pool below was defined by several connected basins of varying heights that created a series of waterfalls. The interaction of sunlight on the rotating colored glass and the motion of flowing water would have produced a reflective and richly animated spatial experience.[35]

The inclusion of water as a component of composition, either on the interior or exterior or both, is one of Goff's most consistent design elements, seen from the 1928 Riverside Studio to the 1982 Los Angeles Museum.[36] His incorporation of water on the interior reached its zenith with design of the Leidig House in 1946. Conceived as a series of circular pavilions built over a naturalistic pool, the interior of the "Lily Pad" House was a secluded place. Designed for amateur gardener Don Leidig, the design expanded Goff's ideas of architectural composition based on dualities of isolated and independent geometric components arrayed in a naturalistic and free-form collage of plants and water. Two undulating buff-colored brick walls with a linear curving ribbon skylight above, set on the side lot lines, defined boundaries at the edges. Between the two walls, and extending to both front and rear, were a series of shallow connected lily pools that would be supplied by water from a well on the property to create the effect of a flowing stream. The pools and the planted areas of trees and shrubs all had free-form edges in counterpoint to the undulating rhythm of the masonry walls. This created a sensuous, curvilinear composition of natural elements, with pink glass walls angled at the front and curved around a mature Japanese cherry tree at the rear. A meandering deck of variable-width wood, providing another distinctive irregular rhythm, was raised slightly above water level to connect a series of circular pavilions. As David G. De Long observed, the pavilions all had very discrete functions and the point of entry into each was fixed.[37] One pavilion was for sleeping; another accommodated bathroom and dressing functions; others were for dining and cooking, with a larger pavilion serving as a gathering space. The pavilion walls varied from opaque to folding screens that might be either open or closed; other pavilions were open platforms with low walls. All had a high circular roof, with a continuous clerestory raised above the primary roof to enclose a collage of the natural world.

The structural system supporting the roof of the Leidig design was equally

distinctive. The central stems in each pavilion were extended as concrete columns to support a tapered beam high above the primary roof. Anchored to the beam were a series of cables connected to the front and rear edges of the overhanging roof. Although the beam above the roof looks like an abstract sculpture with a vaguely animalistic presence as if poised for flight, its profile and direction is a logical structural response. The beam projects upward so as to maintain an appropriate angle for support of the cables as the distance from beam to roof edge increases. The suspended roof would allow uninterrupted views over the garden to the hills beyond. The broad, flat plane of the roof, with a decorative circular motif forming a trellis at the fascia, much like the lily pads

Don Leidig House, Hayward, California, 1946. Project model of exterior. Bruce Goff Archive, Ryerson & Burnham Archives, Art Institute of Chicago.

Don Leidig House site plan. Bruce Goff Archive, Ryerson & Burnham Archives, Art Institute of Chicago.

in the pools of water below, would appear to float in space as it cantilevered over the glass walls below.

Although it remained unbuilt, Goff's proposal for the house rivals C. N. Ledoux's conceptualization of *Inspector's House at the Source of the River Loue* 170 years earlier. In the Ledoux design, with the river flowing through the building and emerging from a circular opening in the façade as a waterfall, the river flow would have been amplified as a dynamic and thunderous force of nature. In the Leidig design Goff proposed using water as a serene and placid element, one that was subdued and reflective. With the pavilions for everyday living raised slightly above water level and cantilevered from a central stem, they had a quality of lightness and an appearance of floating. The Leidig design clearly established Goff's theoretical posture on the role of nature in architectural expression. His conceptualization of the open plan, defined by a series of geometric pavilions juxtaposed against a collage of nature, represents both a synthesis and a significantly individual interpretation of one of the major themes of twentieth-century architecture.

Goff's use of water as an element of design reflects several ideals. It was a way of affirming his conviction that architecture embraces the world of nature. Water has a property of reflectivity, which appealed to Goff. Passage as a journey through space was also a generalized theme Goff explored periodically throughout his career, and a sequence of movement that included water suggested a veiled illusion of floating in a dreamworld like that created in the music of Debussy.

◬

The absence of similar appearance among his buildings gives Bruce Goff's work its distinctive character. His approach to design radically differed from some of his prominent contemporaries—Mies van der Rohe, Walter Gropius, and Le Corbusier—who believed that a predictable identity reflected the ideals of modern society. Goff's buildings do not look alike because of his conviction that they should not. His architectural diversity reflects a belief in solving each individual problem free of any regard for the current fashion of others—or his own previous work. His objective logic and subjective response toward composition, as a duality of reality and imagination, defines a continuity of conceptualization in design.

Goff's finest work represents a skillful integration of form and space with a pervasive sense of unity. He had unique visions of combining one component with another and transforming them, as individual elements, into a new entity rich with meaning. It was not simply the inclusion of a number of separate ideas that gave a quality of originality to a particular building, but rather it was the way he related various parts together to infuse a design with beauty and mystery. His most exemplary works in this regard—the 1974 Ford House, the 1968 Nicol House, and most of all, the museum addition to the Price Studio—were yet to come when in 1946 Goff accepted an invitation to teach architecture at the University of Oklahoma. But the foundations of the language of conceptualization had been set in his early years and during the Depression and World War II. From 1940, with design of the Unseth House, to the 1946 proposal for the Leidig House, a remarkable transformation in Goff's aesthetic values occurred. The earlier design initiated a conceptualization derivative from an ideal of thematic geometric development. The latter represented a creation of dualities—of a man-made and natural world, of delicacy and subtlety—as one of the most imaginative conceptualizations in the history of architecture. It is also of particular importance in Goff's career, for it established a clear pattern of both diversity and continuity in work that followed.

It was the most stimulating experience of my life and I learned that Bruce Goff was the best teacher because he was a perpetual student, and that his function was not only to teach but to inspire.

ROBERT OVERSTREET

Insist on yourself; never imitate.

RALPH WALDO EMERSON

4

TEACHING ORGANIC ARCHITECTURE

When Bruce Goff returned to Oklahoma in 1947 at age forty-three, he had more than thirty years' experience in architecture, notable accomplishments, and clear ideas about the process of design. He came to the University of Oklahoma School of Architecture during a period of expansion following the end of World War II. With few students and only three architecture faculty members in 1945, the school, anticipating growth, was recruiting new faculty. San Francisco architect Fred Langhorst, who had studied with Frank Lloyd Wright at Taliesin, recommended Goff for one of these positions.

Goff was contacted by architecture professor Henry Kamphoefner and by OU President George L. Cross to determine his interest in returning to Oklahoma to teach.[1] Goff's letter of response to Cross was enthusiastic, and he commented that teaching was "not just a job . . . but almost a religion."[2] His lack of academic credentials, however, created some dissension among university administrators.[3] In response, Langhorst, Alphonso Iannelli, and the director of the Chicago Academy of Fine Arts, Ruth Ford, sent letters of recommendation for Goff. Langhorst pointed out that neither Mies van der Rohe at Illinois Institute of Technology, Walter Gropius at Harvard, or Harwell Hamilton Harris at the University of Texas had academic credentials.[4] Richard Kuhlman, a newly appointed professor serving as department chair, wrote to Cross, "There is not a school in the United States that would not consider him a distinguished addition to its staff."[5] Frank Lloyd Wright wrote a brief but succinct letter, stating that Goff was "one of the most talented members of the group of young architects devoted to an indigenous architecture for America."[6] President Cross decided that professional accomplishments were more important than degrees and offered Goff a base salary of $4,800 for a nine-month appointment beginning January 15, 1947.[7] Goff would also receive additional compensation for a summer appointment and could continue his architectural practice. Goff came to OU as one of the highest-paid professors of his time and was appointed chairman of the School of Architecture by OU regents on June 11, 1947, to be effective in September.[8]

Kamphoefner, who had taught at OU since 1937, and Joseph Smay, who had served in the Army during the war, were the only tenured faculty. Kamphoefner, a disciple of modernism, left OU in 1948 to become the dean of architecture at North Carolina State University. Several other younger faculty who had short-term appointments at OU followed him. Upon their departure the composition of the faculty began to change under Goff's leadership, with several significant appointments of individuals identified with organic architecture. In 1949 William S. Burgett left his architectural practice in Hawaii to teach at OU. An admirer of Frank Lloyd Wright and a friend of H. H. Harris, R. M. Schindler, and John Lautner, Burgett was predisposed to the traditions of organic architecture. Mendel Glickman, Wright's structural engineer who worked on projects such as the Johnson Wax Factory, Fallingwater, and the Guggenheim Museum, also came to OU. Glickman taught structures from the standpoint of applied design with minimal focus on theory. In 1949 Elizabeth Mock was appointed to teach history and serve as librarian for the School of Architecture.

Mock, who studied at Taliesin with Wright, authored *Built in the U.S.A.* and *The Architecture of Bridges*, both published by the Museum of Modern Art. William Oglesby joined the faculty to teach Interior Design and Basic Design. Philip B. Welch was at OU as a graduate student and instructor from 1950 to 1953. Welch, an exceptional photographer and enthusiastic studio teacher, was greatly appreciated by the students. In 1951 E. Fay Jones and J. Palmer Boggs joined the faculty. Jones left OU in 1953 to return to his native state and teach at the University of Arkansas, where he also developed a successful practice. Boggs developed a close working relationship with Goff as his structural consultant. Norman L. Byrd and William H. Wilson, an OU alumnus, were also appointed to the faculty during Goff's tenure, and both of them, advocates of organic architecture, worked on Goff's architectural projects at various times. Shizuo Oka, an alumnus and master craftsman in Japanese carpentry, returned during Goff's tenure to teach design studios.

In addition, several young OU graduates, including Joseph Wythe and Arthur Kohara, had short-term appointments. Jack Golden, a fifth-year student, taught Basic Design upon returning to OU after service in the Army. Gail Thomas, Brandon Griffith, and Fred Shellabarger, an admirer of Wright, were appointed to the faculty in 1955.[9] Jerri Hodges, an undergraduate student in philosophy, was Goff's administrative assistant and became a loyal friend for the rest of his life. With this group Goff had a strong supporting cast who were sympathetic to organic architecture and contributed to the direction of the school. The distinguished architects Goff invited to speak at the school also revealed his commitment to organic expression. Frank Lloyd Wright came several times as did Erich Mendelsohn. Lloyd Wright, Richard Neutra, and Alphonso Iannelli also gave lectures.

The school reflected Goff's philosophy of freedom of self-expression, with a pedagogical premise that all individuals had a potential for creativity. The goal was to create a nurturing environment that might help students discover their own potential. As Goff wrote to a prospective applicant, John Lieneweber, "In developing our student's creative ability, we try to give them the necessary means to express themselves [technically] . . . and, to help them find their own aesthetic direction."[10] Goff believed that most schools of architecture were engaged in a "new eclecticism," which allowed them to indiscriminately appropriate ideas from contemporary masters like Mies van der Rohe, Le Corbusier, and Frank Lloyd Wright. It became, in many schools, "the fashion to clan together into one of these three camps, each feeling the other is insane or unclean," as Goff wrote.[11] Such education, Goff believed, could only lead to lifeless imitation. It was critical to distinguish between inspiration, influence, and imitation. Great works of the past, as well as nature, might inspire or influence a design, but the underlying principles must be understood and assimilated to produce an authentic, nonimitative work. "We are not interested in producing disciples of any man but rather in developing individuals with sound principles," Goff declared, and the OU School of Architecture followed suit.[12]

Goff was particularly disdainful of the popular International Style emerging in America during the postwar years of the late 1940s and 1950s. In his view, its expressions were derivative of a continuum of limiting and rigid design principles. Goff was critical of an architecture that relied solely on the expression of a glass wall with an exposed structural grid to sustain visual interest. A glass box, Goff believed, offered only a cold image of anonymity. Furthermore, glass boxes were the same everywhere, with little relationship to specific locations. Finally, they were invariably devoid of any emotional content and diversity of expression that might convey an association with a particular environment or feelings of aspiration.

Goff, however, appreciated the early work of Mies van der Rohe, especially his Barcelona Pavilion, and referred to him as a "master of proportion" in his lectures. Goff's occasional sly reference to glass boxes as "Miesburgers" was not an intended slander of Mies but of his imitators and the presence of so many "glass boxes" throughout America. His comment, which would always bring laughter from an appreciative audience, was analogous to his reference to tract housing in the emerging post–World War II suburbs as "ranchburgers." Like the glass boxes, they were ubiquitous.

Goff was also adamant in his conviction that design derived from predetermined forms was artificial and the antithesis of organic architecture. The *process* of design was critical: to produce imaginative architecture, a composition must grow from a creative impulse from within one's self. This belief was closely related to his insistence on students' individual creative development, and as Goff stated proudly to Lieneweber, "We have the most unusual School of Architecture in the world because here we endeavor to bring ideas out of our students . . . we have no desire to make them little imitations of anyone of the past or present."[13] In a similar vein, Goff assured a prospective faculty member that "we preach no dogma and feel it is just as bad to be modern eclectics as old."[14] Nor did Goff encourage students to imitate him. In response to a 1951 letter from Douglas Haskell, editor of *Architectural Forum*, who sought identification of promising students and recent graduates, Goff responded with the names of twelve individuals with the assurance there wasn't a "little Bruce Goff" among them.[15]

These convictions about individual freedom were ironclad. A visitor to the school once asked Goff how the faculty managed to get such original work from the students. Goff replied, "We leave them alone."[16] He said essentially the same thing when he responded to the father of Robert Faust, a Tulane architecture student who had visited OU and was thinking of transferring. Goff had seen Robert's Tulane drawings and called them "evidence of a real talent but I am afraid that they show signs of interference by teachers."[17] Goff strongly encouraged Faust's father to send his son to OU, as "continuing in his present situation would either lead to open rebellion or conforming at his own expense and would be wasting time for him."[18] In a similar vein, Goff responded to a student in Ecuador who had dropped out of school because of conflicts with faculty over their "silly rules."[19] Goff wrote, "We are trying here . . . to do away with the 'silly rules' . . . and we are striving to perfect a school where each individual has a chance to develop his own creative direction in architecture."[20]

The ambiguity of design was an ever-present issue for the students. They were well aware of Goff's familiar adage: "You can do anything you want to do as long as it is good. There is no *right* solution."[21] They had the freedom to choose, but how did they know what to choose? Goff and other faculty members urged students to trust their intuition. One's initial ideas were usually the best because they were uniquely their own. As an extension of Wright's belief in the "democracy" of architecture, Goff insisted that students had "the right to have their own ideas."[22] Yet they were also encouraged to be curious, try new things, and keep an open mind in conceptualization. No form, color, or texture should be taboo. But as the seed of an idea developed, they should also recognize and understand the order within that idea. The only way one could achieve originality in a design, and thus the potential for richness and variety of expression, was by a critical understanding: order depended upon the disciplined rejection of all that was not true to the idea. It was through this process of discovery that one arrived at an honest expression. This was the meaning of Goff's oft-used statement of design as "discipline in freedom." Ultimately, creativity could only be achieved through intuition, rational thought, and disposing of ideas that did not sustain the order of the initial concept.

The curriculum and pedagogy of the school, accredited by the National Architectural Accrediting Board (NAAB) in 1952,[23] was congruent in many respects with current theories of architectural education in American universities. Goff, and other studio faculty, expected students to address the critical issues of site and environmental response, circulation and functional relationships, structural integrity and materiality, and the formal and spatial composition of their design projects. All required intensive and rational thought during the design process. By the late 1940s most schools had adopted the Harvard model of Walter Gropius with a rejection of historical precedent and theory while emphasizing creativity. Yet the student work produced in many schools tended to be pale imitations of the International Style. Students at OU had the freedom to pursue their own individual expression in a nurturing environment. In 1955 two architecture professors from Tulane University visited OU "to get ideas on how to rejuvenate their school, at the suggestion of the Accreditation Board."[24]

Despite his strong influence upon students' creative development and instructors' teaching philosophies, Goff actually spent little time in the design studio. He believed the studio was the domain of the students, whose ideas he would seldom question. Robert Faust, who transferred from Tulane and graduated from OU in 1956, recalled that he never received a critique from Goff during the design process with one exception: Goff once suggested he extend the form of a curved element in a particular design "to complete the curve."[25] Moreover, Goff would not critique students' work until it was finished. The critiques were then nearly always positive, and he would have something good to say about even the weakest design. The placement of student projects in the display space, however, indirectly revealed his evaluation. There was an unspoken hierarchy within the gallery, with the best works posted in one of several favored independent locations as focal points, and other work displayed in groups along a linear wall. The display thus gave clear indication of both expectations and a sense of direction.

Goff did, however, take advantage of opportunities to publicize the OU School of Architecture, and the cause of organic architectural education, through exhibits of student work in museums and at other universities. The April 1950 biennial meeting of the VII Congreso Panamericano de Arquitectos (Pan-American Congress of Architects) in Havana, Cuba, provided international exposure for both Goff and the school. The U.S. entries to the Congreso Panamericano, organized by the Division of Pan-American Affairs of the American Institute of Architects, focused primarily on contemporary buildings by significant architects and on schools of architecture in the Americas. OU was one of only ten architecture schools throughout the country invited to submit student projects that represented all levels of design studios.[26] Included in the exhibition was a fifth-year project by Blaine Imel, of a Center for Radio, Television, Theater and Music, portrayed as a collage of diverse elliptical forms. Goff himself submitted drawings and photographs of the Leidig House and the Crystal Chapel. A preview exhibition and reception of a sampling of work was held at the AIA headquarters in Washington, D.C. Goff received word that "Oklahoma's panels looked wonderful and stopped the crowd."[27] Goff later wrote to Imel that the OU School of Architecture "carried away top honors."[28]

Even with these honors, both Goff and the School of Architecture gained as many opponents as adherents, with other architects and teachers of architecture offering praise or criticism. Philip Johnson considered Goff one of the ten best architects in America by inclusion on "his list of heroes."[29] But Walter Gropius, head of the Graduate School of Design at Harvard, was "too busy" to come to Goff's lecture when he spoke there.[30] Pietro Belluschi from MIT did attend the Harvard lecture, telling Goff he was writing a book on religious architecture. He believed that Goff, Frank Lloyd Wright, and Erich Mendelsohn were the only three living architects who had "captured the spiritual quality of religion in their work."[31] Yet Louis Kahn angrily denounced Goff's buildings as "an architecture of coke bottles and old locomotive parts."[32] Frank Lloyd Wright said of the school during his visit of 1952, "I myself . . . believed the function of a university to be to awaken the sleepers and the School of Architecture at the University of Oklahoma has encouraged that belief by its teachings. This is already well-established by its own young architect's work which has done more to put Oklahoma in the front rank of educational portraits than anything else it can show."[33] When Philip Welch, a former OU faculty member, gave a slide show of OU student work at the University of California at Berkeley, "The results were a little short of an explosion, with tremendous resistance by most of [the] faculty and upperclassmen with equal receptance [*sic*] by many of the beginning students."[34] Similarly, at a talk in 1968 at Arizona State University two-thirds of the architecture faculty did not attend Goff's lecture.[35] Yet Eero

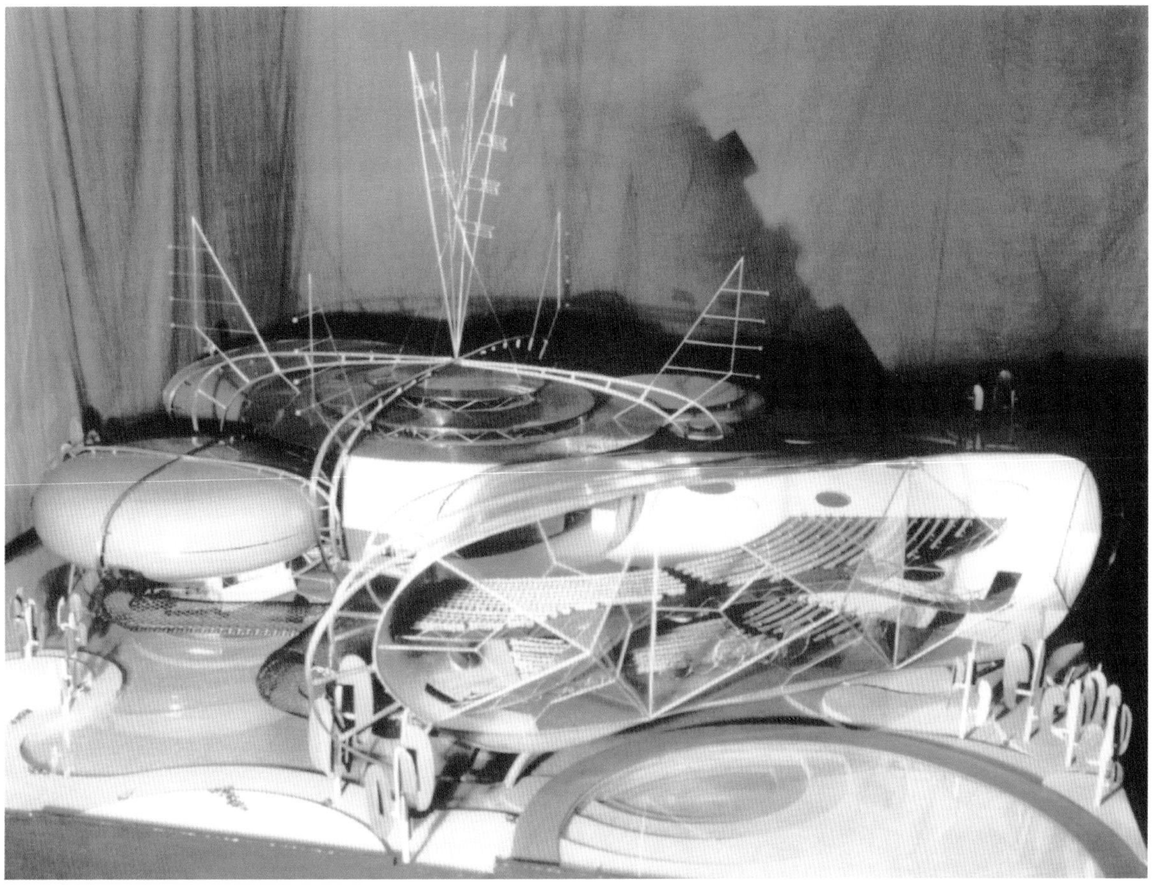

Fifth-year studio project by Blaine Imel. Photograph by Imel.

Saarinen complimented Goff for the fine student work that was being done at the OU School of Architecture.[36] But several years after Goff left the university, a partner in a prominent Tulsa firm still declared, "We will not hire an OU graduate as long as Bruce Goff has any influence there."[37] During one of his several visits to the school, Erich Mendelsohn told the students:

> I had the good fortune to see your work . . . I want to congratulate you, first that the leader of your school is my friend, the brilliant Bruce Goff. Second, congratulate you on your teachers . . . and congratulate you, yourselves that you can work in this school. Because I have seen in my long life many schools of architecture, not only in this country but all over the world. I think it is very fortunate for you to be studying in this School of Architecture.[38]

The exhibition of OU student work at other schools within the region provoked very mixed reactions. John J. Schultz, a 1950 OU graduate who was teaching architecture at Kansas State University, sent Goff a telegram when OU student work was exhibited there in May of 1952:

> academists baffled, hopefuls inspired, doubters convinced, majority pleased, some mad, all upset, many transferring.[39]

Nine architecture students at Kansas State transferred to OU that same year.[40] By 1953 only about one-half of the OU architecture students were native Oklahomans. The others were from forty other states and sixteen countries. Many of them, like Robert Faust, were dissatisfied transfer students. James Gresham later articulated his own dilemma. After two years in the architecture program at the University of Michigan, Gresham transferred to OU in 1949. With nearly all of the Michigan design faculty recent graduates of the Illinois Institute of Technology, they were "true believers that allowed no deviation from the systems Mies [van der Rohe] had pioneered." Gresham characterized his next four years at OU as "nirvana, no constraints, no shibboleths."[41]

Literature on modern architecture during the late 1940s and early 1950s was scant. Although several architectural journals were available, the contemporary work that they published was largely derivative of the International Style. The standard reference book was Siegfried Giedion's *Space, Time and Architecture* with a focus on the development of European modernism as a rational extension of nineteenth-century structural engineering. Giedion built his case on a litany of familiar names—Mies, Le Corbusier, Gropius, and Alvar Aalto—all individuals prominently associated with the emergence of "modernism."[42] Yet there are curious omissions that betray Giedion's bias. For example, there is not a single reference in the book to Gaudí, whom Goff frequently referred to as the "world's greatest architect." The Viennese architect Josef Hoffmann is barely acknowledged, and his work is not illustrated. Giedion abruptly dismisses Expressionism with the comment, "The expressionist influence could not be a healthy one or perform any service for architecture." His characterization of some who "abandoned themselves to a romantic mysticism . . . or built concrete towers as placid as jellyfish" would seem to be a veiled attack on Erich Mendelsohn's Einstein Tower.[43]

Beyond the standard pedagogy of Siegfried Giedion's work, OU students knew about other then-obscure sources because of Goff, who collected books on architecture and art from Europe and Japan. A primary way to achieve inspiration, Goff felt, was through exposure to the other arts. Although an architect must concentrate his energy on his own medium, Goff believed that a knowledge of creativity in other disciplines might serve as "inspiration . . . which can be . . . absorbed to enrich his own work." Such assimilated experiences might enhance one's capacity for a wider range of feeling and allow one to "live through all his senses to really experience life and art and to live and work as one . . . as part of something."[44] He introduced his students to his interests, and shared his remarkable library with them. His personal collection included an extensive array of books on architecture, especially on Wright, Japanese art, abstract European art, and composers whose music inspired him. He also had a collection of the works of French Symbolist poets and artists. Herb Greene recalled that Goff had shown him poetry books of Baudelaire and Rimbaud and the mysterious fantasy drawings of Redon.[45] Goff also arranged for Japanese print dealers to visit the school periodically, and many of the students bought reproductions as prized possessions.

Goff nurtured students' appetite for "aesthetic food" with his own enthusiasm and knowledge of music, painting, sculpture, film, and Japanese art. The music he liked best—particularly Debussy—paralleled his commitment to design with "the idea of the composition growing from the inside out and . . . disciplined into an organic whole that had its own order."[46] Goff shared both his music and ideas on the relationship to architecture with his students, and scheduled extracurricular weekly sessions for listening to music. During the course of an evening session Goff would talk about the music they would hear, particularly the structure and modulations of the composition. He would then turn the lights off and the volume up. On one occasion, when Goff was not present, the music session was interrupted by campus police. An officer burst through the door into the darkened room demanding to know: "What's going on here?" One of the students explained they were just listening to music. The officer, producing a small notebook, wanted their names. The first to respond said he was Claude Debussy and another said he was Arnold Schoenberg. All the students present identified themselves as prominent composers, but they had to spell their fictitious names for the policeman. Jerri Bonebrake (née Hodges) identified herself as Edith Piaf. The officer then left with the admonition to "leave the lights turned on."[47]

FROZEN MUSIC AND COMPOSITIONS

Early in his career, Goff had been attracted to the notion of architecture as "frozen music," a concept advanced initially by both Schelling and Goethe. Goff later rejected that idea as a static concept, recognizing that music involves assimilation through the passage of time while architecture is experienced by movement through space. Yet there were appreciable similarities between the two. Both involved constant changing, and, as Goff wrote, both architecture and music possessed "the elements of invention, rhythm, proportion, balance, scale, orchestration of the media, counterpoint, consonance, dissonance, texture, incident and ornament, all as felt by the artist and composed into an ordered whole."[48] Music, Goff believed, pointed out some of the basic concepts of composition more clearly than architecture. He subsequently developed an advanced design studio course in which he assigned short interpretive projects based on specific design principles, many of which used music terminology.

Goff's abstract paintings, which he referred to as "compositions," were another source of admiration by the students, their diverse expressions rich in color, form, and pattern. In one of his paintings there is a suggestion of a deep ocean environment with a pair of exotic sea creatures with bulging, saclike anatomy. The creatures are vibrant with energy and affirm their presence in a floating miasma. Adjacent is an ominous dark creature with a curved hooklike appendage, a menacing form that appears to have devoured two of the smaller sea creatures or absorbed them by some mysterious process. The two forms are separated by a triangular shaft suggesting a path receding in perspective to a world above. The central creature is visually magnetic with its electrified but ambiguous halo. Is the halo an expression of fright? Or a display of power? The tension is magnified by the dialogue of a horizontal tubular form at the top with a bulging, elliptical form below. Together they push the creatures toward an inevitable conflict as an expression of the malevolent power of nature.

Goff's imagery in his paintings, with their diverse expressions and magnificent craftsmanship, had a great influence on the students. Robert Overstreet, one of his students, commented that Goff's paintings "had music, evoked feelings, emotions, wonder and inspiration." They displayed the same principles of design that Goff discussed in his Architecture Studio. With his paintings students sensed the far-ranging possibilities of freedom in design and the opportunities for creativity through hard work and the process of discovery by doing.

"Composition" was also a term that Goff used in his extensive discussions of architecture. He characterized the meaning of composition as the fusion of all the elements—scale, proportion, rhythm, color, texture, and pattern—that comprise a design. Another of the courses he taught was the Basic Design Studio for beginning students. It was also a required course for transfer students, and the location of that studio, adjacent to his office, signified the importance Goff attached to initial learning. With an introduction of point, line, and plane, Goff encouraged students to follow their intuition and explore the many possibilities of variation. Points, for instance, might vary in size or shape and assume any direction or pattern in the creation of original interpretations. The same ideal of freedom in design determined his discussion of lines and

Facing page, Painting by Goff featuring sea creature–like shapes, from portfolio. College of Architecture Library, University of Oklahoma.

Left, Student painting in Goff's Basic Design studio class.

planes as elements of composition. With the synthesis of these basic concepts, combined with the introduction of overlapping elements, texture, and contrast, led to discovery of the potential of visual artistry. The introduction of color, in both dry and wet mediums, expanded the realization for creative solutions. By the end of the first semester, with Goff's emphasis on composition, students were producing remarkably sophisticated abstract two-dimensional designs.

In 1948, Goff initiated a film series of avant-garde and experimental European films from the Museum of Modern Art's Film Library. Shown on Saturday mornings at the Boomer Theater near the OU campus, the inaugural series included the expressionistic film *The Cabinet of Dr. Caligari,* with its abstract architectonic and sculptural sets, several films by the Surrealist artists

Man Ray, Marcel Duchamp, and Salvador Dalí, and films by directors Hans Richter and Fritz Lang. The film series continued throughout Goff's tenure at OU and for several years thereafter.

The physical environment of the school also contributed to Goff's vision of design education. During the early years of Goff's tenure, the School of Architecture occupied Building #604, a surplus barracks on the so-called North Campus.[49] Constructed for a Naval Aviation School during World War II, these buildings were donated by the federal government to the university in 1946. Separated from the main campus by several miles, the site posed logistic hardships for students who had to commute for nonarchitecture courses. The absence of other distractions, though, offset those difficulties and gave students a quiet, secluded place to work. With the help of his students, Goff remodeled the barracks by placing black fiberboard on the walls for exhibitions and setting up linear compositions of white string to define a series of warped planes at the ceiling. At the end of the hall was Goff's office, marked by a beaded curtain for a door. With these simple abstract touches, an austere environment was transformed into an animated and lively space.

When the school moved back to the main campus, it was assigned to the unpopular yet spacious area beneath the north end of the football stadium. Enthusiastic over additional space to accommodate a growing student body, Goff accepted the challenge the site posed and developed studio space, classrooms, and a gallery where none existed. The exhibition gallery formed an important facet of successful design education, Goff believed. Established in a wide section of a corridor, the faculty ensured that good student work was always on display and was frequently rotated. Although there were occasional concerns that the linear spatial arrangement of studios—like boxcars strung together, with basic design at one end and advanced design at the other—discouraged interaction between beginning and advanced students, faculty efforts to maintain rotating exhibits provided a rich and stimulating environment of ideas. Students could look carefully at projects as a source of inspiration and learn drawing and rendering techniques from one another.

Many of the students during the late 1940s were veterans whose idealism resonated with Goff's optimistic message of design freedom. He taught informally but his lectures were well organized. As he lectured, he would refer to notes written on a partial strip of rolled-up adding machine tape held inconspicuously in his left hand. He could then advance the roll with the slightest of movement of his thumb.[50] Goff was always accessible to students and often engaged them with informal discussions, frequently over lunch at nearby restaurants or during coffee breaks in the Student Union. Though soft-spoken, his capacity to talk for hours was legendary and it was an ability he only shared with Bucky Fuller; the difference is that Goff always made sense. He was quite articulate and spoke in simple declarative English. His train of thought "was extremely ordered and uncluttered, but packed, and he must have had something very close to total recall."[51] His persona was that of a centered individual who projected great confidence in the imagination's potential to create original and authentic work. Even his choice of clothes reflected his countenance: he was always immaculately dressed in a cardigan jacket, often without lapels and of varied colors, paired with slacks and patterned shirts or turtlenecks. He never wore a necktie but occasionally sported a bolo tie. His informal relationship with students established a bond of reciprocal respect and caring. Students who were particularly close to Goff would select a fabric and have a shirt made for him.[52] Similarly, Goff's empathy for the everyday life of students was revealed by his purchase of a winter coat for a student who had none.[53]

ARCHITECTURE 273[54]

One of the courses Goff developed and consistently taught was a fourth-year studio, "Elements of Design," listed as Architecture 273 in the curriculum. The course featured reading assignments of Debussy's "Monsieur Croche, the Dilettante Hater" and Gertrude Stein's "Composition as Explanation" and was defined by a series of design projects usually of one week in duration in which they explored a particular formal aspect of architecture without regard to function. These included the concepts of rhythm; opacity, translucency, and transparency; modulation; balance; theme, variation, and development; incident, terminal, and climax; site relationships; orchestration of materials; ornament; and scale. Goff emphasized that the projects provided both an opportunity to reevaluate the principles of design and to explore those principles individually as a means to learn to criticize one's own work.

Students were asked to prepare a graphic illustration of their own interpretation of each assignment. There was no formula or rules, nor was the project an end in itself. It was simply a time to explore, to reflect, and to learn to use these elements subconsciously. Students were given great freedom in defining the architectural character of each of the projects. Goff encouraged them to stretch their creativity and explore mobile or free forms in addition to geometric forms. "All designs," as Goff said, "even in nature are geometric, mobile or a composite of both. But there must be a reason for the choices you make."

Goff's criticism of the state of architecture extended to his teaching of architecture. In his introductory lecture Goff characterized the essential differences between *organic* and *inorganic* as opposite principles of design. They were like "two religions that were at war with one another." The inorganic (or *synthetic*, as he often said) design process started with preconceived ideas and worked toward a perfection of form. Goff cited the Farnsworth House by Mies van der Rohe as an example of inorganic design, obliquely attacking Mies's well-known epigram, "Less is more," with his own: "Not much isn't enough."

Goff insisted that an organic process of design did not rely on preconceived ideas. He often said that great architecture began with a creative impulse growing outward, through the nature of materials, as directed and ordered by a creative will. Although Goff championed the cause of organic design, he was not dogmatic. He believed that both designs represented the extremes of a continuum and that a design might have elements of both. He made the analogy between simplicity and complexity and suggested that the two concepts could coexist in a building. He also criticized Louis Sullivan, in his search for a rule so broad that it would admit no exception, as being misguided because such a rule did not exist. There were always exceptions.

RHYTHM

Goff gave slide-illustrated lectures on each assignment, drawing from his own vast knowledge of architecture. Invariably he would use analogies to music and often played selections in class to illustrate the relationship to architecture. Rhythm, Goff explained, was present in any building, whether it had organic or synthetic design. It was "the pulse of a composition." But there could be great variations in rhythms. In Greek architecture, he said, there were very subtle changes to correct optical illusions of regular rhythm with an "accelerated rhythm," the columns placed closer together as they approached the corners. Though the concept of regular rhythm was particularly apparent in Wright's work, Goff believed there were many other forms of rhythm. He introduced the musical concept of counterpoint, in which more than one rhythm appeared at the same time. Each existed independently but "would come together at some point" in the composition. Goff suggested there were still other forms of rhythm in music that had application to architecture, such as overlapping, alternate, and parallel rhythms. Even arrhythmic composition, such as the complex music of Bartók and the subtle designs of Gaudí, was possible. Goff also told a story about composer Igor Stravinsky, who, upon hearing a composition of African drummers, rich with overlapping rhythms and counterpoint, said he felt like a schoolboy in his own understanding of music.

Goff continued his discussion on rhythm in music to further illuminate its relationship to architecture. As part of his lecture, he played selected recordings to illustrate the principles of different varieties of rhythm. He played a passage from Debussy's *La Mer* as an example of free-flowing rhythm with modulated changes, and Ravel's *Boléro* with its "steady crescendo build-up of rhythm which breaks down to an irregular rhythm." He played and discussed the "displaced rhythmic blocks" of Stravinsky's *Rite of Spring*, one section's free-flowing rhythm followed by a movement of dominant regular rhythm and then one of irregular rhythm with abrupt changes within a measure. He played Schoenberg's *Serenade*, with its "spasmodic, fragmented and jerky" rhythmic patterns. Goff introduced the concept of rhythmic counterpoint by playing Bartók's Concerto no. 2, a piece with a "dynamic drive of rhythmic fragments repeated irregularly," and Edgar Varèse's *Improvisation for Thirteen Percussion Players* to illustrate a different interpretation of the same idea. Goff concluded this lecture by contrasting the rhythms of music, which were "becoming much more complex and free" while architecture "[seems to] have rigor mortis when it comes to rhythm. We have an opportunity, a challenge, when architecture is freed from being static. We can not only have free forms but free rhythms, which is one of the next big steps in architecture."

OPACITY, TRANSLUCENCY, AND TRANSPARENCY

The objective of this project was to consider light as a primary element of design. The intent was both to explore the effect of light and also to reexamine the meaning of "translucency." Goff used a rather conventional interpretation of the meaning of opacity and transparency: opaque meant a solid form, and transparent meant an invisible form. One of the meanings of translucent was also obvious: a translucent material would allow light but restrict sight. The effect of transparency, realized in the buildings of Perret, was in creating a sense of delicacy to the innovative structure. Wright's Johnson Wax Building provided another example of translucency, with its walls of glass tubing laid horizontally. Goff then referred to Wright's drafting room at Taliesin West as an example of the three concepts' overlap. The opaque stone and concrete base, the translucent white canvas roof, and the transparent small windows created great contrast with the interior but provided a soft uniform light with the canvas's diffusion of the hot Arizona sun.

The other meaning of translucency, Goff said, was one of partial visibility through an opaque mass, much like seeing patches of sky between the leaves of a tree. The use of perforated stone grilles with buildings in India combines

Design of "Regular and Irregular Rhythm," by Howard Alan, a member of Goff's Architecture 273 Design Studio. Color pencil drawing. Photograph by Alan.

mass and translucency. Goff suggested that opaque buildings with a veneer of glazed tile to both reflect sunlight and visually lighten the mass with the use of color, such as buildings in Persia (Iran), evoke a *feeling* of translucency when combined with pools of water. Similarly, the golden domes of the temples of Siam (Thailand) have a high degree of reflectivity, which mitigates their opaque mass and creates an illusion of translucency. Even completely transparent materials, such as plate glass, could change radically depending on the position of the sun. Glass surfaces can at times appear opaque or as reflective as a mirror.

MODULATION

In music the concept of modulation refers to the transition from one key to another. Goff applied this notion to architecture with his conviction that the way one made a transition from one idea to another, or from one plane or surface to another, was an important aspect of design. The concern, Goff said, was to relate "the parts together in a plastic sense . . . together in continuity." Modulation in architecture, could thus pertain to form, color, texture, scale, or the profile of the building against the earth or sky, and could be smooth or abrupt. Goff cited Art Nouveau as an example of smooth, delicate, and gradual modulation of form. The use of "desert crete"—made of large stones from the site that were then placed in concrete walls—as a primary material in Wright's Taliesin West established a strong sense of modulation of the buildings with the site. By contrast, Goff said, Le Corbusier's Villa Savoy provided an example of abrupt modulation with the earth. Pools of water could modulate a building with the ground plane through their reflection, as in Eero Saarinen's MIT chapel or the moats surrounding British castles. Similarly, the battlements on castle parapets provided a rhythmic modulation with the sky.

One of Goff's favorite examples of the potential for modulation was Louis Sullivan's bank in Grinnell, Iowa. The façade of the building, he said, was a masterful composition of modulated geometric terra-cotta ornament juxtaposed over a brick surface. Filling nearly the entire upper façade of the building, the center of the composition was a circular window with an ornamental surround, which was transformed into a rotated square with a superimposed orthogonal square, thence back to a circle again.

Goff did not place a priority on either smooth or abrupt modulation. One was not better or worse than the other. They were simply different from one another, as different as the subtle modulations in Debussy's music and the abrupt modulations of Stravinsky's.

Design of "Opacity, Translucency and Transparency" by John C. Hurtig in the 273 Studio. Color pencil drawing.

Design of "Modulation" by Robert Faust in the 273 Studio. Color pencil drawing. Photograph by Faust.

BALANCE

The objective of this project was to explore the differences between formal and informal balance. The concept of balance was not simply a matter of mass to volume but rather each part of the composition "holding its own with other parts." Aspects of design such as color, rhythms, texture, and scale must also be considered, Goff said.

Formal balance was most often achieved through symmetry, usually upon a major axis. Goff reminded the students that despite this inclination, they must also consider a vertical axis. Informal balance, associated with asymmetry, involved a balance of forms and voids with a visual emphasis on the "felt" center of the composition. He emphasized that neither formal nor informal balance was right or wrong. Different problems required different solutions. Both ideas might even be contained within one another. It was possible to have a symmetrical scheme with asymmetrical elements or an asymmetrical design with symmetrical elements.

In the introduction to this assignment, Goff showed numerous slides of buildings that illustrated both major concepts and various permutations. The choice of buildings is indicative of his range of interests, and his biases. He showed examples from the ancient cultures of Egypt, Greece, Japan, Angkor Wat, and a Mesoamerican temple complex, paired them with twentieth-century American and European architecture, and omitted everything in between. Most of the modern examples, such as Hoffmann's Stoclet Mansion, Mies's Barcelona Pavilion, Le Corbusier's proposed Palace of the Soviets, and Wright's Fallingwater and Taliesin West, involved asymmetry. Goff also commented that he once asked Wright what he believed his greatest contribution to architecture was, and Wright responded that it was "freedom from the tyranny of absolute symmetry."

THEME, VARIATION, AND DEVELOPMENT

The intent of this project was to explore the use of a motif that could be repeated throughout the design, with many variations. It was, Goff said, "a constructive

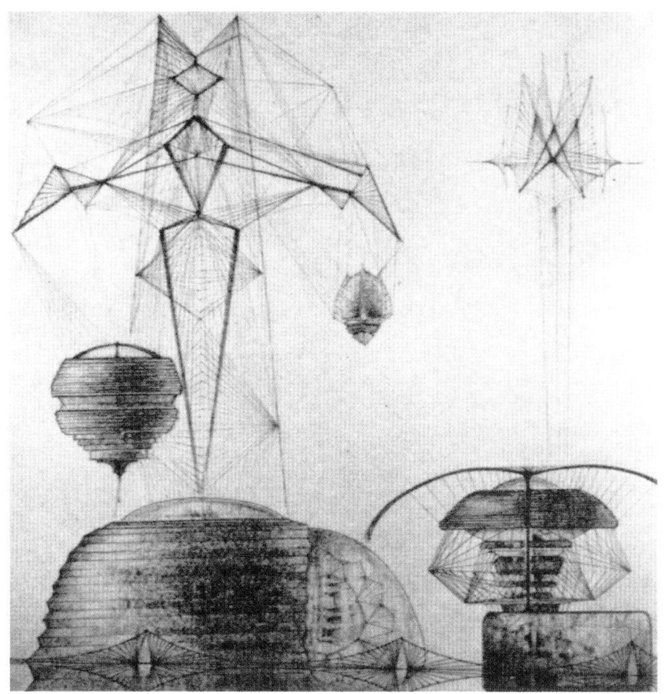

Design of "Balance" by Herb Greene in the 273 Studio. Two pencil drawings. Photographs by Greene.

process that helps create a sense of order in design—a conscious effort." In his introduction Goff used analogies of plant, animal, and mineral forms in nature. For example, a sunflower repeats elements with only a variation in size. The stripes on a zebra are also repetitions but with great variation in width and direction, and their scale changes as they become smaller near the head of the animal. In many crystalline rock formations, the repetition and the variation both become more complex. They possess an even greater variety in form, scale, direction, and color. Goff also made comparisons with musical composition. A composer might establish a theme of only a few notes and then vary it by changing keys and instruments, repeating only parts of the theme or even "turning it upside down." During the lecture, Goff played the second movement of one of Prokofiev's piano concertos as an example.

Goff defined a building's "theme" as the governing idea or motif, which could be repeated throughout the composition and then extended into furniture, windows, and light fixtures to relate all its parts together and establish unity. He alluded once more to the Johnson Wax Building and its circular theme of rounded corners, glass tubing, and circular columns with exaggerated capitals that evoked lily pads floating in the air. The idea underpinning the design, Goff said, was the consistent use of a circular motif to establish a sense of rhythmic motion.

"Variation" meant utilizing the theme as a point of departure in the design, but in a way still related to the theme. For example, one might use an equilateral triangle as a module, which could be elongated, have parts omitted, or be used to form other geometric shapes, such as a hexagon. Goff praised Wright's Price Tower as a masterful composition derived from variations of an angular motif.

"Development," Goff said, was a transcendence of the theme and all its variations, but one that could not have occurred without it. The design, in its totality, thus becomes more important than the theme or variations. Goff alluded to Wright's Hanna House as a design developed from a hexagonal module, yet whose composition was so subtle that the theme was hardly recognizable. Development, Goff said, was the hard part of architectural design and cautioned students that "being consistent is not going to necessarily make it a work of art. Mystery in art starts at the precise moment when our intellect fails to help us."

INCIDENT, TERMINAL, AND CLIMAX

Like he had done in his lecture on rhythm, Goff initiated his discussion of these three terms as elements of a composition that were common to both music and architecture. He defined "incident" as an element of occasional focus that was both subordinate and minor to the overall composition. It was, he said, an accent or special point of interest that might engage one's attention "with a fresh leap of life but not the main show." Goff spoke of "terminal" as a transitional element between one idea joining another. It was a concept closely tied to modulation. "Climax," Goff said, was the most important element of

Design of "Theme, Variation and Development" by James A. Gresham in the 273 Studio. Color pencil drawing. Photograph by Gresham.

the composition and provided a clear and "profound statement of the idea." All of the other elements—incidents and terminals—led up to the climax and sustained the work. Yet there were many possibilities of definition. A composition might have a climax of complex interwoven elements or one of contrast, and could be a serene or an abrupt expression.

Once again, Goff played Debussy's *La Mer* and Ravel's *Boléro* for the students, but this time he highlighted their use of these new terms. *La Mer* had a great variety of incidents with special terminals and a large climax. Similarly, *Boléro* repeated the same theme over and over, with the orchestration providing the incidents and leading to a dramatic dissonant climax.

In architecture he cited the flying buttresses of Gothic cathedrals as an example of defining the central idea. The intersection of the top of the buttress with the tall wall of the nave, modulated with a diminishing scale, provided the visual climax of the building. Another example he used, characterized as a "reverse climax," was the Golden Pagoda of Burma (Myanmar). The large gold-plated, bell-shaped temple was surrounded by a continuum of small-scale ornamental structures of teak, carved and inlaid with colored glass. It was these lower elements, Goff believed, whose intense contrast to the golden bell defined the climax of the design. Examples of modern architecture based upon these design principles included buildings by Gaudí and the Dutch architect Willem Dudok. However, the major part of his slide lecture was devoted to examples of buildings by Frank Lloyd Wright. Although he did not identify specific buildings, Goff provided a very detailed visual analysis of the differences in incident, terminal, and climax, and the interweaving of those elements. He praised Wright's mastery of those concepts, and said Wright had once told him, "Take care of the terminals and the rest will take care of itself."

Goff concluded his lecture with an attack upon a recent multistory apartment building designed by Mies van der Rohe. The design was, he said, the antithesis of Wright's work and had a complete absence of incident, terminal, and climax. There was "nothing to snag your eye" and the only "incident is which of the shades gets pulled down." It was simply "background architecture for anonymous living."

SITE RELATIONSHIPS

Goff initiated this discussion with the admonition that it was essential to understand both the problems and the specific characteristics of any building site. The site would, in part, determine the design. In addition to the obvious conditions of the land contours, climate, vegetation, geology, and zoning restrictions, he emphasized the importance of understanding both the character of the site and the content. The goal, Goff said, was to "handle the site in such a way

Design of "Incident, Terminal and Climax" by Ernest Burden in the 273 Studio. Pencil drawing from the archive in the College of Architecture, University of Oklahoma. Photograph by author.

that the building could not be anyplace else." Even subtle differences could be important. If, for instance, one built a house in the woods, "the solution would be different if the trees were willow rather than oak." Or if a site had ugly surrounding buildings, one could "adjust the color, texture and scale to accommodate the neighbors," Goff said.

He believed that there were two fundamental ways to establish a relationship between building and site. One was blending with the site to make the building appear as if it had grown out of the ground. The other was through contrast. Although the two approaches were opposite extremes, Goff suggested it was also possible to incorporate both ideas simultaneously in a design. Here he mentioned the Katsura Palace in Japan, which contrasts with its site because it is raised above the ground on posts yet also blends with nature through its use of materials.

Wright, he said, had a superb understanding of the site as a design determinant. In much of his work Wright extended walls and terraces into the landscape to establish a serene and graceful relationship with the earth. Yet if he had a site in an industrial neighborhood, such as the Johnson Wax Building, he would develop an introverted design. Moreover, two of his most famous early buildings in Chicago—Unity Temple and the Robie House—had very small, difficult corner sites. Unity Temple turned inwards and the Robie House, without a yard, had raised terraces to ensure privacy. But Wright was at his best, Goff believed, at blending the building with the site. He spoke eloquently of Taliesin West and its "dappled, spotted look" that reflected the desert landscape of sagebrush, cactus, and rock. Even its angular, zigzag elements reflected the environment, drawn from Indian motifs, Gila monsters, and diamondback rattlesnakes.

ORCHESTRATION OF MATERIALS

Goff introduced the lecture by explaining that "orchestration," a term used in music, applied to architecture when one uses a number of materials together in a design. The analogy was related to a tendency to utilize the sound of individual instruments to create and sustain a mood. As a result, Goff said, the orchestration in music had become increasingly translucent. He cited Debussy's *Prelude to the Afternoon of a Faun* as the first clear statement of a new kind of orchestration, with the individual instruments expressing a feeling integral to the piece as a whole.

Instead of instruments, then, building materials were the architect's medium. The ideal was to use materials for a definite reason—whether

Design of "Site Relationships" by James H. Gardner in the 273 Studio. Color illustration. Photograph by Gardner.

utilitarian, structural, or aesthetic—and to sense the importance of each, even as together they expressed an overall effect. Goff cited Wright's Dana House as an example of extraordinarily skillful orchestration. Built of brick, stone, shingled tile, leaded glass, copper, wood, and a stamped decorative frieze, one is less aware of the individual materials than of the total concept.

The goal was thus to transcend the nature of the materials individually, for they were simply "a means to an end rather than an end in itself." There were no rules, Goff said, and there should not be any limit to the number of materials in a design. The hazard of using only one material was monotony, and the danger of using too many materials was a chopped-up appearance. He suggested "it was better to see how few materials one could use together well, rather than using many." Goff urged students to learn as much as possible about all building materials because of their enormous variety: "It is easy to get lost in the nature of the material rather than what we are saying with the material." Goff suggested that ideas about the orchestration of materials are constantly changing and one must experiment "even if you make mistakes. Don't be afraid to take risks."

ORNAMENT

Goff began with the comment that most modern architects considered ornament on buildings taboo "so we should consider it." That single introductory statement reveals a great deal about his posture on design. Yet while Goff was at odds with current architectural fashion, he also genuinely believed that there were reasons to utilize ornament. His comment also reinforces his conviction that there were no taboos in design and that he, and his students, must have freedom of imagination.

Although ornament was used in earlier times, its primary function was symbolic. Painting, sculpture, mosaics, and frescoes were used to represent a religious or political concept or record a historical event. But as Goff said, beauty was their by-product. Ornament became a way to modulate a building's scale, and it offered visual relief of uninteresting surfaces, adding a decorative element and giving definition to the entry. It was for this reason, Goff insisted, that ornament was important in building design: it offered the opportunity to establish a hierarchy of scale. It should "reward you as you approach" the building. But, he cautioned, ornament must be integral together with the surface.

Goff showed slides of buildings in India, Siam (Thailand), and Burma (Myanmar) where ornament was used as texture, covering entire surfaces. Initially the texture appears very complex, he said, but upon closer inspection the organization of "sculptures within sculptures" conveyed a sense of simplicity.

Similarly, the work of Mies van der Rohe "appears very simple but in reality it is complex because it took such a struggle to create it. Don't let the appearance of simplicity or complexity fool you until you get to know it." He also showed slides of vernacular buildings in Africa and a grain-storage structure in Sumatra. He alluded to Sam's Tower in Watts, Los Angeles, which was not a building at all but a three-dimensional ornament. Goff's twentieth-century examples included buildings by Gaudí that used "ornament as texture," the Glasgow tearooms by Charles Rennie Mackintosh with their ornamental chairs and light fixtures, and work by both Sullivan and Wright. He particularly admired the ornament of Sullivan because it was integral with the surface and "not tacked on." He mentioned Wright's Coonley House as an example of a more restrained ornament through its subtle leaded-glass details and the muted burnt-orange color of the tile. Also, he praised Wright's Taliesin West for the composition in its totality of form, color, and texture as being "ornament for the desert."

SCALE

Scale, Goff said, involves the relationship of the parts in a composition to one another. Scale is "a modulus of measurements" but is not the same as proportions. Elements of a façade could be proportional to one another with little regard for scale, as in the case of a monumental building with large scale but entry doors at a small scale. Though monuments in urban parks and plazas are often appropriately larger than life, their parts are related to one another in terms of scale. Among artisans, Goff believed that their use of proportional systems, such as the Golden Mean, was "an outgrowth of their sensitivity to scale." Goff also alluded to the sense of intimacy in classical Japanese architecture, especially in the case of temples, houses, and gardens. Architecture that was in scale with people thus expressed their culture. He also praised Le Corbusier's development of the "Modulor" proportional system as a means to address issues of human scale in design.

In his lecture Goff emphasized that an architect must be sensitive to the scale

Design of "Orchestration of Materials" by Robert Faust in the 273 Studio. Color pencil drawing. Photograph by Faust.

of a particular environment, especially in an urban context, as surrounding buildings might influence design decisions. Goff also said that one must consider the function of the building when making decisions about scale: "The scale of a jewelry store would be very different from a building that sold tractors." There were times when scale should be very intimate, and the more the "scale is fragmented it becomes more intimate." For design problems where one needed a range of small, intimate scale coupled with large, impersonal scale, "[the] key is variation in scale."

Goff again used analogies to music in his discussion of scale, posing two extremes. Wagner's operas had an overwhelming, grandiose scale, while Debussy's pieces had an intimate sense of smaller scale and intimacy. The same principle could be applied to architecture. Ultimately it was an issue of artistic judgment and of "individual interpretations of ideas about scale."

The Architecture 273 studio represents a unique approach to design education. Students responded with imaginative architectural interpretations of Goff's aspects of design, creating illustrations of extraordinary quality. Their work reflects a conceptual abstraction of a single idea devoid of any functional context. The intent was to explore potential realizations of design elements as an adventure in the realm of the imagination. Although he joked with students about a speaking engagement at another university and his anticipation that someone would ask if "OU students wore long robes and spoke in tongues," Goff was very clear when he told his students that "being free isn't enough and you must have discipline." One must seek "discipline in freedom," as Debussy said, to give order and coherence to design.

The content of the 273 studio did vary from time to time. A principle of design considered one year might be omitted the following year, or a new one added with different expectations. For example, one year Goff gave a separate assignment on "counterpoint," which had been previously combined with "rhythm." In spite of his aforementioned casual, friendly relationship with students, Goff could be a demanding professor. In his 273 lectures he reminded students of his expectation that they attend the afternoon-long design studio three times a week, along with the special music sessions on Wednesday evenings. However, if a student missed class for some other conflicting event, such as a special lecture in another discipline or a concert, Goff was prone to say, "Don't let school get in the way of your education."[55]

⟁

After Goff left the university for full-time practice in 1955, he continued to teach elements of his design studio to apprentices who had not studied at OU. Nelson L. Brackin, a graduate of Auburn University, worked with Goff in Tyler, Texas, from

Design of "Ornament/Elaboration of Architectural Space," watercolor, ink, color pencil by John Davis in the 273 Studio. OU College of Architecture Archive. Photograph by author.

June 1975 through September 1978. Goff provided a series of exercises modeled from his 273 studio and with each assignment he played recordings of music to expand his discussions of the concepts.[56]

During his time at OU, Goff created an architectural education program that reflected his ideals. His lectures during the early years of his tenure were primarily discussions of specific concepts of design, which gave form to his own architectural visions and, as such, they provide insights into Goff's rich and varied expression. Goff taught what he knew and believed about architecture. In this sense, both *what* and *how* he taught informed his convictions and values about a process of design.

Facing page, Design of "Orchestration of Materials" by Robert Faust in the 273 Studio. Color pencil drawing. Photograph by Faust.

A masterpiece must have the quality of *surprise,* to engage our attention, and of *mystery* to hold our interest. It must be complete in itself with its own character of disciplined order, no matter how "free" it may seem.

BRUCE GOFF

The final form tends to be built up as a composition of clearly differentiated parts, each contributing its individual detail, while maintaining harmony with a larger whole.

HERB GREENE

5

PROFESSIONAL PRACTICE AT OU

There was a symbiotic relationship between teaching and learning for Goff, as he was a source of inspiration who was in turn inspired by student efforts. His new and refreshing ideas generated enthusiasm among his students, especially as projects by Goff began to move from design to construction. Local and national press coverage of his buildings, and of the school, intensified his vision of new directions in architectural education and stimulated students and fellow faculty members to follow suit. As Goff encouraged imaginative solutions, he too was encouraged by students' commitment to creativity. Goff's time at OU provided an opportunity to share his ideas about architecture and the flexibility of his schedule allowed him to continue his professional practice.

As a result, Goff's OU years proved to be one of the most productive times of his career, and he produced some of his finest work as a professor of architecture. Buildings he designed from early 1947 until his departure in late 1955 exhibit a remarkable sense of diversity. Yet it is the continuity of values in conceptualization that relates these designs to subsequent designs in his career and that informs their premises. It is this duality that authenticates his body of mature work.

△

Goff's first commission after his return to Oklahoma was a house for H. E. Ledbetter, which he received upon recommendation by his colleague Henry Kamphoefner. Designed in 1947 and built the following year, the site's convenient location two blocks west of the OU campus meant Goff's students could observe firsthand the sequence of construction. This major opportunity for students to witness an imaginative design come into being undoubtedly increased Goff's credibility with them, both as a creative designer and as one who could solve the practical problems of building with great authority.

The house is a composite arrangement of geometry, combining rectangular and circular elements with undulating, meandering forms. The façade of the trilevel design is a collage of several differing components, with irregular sandstone walls laid in a random ashlar pattern. The walls contrast with a rhythmic band of glass set above a cantilevered band of corrugated sheet-metal storage cabinets. Two metal discs, serving as a carport and garden shelter, are suspended from steel frames rising above the cornice.

The Ledbetter House has an oblique reference to the earlier Leidig project, but its client-specific solution was quite different. The Ledbetters wanted large rooms, lots of natural light, and minimal hallways. The building site was small: a corner lot with a three-story limestone fraternity house across the street that was "as big as a barn and the house next door the size of a postage stamp."[1] The budget was modest as well.

In the Leidig House the masonry walls defined the edges of the composition to establish boundaries. In the Ledbetter House the walls serve the same purpose but also establish zones of activity, defining the driveway, the entry, the garden, and the house itself. The undulating, eroded sandstone walls establish a dominant theme tied to Goff's philosophy of organic architecture: he wanted the stone to appear as it would in its natural state. The wall defining the rear elevation of the house erodes into the landscape, partially enclosing a garden as it disappears into the ground. It then reappears, from a different point, to merge again with the house. It suggests a state of nature, a world of earth and stone where both house and garden, as extensions of one another, become united.

Another dominant theme, that of highly polished and machined geometric forms, contrasts with the free-form stone walls. Solving the problem of the site's size, Goff precisely arranged these compositional elements with a gradation in height, so that a lower form always appears in front of a higher form. The gradation transitions from the principal part of the house, a one-story-tall form farthest from the street, to the smaller one-story-tall kitchen, the suspended carport, and the semicircular reflecting pool at the edge of the sidewalk. Goff created very clear hierarchies of form and scale corresponding to the function of each element, and his organizational strategy conveys their meaning.

Goff then modulated the façade by establishing a rhythm of repeating components, contrasting with both solid, anchoring elements and light, floating elements. The large panes of fixed glass, set in a sawtooth pattern, create a prominent rhythm across the facade of the house and contrast with the undulating sandstone wall. Goff enriched the sawtooth rhythm with a decorative pattern of translucent glass ashtrays, inset in pierlike mullions of wood, as a counterpoint. By light of the moon or sun, the ornamental ashtrays sparkle like prisms. The assemblage of deep mullions with angled glass was not solely for the sake of visual expression: Goff set each pane at an angle so they would not reflect a large limestone fraternity house across the street.[2]

The contrast of anchoring versus floating elements is quite pronounced in the Ledbetter House. Attached with cables to frames above the cornice, metal discs seem to hover in the air in both the garden and the carport. The roof over the kitchen and the main part of the house is tapered on the top so that the edge of its deep overhang becomes very thin. This in turn magnifies the discs'

Following spread

Left, Ledbetter House, Norman, Oklahoma, floor plan. Designed by Goff. Drawing by Lucia Lee, OU College of Architecture, Design and Research Center. Courtesy College of Architecture, University of Oklahoma.

Right, Ledbetter House, façade. Photograph courtesy of Robert Goins.

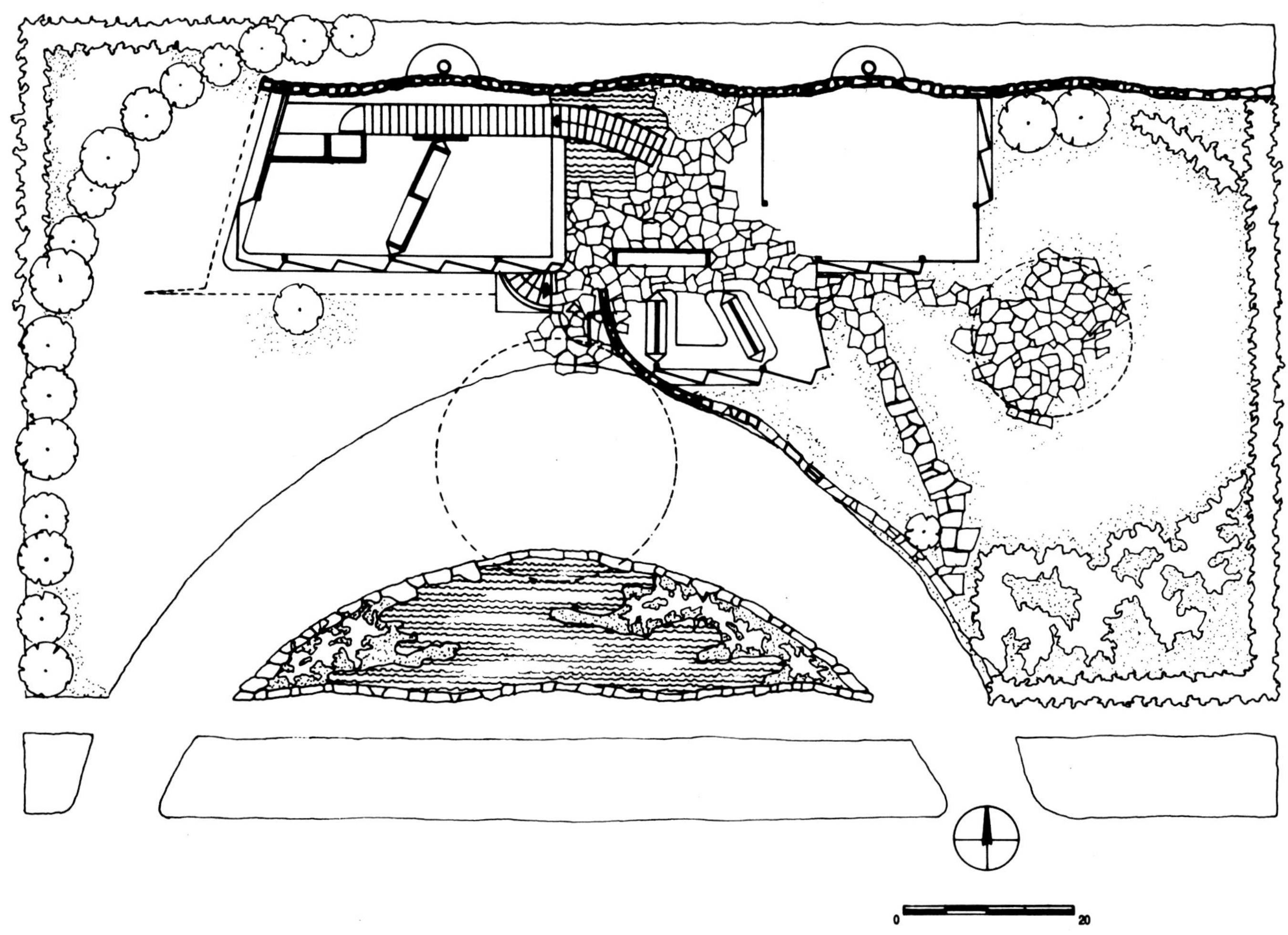
0
20

Ledbetter House, façade detail.
Photograph by author.

sense of lightness to the composition. In his designs, Goff developed many variations of this subtle expression and its creation of illusory planes and lines that appeared to float in space.

The interior of the Ledbetter House is similarly rich in detail, with an open plan that defines three distinct zones: the entry, kitchen, and living room at ground level; bedrooms one-half level above; and an alternate living space below the bedrooms. The corrugated metal wainscot cantilevered into the entry makes apparent this trilevel spatial concept, just as it does on the façade. Forming a balcony for one of the bedrooms, the wainscot separates this zone from the entry. The ramp curving from the foyer to a corridor adjacent to the undulating sandstone wall serves a similar function. It invites but also separates; it defines a distinct zone, one that is private yet visually accessible.

Other features of the large entry foyer speak to Goff's philosophical dedication to architecture in harmony with the natural world. Fountains concealed in the sandstone wall splash into a pool under the foyer ramp. Seeping into

Left, Ledbetter House, façade and canopy. Photograph by Keith Rinearson.

Right, Ledbetter House, interior. Photograph by Keith Rinearson.

and falling from the stone wall into an irregular-shaped pool, its edges thick with plants, this element evokes a secluded forest glade. The sight and sound of the water, combined with sunlight from the ribbon skylight separating wall and roof, animates the composition. The meaning is clear: architecture is an extension of nature and it is of the realm of sky, earth, and water. But in Goff's ideal, architecture also embraces a manmade world. In the Ledbetter House, the precise geometric forms of metal float and contrast with meandering stone walls as an anchoring element. It is the visualization of these two realms, contrasting with one another yet joined together, which reveals the imaginative celebration of dualities so often apparent in Goff's architecture.

The house became locally known as "Calamity Corner," according to Mrs. Ledbetter, because of the number of curious onlookers both during construction and after completion.[3] On May 2 and 3, 1948, an open house was held as a fundraiser for the Norman Spastic Paralysis Institute.[4] The event brought more than 13,500 people to the house and raised $2,100 for the institute. In addition to local attention, *LIFE* magazine featured the house in its June 28, 1948, issue, in an article about the open house and titled "Consternation and Bewilderment in Oklahoma." Today, the Ledbetter House is listed on the National Register of Historic Places.

Goff's design of the Hopewell Baptist Church in 1947 extended another theme of a symmetrical prismatic form defining an enclosed interior volume with a vertical axis. Pastor D. B. Hoskins and J. L. Thomas, a production foreman for a local oilfield drilling company and member of the congregation in the rural community of Deer Creek, west of Edmond, approached Goff for the design of a new church. They had little money, stacks of donated oilfield pipe, and a construction crew comprised of congregation members. They requested a concrete block building with a pipe roof that might be fabricated by welders in their congregation. Goff suggested they use the salvage pipe for the entire structure. His two-level building design incorporated the concrete stairs of their existing wood-frame structure and included a sanctuary for three hundred people positioned on an upper level above classrooms. Defined in plan as a dodecahedron (twelve-sided), the building rises eighty feet to the top of the skylight as a monumental prism set upon a flat, treeless plain. Sheathed with red hexagonal shingles, a reference to the red earth of western Oklahoma, and framed with tapered silver-painted Warren trusses fabricated from welded sections of four-inch drill stem, the building became known locally as the "Tipi Church" as its form, from a distance, resembles the cone-shaped dwellings of the Plains Indians. Built by the congregation in evening shifts, they named each of the twelve trusses for one of the disciples of Jesus as they were built and attached to the circular compression ring at the top of the prism. The last truss, which proved the most difficult to attach, they named "Judas."

The exterior walls of the lower level of classrooms, with a wainscot of corrugated metal capped with a narrow band of continuous windows, are recessed but canted outward at the top. They slope at the same angle as the sanctuary but in the opposite direction. The overhanging form above creates a strong shadow line, which mitigates its massiveness and bulk. Similarly, the skylight at the apex of the sanctuary has other meanings beyond the obvious function of lighting the interior. The articulation of glass and converging steel trusses amplifies the structure's autonomy.

Topped with a glass disc, the skylight could be raised pneumatically for ventilation. A 35-foot-long chandelier, made of fluted metal cake pans and glossy plastic tea coasters, was suspended from the apex to magnify the presence of a vertical axis. The convergence of the dramatic symmetrical space creates an association of inspiration and mystery. Looking upward, one loses the sense of both scale and distance in an endless space reaching to the clouds.

Goff's use of ordinary vernacular objects in architectural design, such as cake pans transformed into light fixtures, is similar to the American composer Charles Ives's incorporation of a motif from an Episcopal hymn or passages from patriotic songs in his musical compositions. For both Goff and Ives the vernacular served the same purpose: creating original works that referenced the reality of everyday life. In the Hopewell church, the use of a common kitchen object also suggests a dynamic of contemplative opposites, as the stark simplicity of the monumental space converges to the skylight and guides the eye to upward. Yet as containers of food, the fluted cake pans are suspended on the central axis reaching down to the congregation below in a subliminal gesture to worldly necessities. Together they serve as a metaphor for the reality of secular life.

Hopewell Baptist Church is significant in several respects. It represents an idealized conception of centroid geometry with a direct correspondence between exterior form and interior space. It was the first major building constructed that clearly established a design typology for Goff. Conceptually, it became a prototype for many variations of designs in subsequent years. The building, listed on the National Register of Historic Places, is also a testament to the tenacity of those who sacrificed their evenings to build the church, as

Following spread

Left, Hopewell Baptist Church, Edmond, Oklahoma. Plan drawing by OU College of Architecture, Design and Research Center. Courtesy College of Architecture, University of Oklahoma.

Right, Hopewell Baptist Church, façade. Photograph by author.

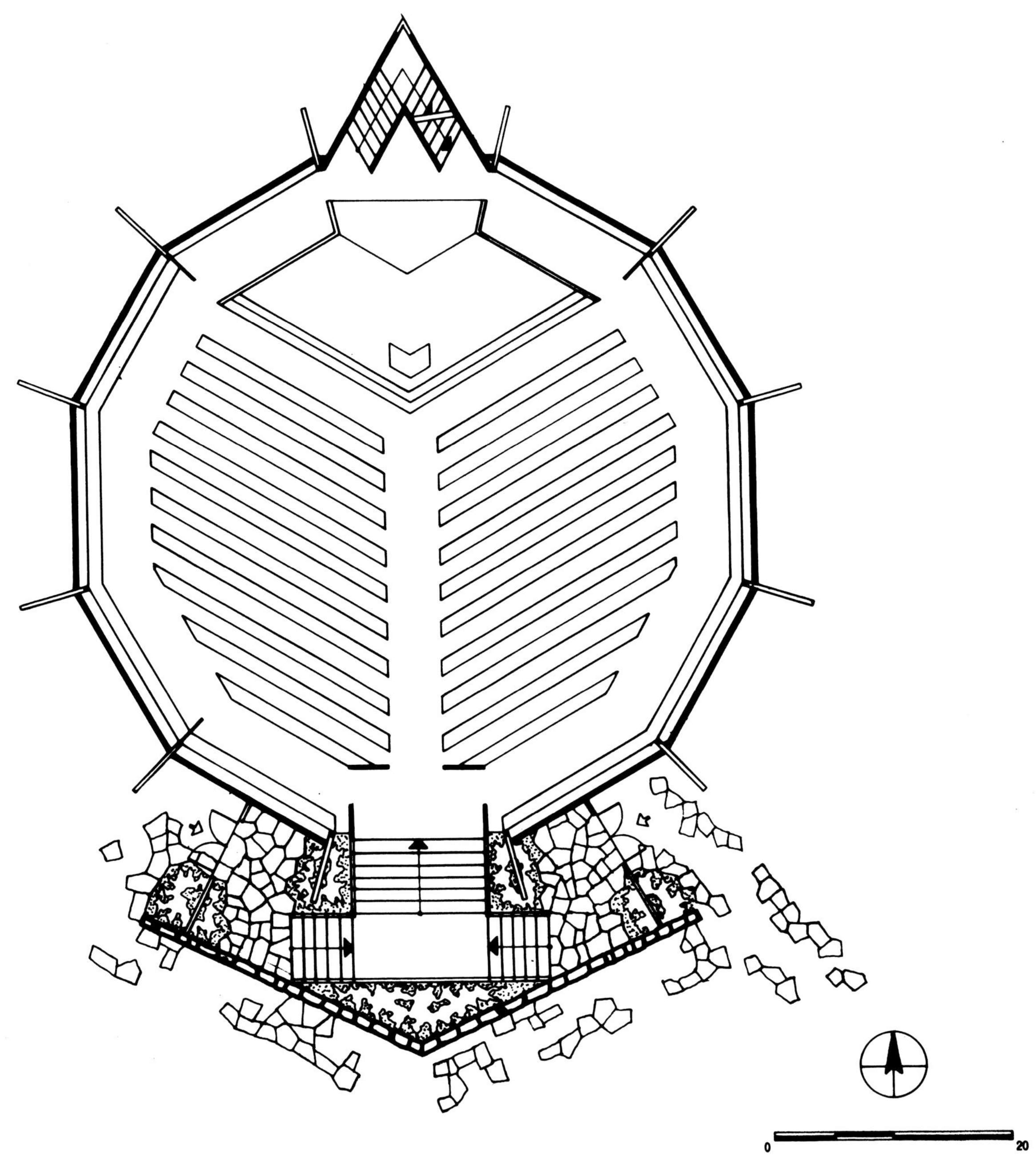
0
20

Left, Hopewell Baptist Church, structure detail. Photograph by Robert Bowlby.

Right, Hopewell Baptist Church, interior. Photograph by author.

it took four years to complete. It was also fortuitous that the congregation had Goff as its architect because of his Navy experience with low-budget buildings that utilized surplus materials. In response to *Architectural Forum*'s request for information about Hopewell manufacturers and suppliers, Goff wrote the editor, "There is very little that can be filled out on the form . . . as practically everything here was home-made out of grocery store materials."[5] Upon completion, the Hopewell Church was frequently pictured in Oklahoma newspapers, trade journals for manufacturers of steel and Styrofoam, architectural journals, and books on Goff, and it also appeared in a 1955 *TIME* magazine essay on church architecture. However, Goff later became dissatisfied with some modifications such as a "big air conditioner they stuck on the back."[6] The modification dramatically altered the angled projecting stair to the choir loft.

Goff's next major project of 1947 was a house for Ruth and Albert Ford of Aurora, Illinois. Robert Overstreet, an OU architecture student who prepared the construction drawings and built a framing model of the structural concept, later said that Goff characterized Ruth Ford as a "woman who wore big bracelets and African jewelry. She liked big, rounded forms and exotic things and her favorite color was red-orange."[7] Ruth wanted a centralized ensemble of hearth, kitchen, and workspace as the center of her world. Conceptually, the Ford House represents another variation of building design defined as a primary geometric shape with a corresponding interior volume. It also represents Goff's acknowledgement of the client, of whom and what she was, believed, and wanted.

The Ford House reveals Goff's skill in visually combining several elements to create an interior focal point. Both the convergence of structure and an array of elements positioned on the house's vertical axis reveal its prominence. The spatial arrangement evolved from the specific desires of his client. In addition to the central location of her hearth and work area, Ruth Ford wanted a large space to display her paintings and to entertain. At the very center of the space, a large recessed circular area surrounding a copper mast serves several functions. The mast serves as the major structural support for the ribs of the dome, a zoning device between kitchen and conversation area, and a fireplace and the armature for the cantilevered circular studio above. Collectively, the mast becomes the visual magnet. Surplus steel Quonset hut ribs painted bright red-orange frame the space's primary hemispherical form. Cutting one-third of the length from each rib extended their curved surface in a downward direction, as the ribs converged to the central axis. One segment of the dome opens to a screened outdoor room, providing a source of natural light. A flat roof connects two smaller partially domed bedrooms to the primary form.

With the exception of the outdoor room, the exterior materials include a band of cannel coal at the base, laid in a random ashlar pattern with white mortar decorated with marbles. The coal wall, inset from the outer shell, provides concealed ventilation shutters. The curved surface of the shell above, wood-shingled and stained dark green, converges to the central skylight and reveals the intersecting pattern of ribs. The connecting flat-roofed areas also have a curved surface on their underside, the fascia merging with the soffit and covered with one-inch-wide jute rope. A free-standing wall of coal with randomly spaced curved and circular openings partially screens the house from the street. Goff told Overstreet that Mies van der Rohe had once proposed using coal as a masonry material.[8]

The interior surface of the dome is clad with cypress boards laid in a herringbone pattern above the low coal wall. The congregate space has three different levels: a ring of undifferentiated space at the perimeter surrounds a recessed seating area at a lower level, which faces a central copper-hooded fireplace with an open kitchen behind. A cantilevered circular platform, which served as Ruth Ford's studio, is aligned on the axis and also projects into the outdoor room.

Built with meticulous craftsmanship by OU architecture alumnus Don A. Tosi, the Ford House's continuity of curving major and minor forms also has

Following spread

Left, Ruth and Albert (Sam) Ford House, Aurora, Illinois. Plan drawing by OU College of Architecture, Design and Research Center. Courtesy College of Architecture, University of Oklahoma.

Right, Ford House, construction, 1947–50. Bruce Goff, architect; photograph by Eliot Elisofon. Bruce Goff Archive, Ryerson & Burnham Archives, Art Institute of Chicago.

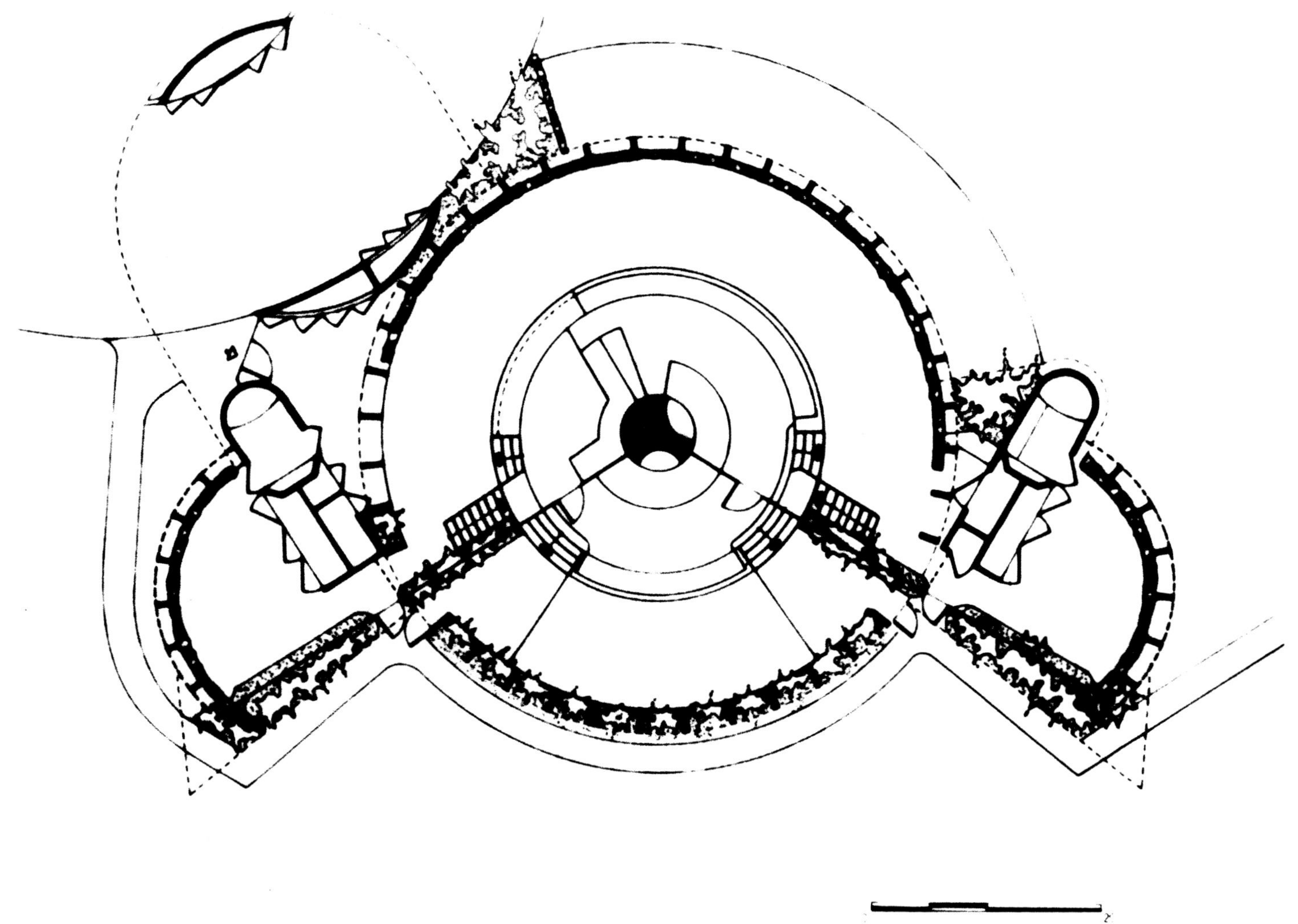

Ford House, façade with free-standing coal wall. Photograph by author.

a strong sculptural presence, ornamented with animalistic "tusks" supporting the carport and the independent perimeter wall of coal that, as an element of the earth, defines a boundary. The design also has clarity of functional purpose, its visualization of public and private areas indicated by the forms' variation in size. The contrast between the red-orange steel ribs, dark green shingles, and black coal provide a clear expression of structure, as the ribs emerge from the earth to disappear beneath the shingled skin of the wall-roof continuum and appear again at the apex.

A gradation of texture and pattern, from the large, randomly placed coal at the base to the precise pattern of converging structure at the skylight above, also contributes to a hierarchy of scale. Similarly, the use of jute rope to connect

Ford House, exterior view of "outdoor room" and bedroom modules. Photograph by author.

forms on the overhanging soffit/fascia of the flat roofs intensifies the association of a finely scaled directional pattern belonging to the realm of the upper part of the composition, much like the leaves on a tree. As Overstreet recalled, Ruth Ford "liked the use of jute rope on the fascia because of its association with African art and walls made of coal appealed to her because it was something unusual."[9]

The Ford House is a clear visualization of ideas Goff discussed in the 273 studio on the importance of a gradation of scale. Goff later commented:

> I like buildings that add up to a very impressive whole no matter what is going on to make them as they are. As you come nearer to them and closer . . . they reward you for your interest by giving you ornament or some incidence that relate with people more. In nature you can see the

Ford House, interior view of skylight and intersection of curved ribs to the mast. Photograph by author.

tree as a whole shape from a long ways off but when you get closer to it then you can see the various branches and the leaves and spaces in between that the sky shows through. And then if you climb into the tree you get still another experience of spatial containment.[10]

The Farnsworth House by Mies van der Rohe, which also had a steel-framed structure, was under construction at the same time as the Ford House on a site about ten miles away. When Mies stopped to see the Ford House he commented, "Bruce Goff is a good architect but no one should try to imitate him."[11] Shortly after its completion, the Ford House was featured in *Architectural Forum*, *Popular Science*, and *LIFE*.

Above, Ford House, interior. Photograph by Eliot Elisofon. Bruce Goff Archive, Ryerson & Burnham Archives, Art Institute of Chicago.

Following spread

Left, Julius Cox House, Boise City, Oklahoma, 1949. Plan drawing by OU College of Architecture, Design and Research Center. Courtesy College of Architecture, University of Oklahoma.

Right, Cox House, façade. Photograph by author.

Two houses of 1949 and 1950 contrast with the Ford House with their rectilinear plan geometry and subdued palette of materials. The 1949 Julius Cox House and its 1959 addition, in Boise City, Oklahoma, obliquely reference the scale of Frank Lloyd Wright's Usonian houses. Cox's son served in the Navy with Goff and recommended him for the project.

The expression of the Cox House is that of a series of independent masonry masses paired with a reverse batter of tan-colored brick bands and capped with a double course of pumice. Glass walls separate the different masonry forms. The roof planes, appearing at three different levels, are flat with deep, overhanging roofs and a thin fascia, and are similarly separated from the masonry

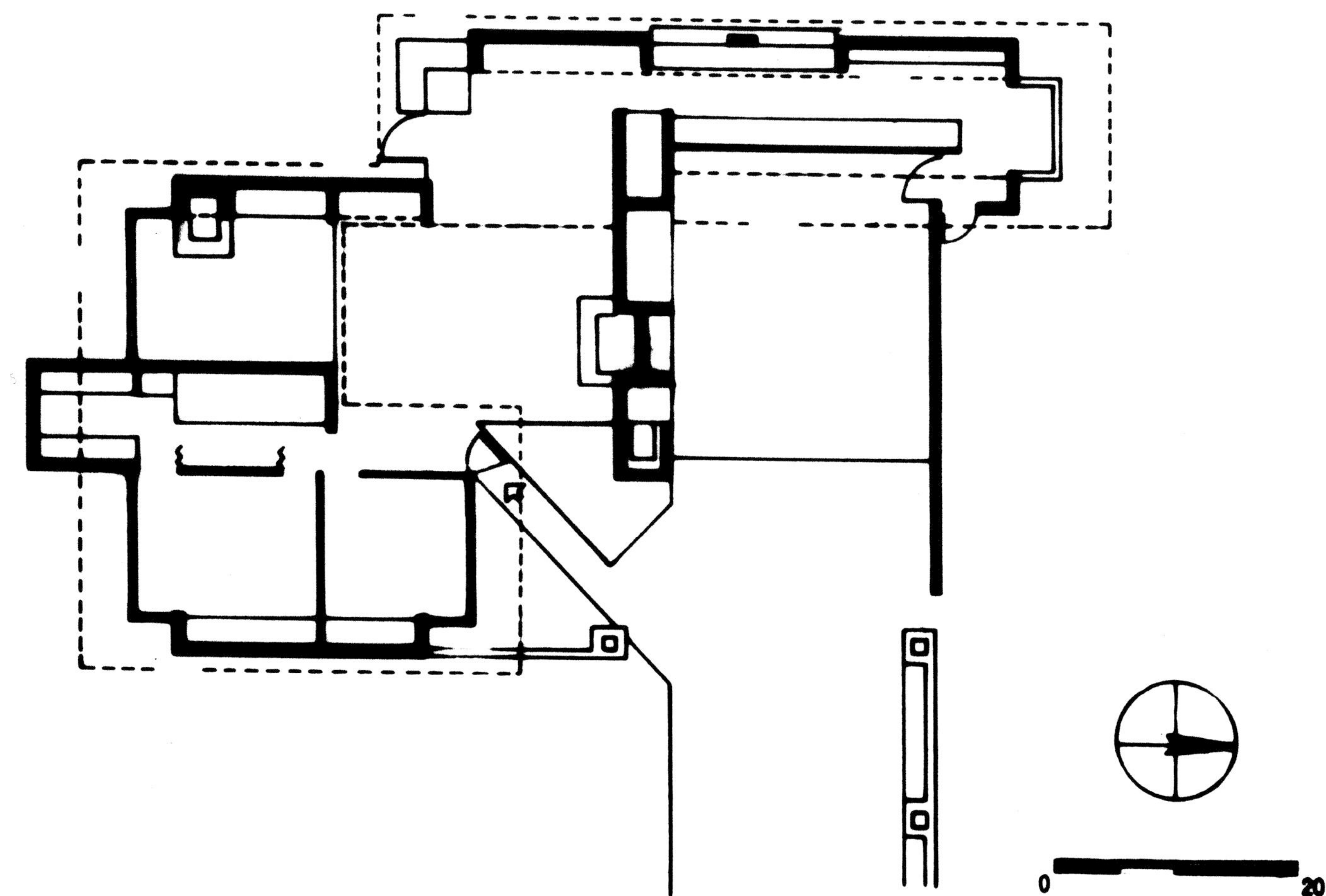
0
20

by clerestories and high windows. The roof was constructed of modular, precast concrete units manufactured with the trade name of "Flexicore."[12] Each of the long-span pretensioned units measures twelve inches wide by six inches deep and two cylindrical voids run the length of each unit. The roof is supported at the perimeter by steel trusses, fabricated in Cox's farm implement dealership shop and infilled with glass. With this arrangement of cantilevered roofs Goff created an illusion of thin, hovering planes with circular openings in the Flexicore fascia forming a decorative rhythm.

The major elements of the Cox House—modulated opaque walls for privacy, transparent walls for natural light and views, and linear structural components of the enclosing roof planes—all have a sense of independence. Each element defines a different visualized purpose. Collectively, they create a composition of repose and project an association of relatedness to the flat Oklahoma Panhandle landscape. Although it was an imaginative expression of structure, Goff was disappointed that the steel trusses were infilled with glass. His design specified that the trusses would be set behind the clerestory of glass to visually separate the roof from the wall and magnify the autonomy of forms.[13]

Given to the Cimarron County Historical Society after Cox's death, the building currently houses the society's administrative offices. A large abstract depiction of a dinosaur, built of CoreTen steel, was later erected adjacent to the house as a reference to the popular dinosaur tracks on nearby Black Mesa. The rusted stylized sculpture, taller than the house, projects a cartoonlike image. Its presence compromises the visual integrity of the house and problematizes its possible inclusion on the National Register of Historic Places.

The 1950 house for J. D. Wilson, Goff's commanding officer when he was stationed at Camp Parks, California, was similarly derivative of a geometric conceptualization of rectilinear elements. Its design of fourteen-foot modular cubes arranged in an interlocking stepped pattern was unique for Goff, as there was neither a hierarchy of form nor a focal point in the composition, with one subtle exception. A diagonal glass wall in a reflecting pool, placed so the exterior basin of water extended into the interior of the house, modulated the repetition of the cubic forms. In its totality, the pool defined a module, with a fireplace terminating the interior corner. The fire would always be seen in the context of water, creating a fusion of two elemental but opposing forces of nature. Goff developed this feature in several subsequent projects.

Built in Pensacola, Florida, on a flat bayside site of pine trees, the building's orientation took advantage of the prevailing wind for cross-ventilation and provided views of both ocean and trees. A welded frame of surplus boiler tubes, fabricated on the site by Ray Cobb and OU alumnus Rex Slack, structurally defined each of the beveled-edged modules.[14]

The vertical bevels were fitted with jalousie windows for ventilation, while the horizontal bevels at the top were filled in with translucent plastic to subdue the sunlight. The bottom horizontal bevels raised the modules above the ground as a precaution against flooding and their shadow line visually lightened the composition. Although some of the exterior walls were composed entirely of glass, the module's primary walls were clad in redwood siding, laid in a concentric pattern on both the exterior and interior. With the structural frame giving edge definition in the beveled reveal, the pattern amplified each cube's separation. Although the house was destroyed by fire in the 1980s, it was a building of extraordinary craftsmanship and one of precise order and logic that paired well with the client's distinguished military career.

Above, Wilson House structure with Jack Golden visiting construction site. Photograph courtesy of Rex Slack.

Following spread

Left and center, Wilson House, exterior and interior.

Right, Wilson House, Pensacola, Florida, 1950. Plan drawing by OU College of Architecture, Design and Research Center. Courtesy College of Architecture, University of Oklahoma.

In March 1949, President Cross asked Goff to design a student religious center on the OU campus. His proposed design, which became known as the Crystal Chapel, generated enormous enthusiasm and loyalty among students. However, preliminary design drawings were received with ambivalence when shown to a prospective donor the following month. Goff continued to develop the design, though, completing final presentation drawings and a model in March 1950. The major components of a chapel, an education and activities building, and a chimes tower defined the design.

Recalling the imagery of German Expressionism with its vision of translucent crystalline geometry, the prismatic chapel extended the theme of a

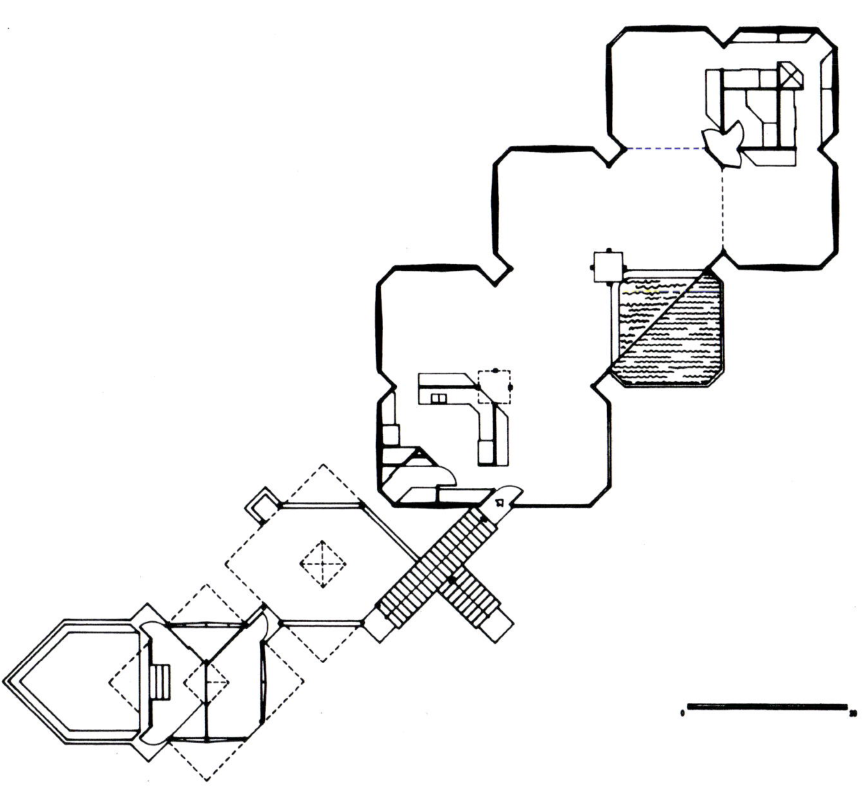

symmetrical form with a vertical axis. Three conjoined diamond-shaped surfaces formed a seventy-five-foot-tall volume, where extensions of triangular planes defined three radiating wings set in a hexagonal pool of water. An aluminum structural grid of diamond-shaped modules defined the roofs of the continuum, with the diamonds to be filled with three-layer prefabricated panels of pink-colored plate glass on the interior, a middle layer of pink fiberglass for both light diffusion and insulation, and an exterior layer of stainless steel wire glass. Goff sought an effect of rose-colored translucency within the tall prism. The chapel would then be fitted with tubular cold cathode lights adjacent to the structural members, so that the form would have a lacelike pattern at night. The faceted panels of the chapel would also be highly reflective in sunlight, and the crystalline form would be further magnified by surrounding pools of water.

Goff envisioned a chapel supported by a base of triangular piers of unpolished pink Oklahoma granite, set in a reflecting pool that extended to the interior. Panels of "Gemmeaux," a decorative French art glass made by sealing fragments of colored glass with transparent plastic glue between two sheets of plate glass, would act as walls between the piers. Robert Overstreet, who built the model of the project, said Goff wanted the images of the Gemmeaux glass to suggest abstract evil and diabolical forms.[15] On hot days, the water level of the pool could be lowered to allow water-cooled breezes to sweep into the interior and exit via a vent at the apex. Arranged around a central hexagonal-shaped glass floor light, which also served as the ceiling for a study at the lower level, the interior of the chapel would seat three hundred. Goff wanted to suspend decorative chains of silver and glass from the apex of the prism to amplify its vertical interior axis. Roof planes at one corner of the chapel would be completely transparent to allow full view of the chimes tower upon leaving. The 150-foot spire, with its pink granite base and "wings" of aluminum and glass at the top, would be visible for miles over the Oklahoma landscape. A smaller activities building, set independently to one side of the chapel, was to be similarly clad in faceted glass panels.

Above, Crystal Chapel model for University of Oklahoma, project built by Robert Overstreet. Photograph courtesy of Bruce Goff, 1978.

Left, Crystal Chapel, interior drawing by Herb Greene. Photograph courtesy of Bruce Goff, 1978.

The Crystal Chapel was a design of great repose and dignity, a superb manifestation of Goff's architectural imperatives of "modulation" and "theme, variation, and development."

Architectural Forum published the project in July 1950. The writer of the *Forum* article included a comment by an unidentified colleague of Goff, who referred to the design as "this great pink crystal, symbolic of Oklahoma's religious life laced with the sky, luxuriant with water, its hundreds of facets touched with glitter by day, mysteriously radiant by night."[16] Photographs of the model were also published in *Sooner Magazine* and local newspapers, both of which generated considerable discussion over the presence of contemporary architecture amidst the university's existing Gothic buildings.

Meanwhile, Mr. and Mrs. Fred Jones, a prominent family of Oklahoma City, met with President Cross early in 1951 to discuss a donation to the university for construction of a nonsectarian chapel. The project would act as a memorial for their son Fred Jones, Jr., who had died in a plane crash in December 1950. Though the Jones family appreciated Goff's genius, they believed a conservative and restrained design would be more appropriate for the campus. They engaged Parr and Aderhold of Oklahoma City to design the chapel. A photograph of their prospective design, which resembled an English church with a tall steeple, was published in the student newspaper prior to the groundbreaking ceremony scheduled for February 2, 1953. In the weeks following, the earlier debate on propriety found new life with an outpouring of protests against the rejection of Goff's design. OU architecture students wrote to prominent architects throughout America to enlist their support for Goff's Crystal Chapel.[17] Many responded. The distinguished William Wurster of California wrote that Goff's chapel would be one of the "outstanding buildings of our time." Frank Lloyd Wright commented that the more traditional Parr and Aderhold design was not surprising for "an educational system geared to please patrons. . . . The University loses, not the students."[18]

The Jones family vacillated over the chapel's concept and, some years later,

President Cross redirected their support toward the construction of a new art museum. But Goff's design was not forgotten. Beautifully crafted and rich in detail, the model was so realistic that published photographs were often mistaken for an actual building. It was not uncommon for architects visiting the School of Architecture from abroad to inquire as to the exact location of the Crystal Chapel, even twenty years after its initial design.[19]

The 1950 Bavinger House in Norman, Oklahoma, represents one of the finest examples of Goff's mature work. With its response to the wooded site, a predominant use of native stone, and a fluid continuous space of spiraling geometry reaching into the sky, the house epitomized his philosophical commitment to architecture as a vision of the natural world. The Bavinger House is a logarithmic spiral, built of rubble stone which appears to emerge from the earth and wrap around a central mast over fifty feet tall. Built next to a stream that was dammed to create a small pond, the house is set into the side of a low hill. Defining the locus of the spiral geometry, stainless steel airplane struts suspend the roof's warped plane from the mast.

Suspended circular "bowls," some with fishnet walls, fill the interior in arrays that create rooms for specific activities.[20] The spoon-shaped bowls, each with an attached copper-covered cylindrical closet, have a fixed radial relationship to the central mast and establish a rhythm at regular intervals as they ascend in tiers three feet apart. The pattern of forms defining the house is thus a composition of two related but different geometries: the logarithmic spiral enclosing the volume is asymmetrical as a form in motion, while the smaller circular pattern defining individual spaces is repetitive and static. But both originate from a common point and both can be defined mathematically. The pattern of radiating struts supporting the roof further emphasizes the mast's function as a point of the two geometries' origins.

Contrasting with the precision of the two geometries, a profusion of plants and pools of water enriches the interior and defines the lower level. Excavated into the side of the hill, the curved wall is terraced on the interior to create a series of irregular stepped planters. Climbing plants extend up the rock-faced wall toward the ribbon skylight at the spiraling wall's perimeter. Other planted areas are set in the floor itself, with meandering flagstone paths weaving between lush plants, terraces, and goldfish pools. Much of the lower level of the house is treated as a naturalistic garden with "rooms" floating above.

The design evolved from the client's dissatisfaction with conventional tract housing. OU art professor Eugene "Gene" Bavinger and his wife, Nancy, asked Goff to design a house they could build themselves, with a large open space that could immerse them into a world of nature. Nature had formed the expression of Gene Bavinger's abstract paintings throughout his long career.[21] Bavinger purchased an outcropping of surface rock on a farm about three miles from the building site. Known locally as "ironrock," it is a very hard and dense sandstone containing barite crystals. With the help of architecture students—and dynamite, sledge hammers, and a flatbed truck—the rock was broken up and hauled.

Facing page, Gene Bavinger House, Norman, Oklahoma, exterior. Photograph courtesy of Bruce Goff, 1978.

Building the 96-foot-long rock wall was another monumental job, requiring two hundred tons of rock. Designed as a cavity wall with steel reinforcement, the curved wall's shape and height required placing the rock on both exterior and interior surfaces with extensive scaffolding. Assisted by twenty-eight architecture students who mixed the mortar and helped with other phases of the work, Bavinger personally laid all the rock.[22] By taking part, the OU students were able to witness the architectural process in its entirety, from the design's origins with Herb Greene's exquisite drawings to the opportunity to participate in construction and the detailing process of this unique and important twentieth-century building. The house required five years to build and is as much a testament to Bavinger's endurance as it is to Goff's creativity.

Design of the Bavinger House represented, in part, a synthesis of ideas from the earlier Leidig project. In both, a collage of plants and pools of water forms the lower level of the structure. Both designs also juxtaposed circular elements to define specific activities within the larger space. However, in the

Leidig design Goff placed these elements of varying size on a single level in a random pattern but arrayed elements of the same size at different levels in a repeating pattern in the Bavinger House. Vladimir Tatlin's 1920 Monument to the Third International may also have influenced the Bavinger House with its use of geometric elements suspended within an enclosing spiral form. German Expressionism could also have been a source.

Above and facing page, Bavinger House, plan drawing and interior drawing by Herb Greene. Courtesy of Bruce Goff Archive, Ryerson & Burnham Archives, Art Institute of Chicago.

Although these influences may be present in the Bavinger design, collectively they represent only an inspirational point of departure for Goff's imagination. His interpretation remains unique and in several ways extends the precepts of organic expression. The Bavinger House provides one of the best examples of Goff's propensity to give each design component a sense of autonomy as an element of a larger composition. Wall, roof, and structure are clearly independent elements, and visualization of a separate geometric pattern for specific activities enriches their composition. Goff created formal hierarchies with the series of circular elements within a space that is fluid and continuously modulated. The sense of spatial movement defined by the spiraling form draws one into the space. As the relationship between walls, floor, and ceiling constantly changes, the direction of the flow of space becomes more powerful. Where the walls merge closer together, the distance between floor and ceiling expands. Projecting into this space, the circular bowls spiral upward, consistent with the direction of the enclosing form, but are static in their relationship to the central point of origin. Rounded at the bottom and covered in ochre-colored carpet, with a Plexiglas dome from a World War II bomber as a light fixture, the bowls are accessible by stairs attached to the interior wall of the spiral as it converges. The lowest bowl, located at the wide part of the spiral nearest the entry, forms a conversation area raised slightly above the floor.

The next highest bowl, suspended in space from the joists above, is a sleeping area with walls of fishnet and sheer curtains, the mattress recessed into the floor and covered with a bedspread of carpet. The next two bowls, still higher, function as sleeping areas for children and are similarly defined. The uppermost bowl, which extends beyond the primary spiral wall, is enclosed with glass to serve as Gene Bavinger's painting studio. With this design of two independent but sympathetic geometries, Goff created a dynamic space and a composition of visual tension—one of a solid anchoring element emerging from the earth and contrasting with light, frail elements floating in space.

Even with the mathematical logic in the precision of these two geometries and their relationship with one another, the specific translation of form into architectural reality is critical. With its walls of rough natural stone thrusting upward out of the earth in a setting of woods and stream, Goff's translation is an ode to nature—a transcendentalist vision of nature as the mediator between the imagination and reality. The highly irregular glazed openings in the spiral wall suggest a geological formation of natural voids, like the entrance to a cavern. This foreshadows the interior of the house, whose landscape of plants and water also has a cavelike quality. The expression of nature even pervades the details, such as the mullions of saplings in the glass-walled studio, and sustains the building's poetic image. The use of unorthodox materials in the design also reflects logical creativity in the effort to address specific problems of economy, structure, and aesthetics. An oilfield drill stem was utilized as the central mast because it was a surplus item and could be purchased at low cost.

Similarly, the stainless steel airplane struts were surplus items that addressed a structural problem. But their other purpose, as a suspension system, was to sustain Goff's aesthetic ideals: the warped roof plane became a dynamic, sinuous ribbon twisting skyward as an independent component; the weblike quality of the struts further magnified the illusion of light and delicate elements belonging to the realm of the sky; and the reflectivity of those components, amplifying their linearity, provided still another dimension of contrast with the massive walls. In the same way the blue-green glass cullets, incorporated as clusters in the curved rock wall, fulfilled multiple purposes. As a byproduct of glass manufacturing, they were inexpensive waste material that Goff's imagination transformed into objects of great potential. The cullets approximated the size and form of rock for the masonry walls, and their translucency and brilliant blue-green color provided a reflective counterpoint with the dark, matte finish of the iron rock.

The Bavinger House, with its rough stone walls ascending into the sky, responds to the character of the gnarled blackjack oaks as a song of praise for the natural world. It also reflects the athletic presence of its client, a man whose rugged facial features and muscular torso led Goff to comment that "he looked like a burly truck driver."[23] A design of great originality, the Bavinger House also represents a comprehensive manifestation of Goff's aesthetic ideals expressed in his 273 studio. Later he expanded on the notion of a "continuous present" in the Bavinger House:

> I wanted to do something that had no beginning and no ending as a fluid collage. Gertrude Stein says we begin again and again; this house begins again and again. She talks about the sense of not being in the past, present or future tense, but in the "continuous present." I was thinking in those terms.[24]

Yet upon completion of the house, initial coverage in *LIFE* magazine was disappointing. Goff characterized the article as a "fiasco as far as explaining the house to people who have not seen it, for the people who have seen it consider the article quite inadequate."[25] In response, composer and OU dean of fine arts Harrison Kerr wrote a caustic letter to the editors of *LIFE*, suggesting their coverage was a wasted opportunity: "faced with something new that has not yet been stamped 'approved', LIFE takes refuge behind a murky veil of provincial snobbishness and usually reduces its comment to the level of a sophomoric

Left, Bavinger House, interior construction, 1950. Ryerson & Burnham Archives, Art Institute of Chicago.

Right, Bavinger House, interior construction, 1950. Ryerson & Burnham Archives, Art Institute of Chicago.

Facing page, Bavinger House, exterior.

wise crack."[26] But the tide of recognition changed and the Bavinger House was added to the National Register of Historic Places in 2001. It is one of Goff's best-known designs and has been included in numerous articles and books on architecture. In 1987 the house was awarded the prestigious Twenty-Five Year Award of the American Institute of Architects, recognizing its enduring contribution to American architecture. The citation reads: "It spirals joyously into the Oklahoma sky, cut loose from the earth by a mind as free as the prairie landscape, a celebration of the spirit of man and nature united in architecture." Unfortunately, the house's heir and owner had difficulty securing funds for rehabilitation and destroyed the Bavinger House.

Extending the circular theme of the Bavinger House, in 1952 Goff also designed a house for the John Garvey family of Urbana, Illinois. A music professor at the University of Illinois, Garvey wanted a house where he and his wife, also a musician, might give performances for small audiences yet also practice inde-

pendently. The plan of the Garvey composition is also a fluid collage of circular forms with smaller elements arrayed asymmetrically within a larger symmetrical form. The larger form curves outward from a circular basin of water in a central garden, and open-web metal ribs define its structure. The cylindrical form of a glass curtain wall, placed at the horizontal tangent point of the ribs, supports them. Beyond this point the ribs cantilever to extend the curve downward at the perimeter. The symmetrical form, resembling the geometry of a morning glory flower, would be clad with metal fencing material and sprayed with transparent plastic. Goff wanted irregular hanging edges to contrast with the ribs' smooth plastic skin. Water would flow from the tangent point of the ribs and over the plastic into the basin below, providing a cooling effect for the garden and for a circular music room and living space enclosed with domed plastic roofs. In winter, the water would freeze and provide insulation. This seasonal effect also would provide variations of translucency.

Functioning as rooms with skylights and built-in furniture, the aluminum spheres would be supported at their midpoint in the cylindrical glass wall by an armature. Defined as a square with curved sides (a motif referred to by Goff and students alike as a "squircle") and incrementally spaced radial members, the spheres and supporting armature would give an effect of opaque forms suspended in space. At the entry level a transparent helical circulation tube would ascend upward to the spheres, arrayed in a regular rhythm at different levels on the tube's exterior side. The spheres would define a kitchen, bedroom, bath, two additional bedrooms, and a study positioned directly over the entry. Opposite the kitchen would be a dining room sphere, on the interior side of the helix, with a transparent dome to relate it to the enclosed garden. A plastic canopy served as the carport, and a semicircular plastic fence inset with a rhythm of spherical planters in smaller "squircle" armatures defined the driveway.

Clearly linked to the earlier Bavinger House, the Garvey design also acts as a study of Goff's "opacity, translucency, and transparency" concept. In one sense it represents the Bavinger House turned inside out. At the Bavinger House, the opaque outer shell spirals into the sky. In the Garvey design the protective shell would be translucent and converge into the earth. The "rooms" within the Bavinger House are open and transparent but in the Garvey design they were exposed to the exterior as opaque spheres. It was a design of contrast, and Goff wanted an expression "less rooted to the ground . . . toward a more athletic and lighter understanding of architecture."[27] The opaque spheres concealed and contained activities of private living, yet the total architectural composition, including its passage through space, was open and revealed instantly. The Garvey design represents yet another interpretation of dualities, of visual integration of opposites, in defining creative architecture. There were familiar idealized components in the composition, including the ubiquitous element of water, but it was on the roof—a flowing stream in the sky—rather than earthbound. The transformation of a flower into a translucent shelter with exotic

House for the John Garvey family, Urbana, Illinois, project, 1952. Drawing by Herb Greene. Ryerson & Burnham Archives, Art Institute of Chicago.

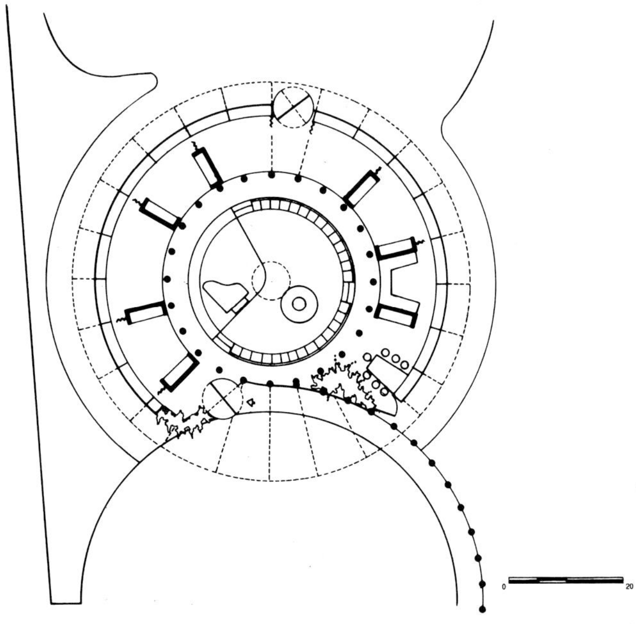

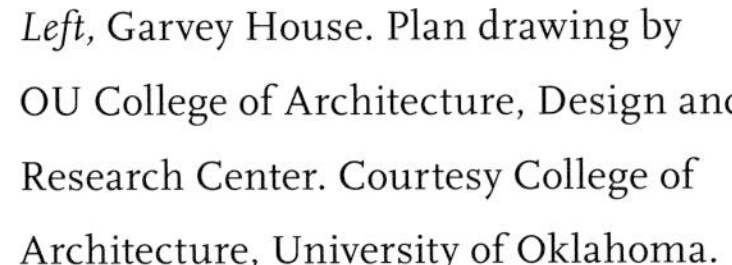

Left, Garvey House. Plan drawing by OU College of Architecture, Design and Research Center. Courtesy College of Architecture, University of Oklahoma.

Right, Garvey House, interior, 1954. Ryerson & Burnham Archives, Art Institute of Chicago.

spherical fruit as rooms creates a sense of interrelatedness with nature.

Though this version of the design remained unbuilt, its presence on paper has direct reference to Emerson when he wrote: "The feat of the imagination is in showing the convertibility of everything into every other thing."[28] Goff, however, was ahead of contemporary technology. A warranty limitation on the membrane of transparent plastic sprayed on wire and excessive fabrication costs of the spherical rooms created problems. There were also structural problems. The absence of a tie ring at the ends of the curved metal joists cast doubt on the sustainability of the design. Aware of some of these problems, Goff abandoned the design and developed a second, greatly simplified scheme in 1954. Defined by a circular plan with a low-pitched conical roof and earth-bermed exterior walls, the design recalled earlier themes of centroid plan geometry with its interior arrangement of public space at the center and private functions at the perimeter. The floor of the central area is embedded into the earth three feet below grade and defined at the perimeter by a ring of built-in seating/storage units. The arcade of columns, built of concrete sewer pipe with the bell-shaped ends butted together, amplifies the circular theme and separates public from private space.

The 1955 design of the John Frank House in Sapulpa, Oklahoma, extended Goff's vision of composite geometry with a linear segment of an arc penetrated radially by subordinate forms. Built near the crest of a heavily wooded hill in a post–World War II suburb, the house's broad curved terraces form a cascading, monumental base for the facade of barrel-vaulted terra-cotta tile. Punctuated with a rhythm of deeply recessed windows, the pattern-rich façade, harmonizing in color with the stone of the terraces and branches of the many trees, is cantilevered over a recessed foundation to create a shadow linc. A radial form with a rounded end clad in brick penetrates the façade, finished with a light-green glaze and weeping mortar joints. Although the top surface of this form is the deck for a swimming pool, seen from the street the form is simply an abstract element contrasting in color with the curved wall of roofing tile. Collectively the façade ensemble of the two components is one of mystery.

The house is entered from a courtyard at the rear, and the elevation of that exterior wall is also abstract but with a very different scale from that of the façade. A glass curtain wall of multicolored decorative tile, set behind a narrow reflecting pool terminated at both ends by two bathrooms projecting into the courtyard, is its principal component. Like the walls of the swimming pool extending from the façade, the symmetrical rounded bathrooms are also finished with a green-glazed brick. At the midpoint between their forms, a bridge crosses a pool of water to the entry. Goff amplified the entry with a pair of planters mounted on the bathroom roofs. Constructed from the ends of steel boiler tanks and raised above the roof surface, the planters also serve as exterior lights for the courtyard and as skylights for the bathrooms.

Following spread

Left, John Frank House, Sapulpa, Oklahoma, 1955. Plan drawing, OU College of Architecture, Design and Research Center. Courtesy College of Architecture, University of Oklahoma.

Right, Frank House, exterior.

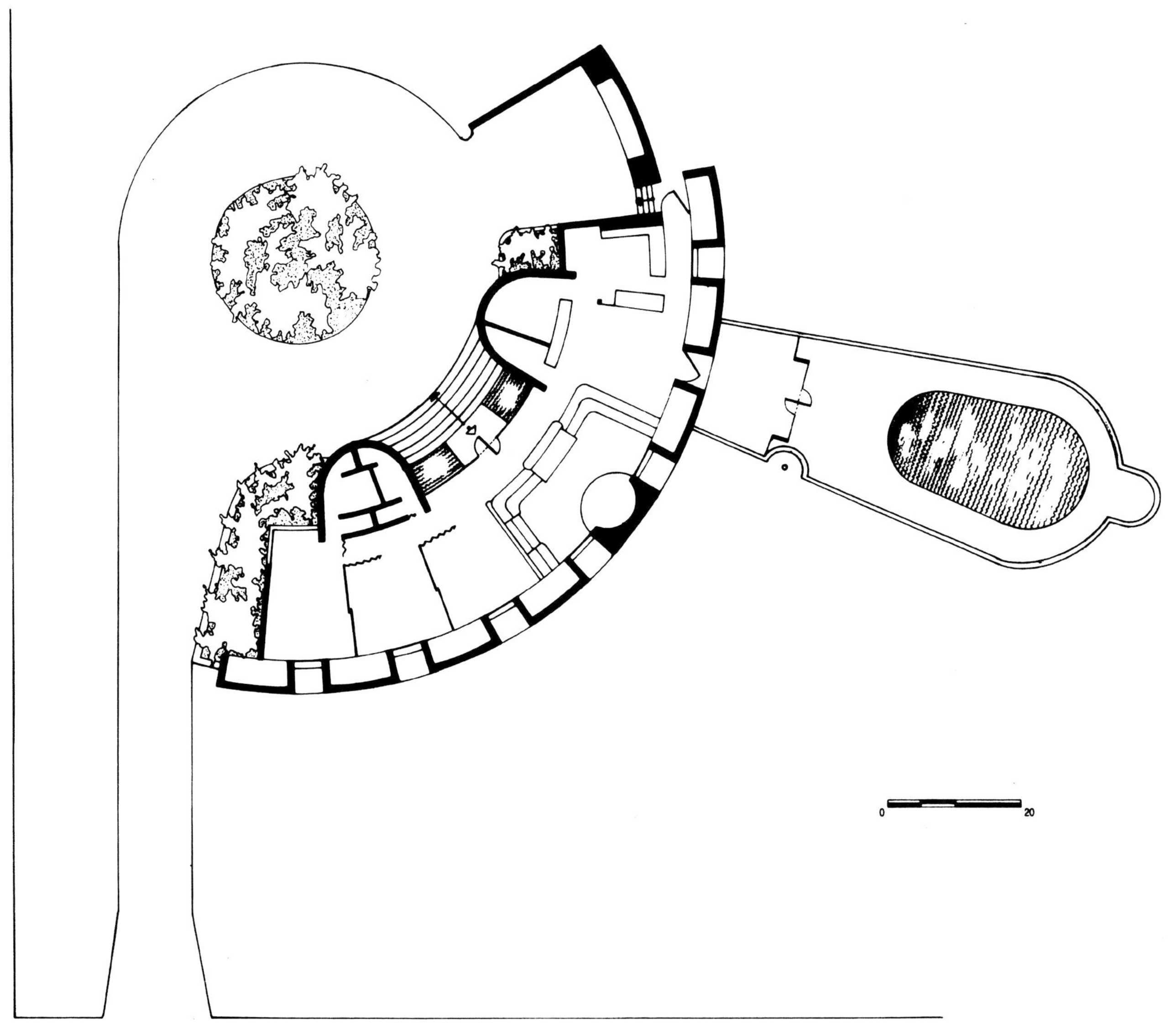
0
20

The interior of the Frank House is a curvilinear sequence of spaces, with an open plan arrangement defining the kitchen and dining area at one end and a large living area opposite the entry. The recessed floor in the living area has built-in seating on three sides, which faces a cone-shaped fireplace of tiled units, also glazed light green, with the tall chimney penetrating a skylight. Adjoining bedrooms occupy the other end of the linear curving plan. Folding wood partitions act as bedroom walls, defining a corridor adjacent to the tiled curtain wall, and the radial walls between bedrooms are sliding partitions. With all the partitions opened, the interior becomes a single space. Goff achieved this openness by placing the service elements at the perimeter on both sides of the arc. The bathrooms, defined visually as abstract forms, project into the courtyard while closets line the outer curved wall of the facade between a rhythm of windows set in deep reveals.

Goff's client was the owner of Frankoma Pottery, which manufactured dinnerware that incorporated western motifs such as cactus, wagonwheels, cattle brands, and Indian themes. All of these ceramics were glazed with one of several standard Frankoma colors. Goff collaborated with his client, who had formerly taught ceramics at OU, to glaze the brick in a light-green color, which was one of the popular colors Frank used on his dinnerware. Goff also utilized Frankoma glazes of contrasting colors in the design of decorative tile on both the interior and exterior surfaces of the glass courtyard wall. The circular motif of open voids in the lacelike tile allowed both natural light and partial vision. The tile units, and glazing for the brick, were all manufactured at the Frankoma Pottery plant.

Listed on the National Register of Historic Places, the Frank House represents an expression of clarity in functional organization. It also extends a fundamental tenet of organic architecture in addressing specific issues of site and client. By using masonry units glazed with Frankoma Pottery colors, Goff embraced the very livelihood of his client with the design. He created a building of both repose and dualities, an expression of ruggedness and protection and

Facing page, Frank House, exterior. Photograph by Robert Bowlby.

Frank House, tile at courtyard entry. Photograph by author.

another of delicacy and intimacy. The design represents a close collaboration with an artist whose creativity Goff respected and, like much of his best work, was a design of specificity rich in meaning.

In later decades, Goff told his old friend Jerri Hodges Bonebrake, "The happiest years of my life were those when I was at OU."[29] Buildings and unbuilt projects of the university years brought Goff national and international acclaim as an architect and recognition as a creative innovator in architectural education.

Although he was widely respected on the OU campus, Goff resigned in December 1955, citing "ill health" as the reason for his departure amid personal controversy.[30] He tried to convince visionary architect Paolo Soleri to apply for a teaching position at OU. Soleri, an Italian who studied with Wright after he emigrated from Italy in 1947, would later become widely known for Arcosanti, an experimental community in Arizona he designed and based on ecological principles in a composition of diverse geometric forms. In his letter to Soleri, Goff reiterated that the goal of education was to develop the creative individual "with the best coordinated technical and aesthetic help . . . so that one might solve practical problems with imagination as a complete Architect. And discipline must be sought in freedom."[31] Soleri, however, did not want to leave Arizona. Goff then encouraged Herb Greene to return to OU. Greene joined the faculty in September 1957 to become an inspirational and respected teacher through extension of the ideals of organic architecture. The freedom of self-expression, initiated by Goff and continued by Greene and other faculty members, provided a continuing direction for the School of Architecture—and for Goff's later work as a practicing architect in Kansas, Oklahoma, and Texas.

Talking to Bruce Goff was like talking to yourself in the mirror. I asked him if it [a feature of the design] should be painted red or black. He responded it should be both.

JOE PRICE

Every mind is different; and the more it is unfolded the more pronounced is that difference.

RALPH WALDO EMERSON

6 A CONTINUING PRESENCE

Although Goff left OU in December 1955, he remained in Middle America for the rest of his life. He located his office first in Bartlesville, Oklahoma, then moved to Kansas City, Missouri, and finally to Tyler, Texas. During nearly three decades of professional practice in those communities, all of his significant constructed buildings, with the exception of a Bartlesville church education building and a Los Angeles museum, were single-family houses. As a sole practitioner who never sought clients, Goff's economic circumstances varied. There were times of intense productivity with many commissions, but at other times he had little work.

Goff continued to pursue earlier themes but his best work introduced original interpretations that invariably reflected the aspirations of the client and attributes of the site. There were, however, some generalized concepts that were dominant during the later phases of his career. During the Bartlesville years, some designs emphasized the complex arrangement of composite geometry and asymmetrical compositions. In Kansas City, some houses show greater restraint in their use of multiple building materials defining the exterior form, while others show more reliance on ornament as an element of composition. Finally, in his Tyler years, Goff's major design achievement was a museum with varied form, color, pattern, and texture that masterfully synthesized his architectural ideals.

BARTLESVILLE, OKLAHOMA, 1956–1964

By January 1956, Goff had established his combined office and living space in one of Price Tower's newly completed two-story apartments. Goff knew the H. C. Price family, and it was on his recommendation they commissioned Frank Lloyd Wright to design the tower for their corporate headquarters. Shortly thereafter the elder Price had Wright design a winter home in Arizona and H. C. Price, Jr., engaged Wright for a family home on "Starview Farm," a Bartlesville rural acreage owned by the family. Youngest son Joe Price, who studied engineering at OU during the early 1950s, sought Goff to design his own bachelor house, seeking a place of escape where one could "sit on the floor."

Goff's first design for Joe Price in 1953 was unlike anything he had ever produced. It was a series of dissonant and angular fragmented forms set on pedestals cascading down the side of a hill. Goff referred to the design as a "studio" since it combined living quarters with space for Price to pursue his interest in photography. Curious about Goff's design, on one of his visits to Bartlesville Wright asked to see the drawings. He disapproved of the project's anticipated costs, writing Goff a patronizing letter of criticism that referred to the design as "hocus-pocus for an opus."[1] The project was not built.

When Price approached Goff for a second design in 1956, he requested the use of modular planning, believing it might help control costs. Although Goff thought Price's request was due to Wright's objections to the aesthetics of the initial design, the second schematic was warmly received by Price. This initi-

ated an enduring friendship between the two men, as Goff was not only the architect for Price's house but also encouraged his interest in collecting Japanese paintings. They later traveled together to Asia, and Price commissioned Goff to design the last major project of his life, the Pavilion for Japanese Art at the Los Angeles County Museum of Art.

Built on the Starview Farm property, the Joe Price Studio represents Goff's most opulent house design. With major additions in 1966 and 1974, the house in its final form was a composition of both great diversity and continuity. The initial design of 1956 featured a floor plan in the shape of an equilateral triangle with extensions at the corners that formed a pinwheel arrangement. The triangular shape defined a large open volume, and each of the corner elements provided space for separate activities: the entry under a cantilevered carport; a screened porch; and a bedroom with a cantilevered bed. A series of paired, elongated hexagonal units served as transitional elements for passage between

Above, Joe Price House, Bartlesville, Oklahoma, project, 1953. Courtesy of Bruce Goff.

Following spread

Left, Price House, studio plan. Drawing by Irene Fatsea, Design and Research Center, OU College of Architecture. Courtesy College of Architecture, University of Oklahoma.

Right, Price House, porch detail. Photograph by author.

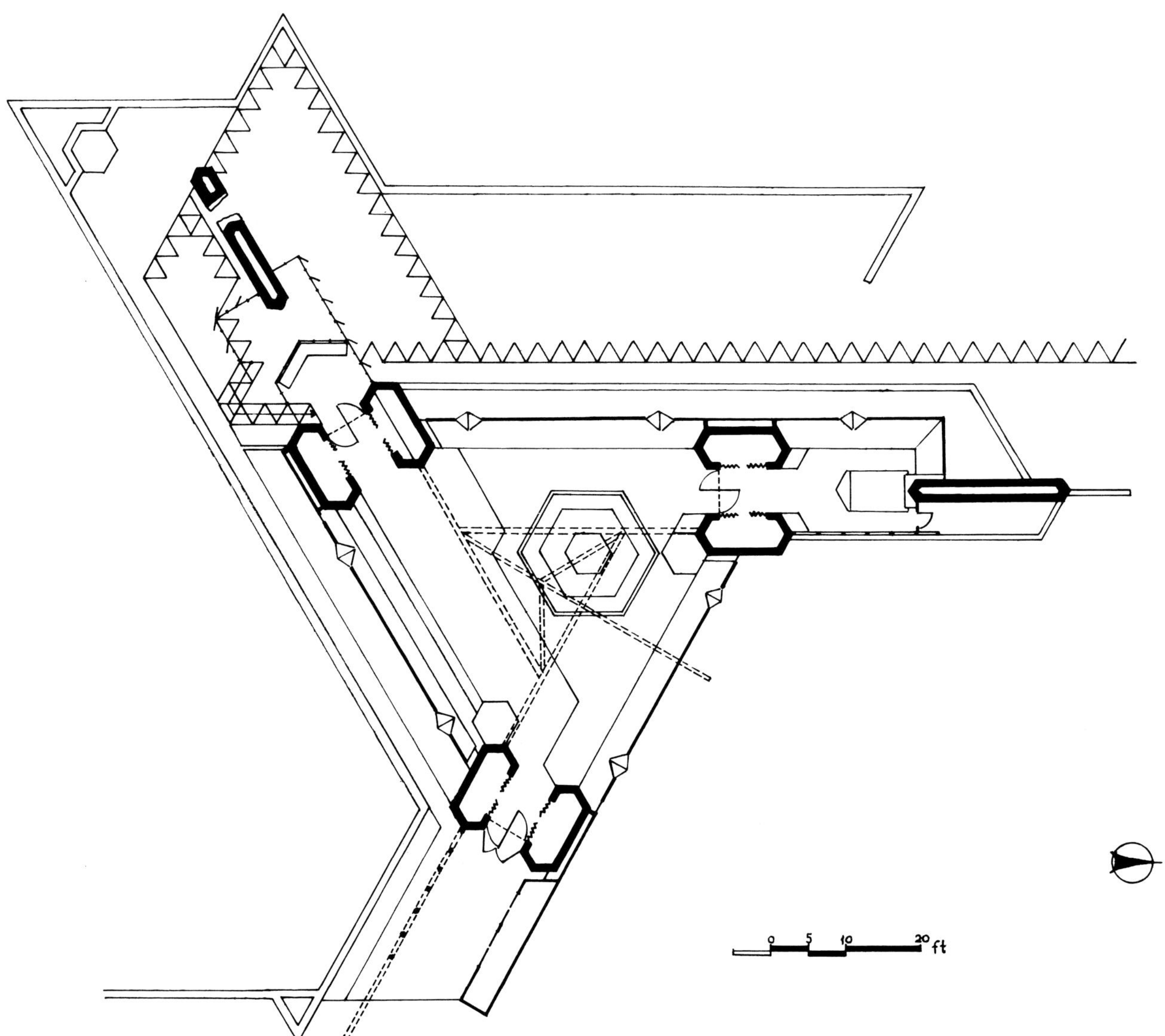
0
5
10
20 ft

the primary space and the secondary spaces at the corners. These elements, too, had different functions. Units adjacent to the entry defined closets, the ones next to the bedroom defined a bath and another closet, and the units nearest the screened porch provided minimalistic kitchen facilities.

The large triangular form's exterior walls sloped outward from their foundation to join the pitched roof planes. Constructed of structural wood decking, both roof and walls were covered with reflective gold-anodized aluminum that amplified the form's crystalline quality. These aluminum pinnacles thrust upward from the cornice at an inverse angle to the slope of the roof. When asked about these elements in 1982, Goff said that he "wanted to make an interesting profile against the sky."[2] The paired service units at the corners were veneered with anthracite coal laid in an irregular pattern and interspersed with blue-green glass cullets. Although the three extended elements at the corners of the primary form were all treated differently, it was the two-story screened porch with a water feature that was of greatest complexity and variety. The ground declined steeply from this corner to define two levels, one congruent with the main floor of the house and a lower level terrace with a pool of water containing goldfish and lily pads. The pool, which also extended inside the screened porch, was bifurcated by a large pier of coal that projected upward at the outside corner like the prow of a ship. Heavily encrusted with glass cullets, the pier's irregular opening framed a bronze statue of a phoenix. Water emanated from concealed sources in the masonry to splash into the pool below. A vertical trellis, made of cast aluminum triangles and painted muted red, shaded one wall of the screened porch and appeared to rise from the pool of water.

Exposed, laminated wood beams framed to the service units in a pinwheel configuration defined the roof structure and sustained the theme of triangular geometry. Primary structural beams were painted black with secondary beams, at the perimeter of the prismatic volume, painted turquoise. The perimeter beams also served as the armature for a continuous cove, edged with gold aluminum strips embossed with a triangular motif, for concealed lighting. Beams framing the screened porch, bedroom, and a large clerestory at the apex of the principal space were dramatically cantilevered, each terminated by a triangular ornament. Gold-anodized aluminum finials, set at an angle, rose from the top of the coal-covered service units to further enrich the profile of the roof.

The opulent interior featured a rubbed gold finish on the exposed wood ceiling and a floor mostly covered by thick white shag carpet that extended up the sloping walls. A recessed conversation area, hexagonal in shape and also covered with the carpet, was offset from the locus of the geometric form. The carpet on the floor, walls, and recessed area was underlaid with a two-inch-thick foam rubber pad to provide a soft surface for sitting. Dozens of colorful pillows provided the primary furnishings. In the center of the hexagon, a recessed cabinet concealed a bar and the controls for audio equipment that could be raised hydraulically. The cabinet had a mosaic-tile surface with a brilliantly colored design of variations on a hexagonal-triangular theme.

Small diamond-shaped windows in the primary space featured interior shutters. In their open position the shutter surfaces were faced with purple mirror, but the opposite side was carpeted. When closed they formed a continuous surface and sealed the space to any exterior. At the centroid of the triangular volume the roof was modulated with a clerestory set in an angular hood, its interior surfaces covered in goose feathers. Planes of transparent plastic strips that were suspended into the space below animated the ensemble.

Tall, center-pivoted doors positioned between the three service units defined entries into the main room. Built of mahogany with an inset glass panel repeating the elongated hexagonal shape of the service units, all three doors had an abstract mural attached to the glass. Each door had a different design of various colors and materials, but all were geometric variations on a triangular theme.

In 1966 Goff designed an addition to the house to provide space for Price's growing collection of Japanese paintings of the Edo Period (1615–1865). Price had recently married and also needed expanded living space. The major element of the addition, a museum, represented Goff's finest achievement in

Price House, interior. Ryerson & Burnham Archives, Art Institute of Chicago.

Above, Price House, cabinet with mosaic tile top. Photograph by George W. Lewis.

Following spread

Left, Price House, mural on one of the three glass doors defining entry into the main room. Photograph by Tamera McCuen.

Right, Price House, detail of clerestory set in an angular hood mounted on the roof. The interior of the surface is veneered with goose feathers with strips of hanging plastic set in motion by movement of air within. Photograph by George W. Lewis.

assigning multiple meanings. Set to one side of the original house's entry, the museum connected with a narrow space containing a kitchen, dining area, and small bathroom. Sliding glass doors from the dining area overlooked a teak deck and Japanese garden enclosed by low walls of coal and glass cullets. The museum floor plan was a variation of the earlier triangular theme, but its clipped corners formed a hexagonal shape with unequal sides. Attached at the midpoint to each of the three major exterior walls were elongated hexagonal units similar to the service units of coal in the original house. A hipped roof of gold-anodized aluminum, with deep eaves and a triangular skylight joining the roof planes at its apex, enclosed the museum.

A muted color palette of materials greatly subdued the symmetrical prism of the museum's interior. Dark-brown refrigeration cork sloped to the apex of the ceiling, in bands separated by gold mosaic tile inserts. The hexagonal units on the exterior walls were finished with off-white silk on their interior to serve as *tokonomas* for hanging paintings. The adjoining glass walls' inside surfaces

Plan of museum in Price House. Drawing by Irene Fatsea, OU College of Architecture, Design and Research Center. Courtesy College of Architecture, University of Oklahoma.

were lined with sliding *shoji* screens and covered with Japanese rice paper to diffuse the light. Three free-standing teak cabinets, set on a raised platform to suggest an inner space distinct from perimeter spaces, provided additional surfaces for display of paintings. They also served multiple functional purposes: one was a storage area for paintings; another concealed a hidden stair to a space below; and the third was used as a closet for a perimeter space that became a sleeping area at night. Futons, stored during the day, could be laid on the floor

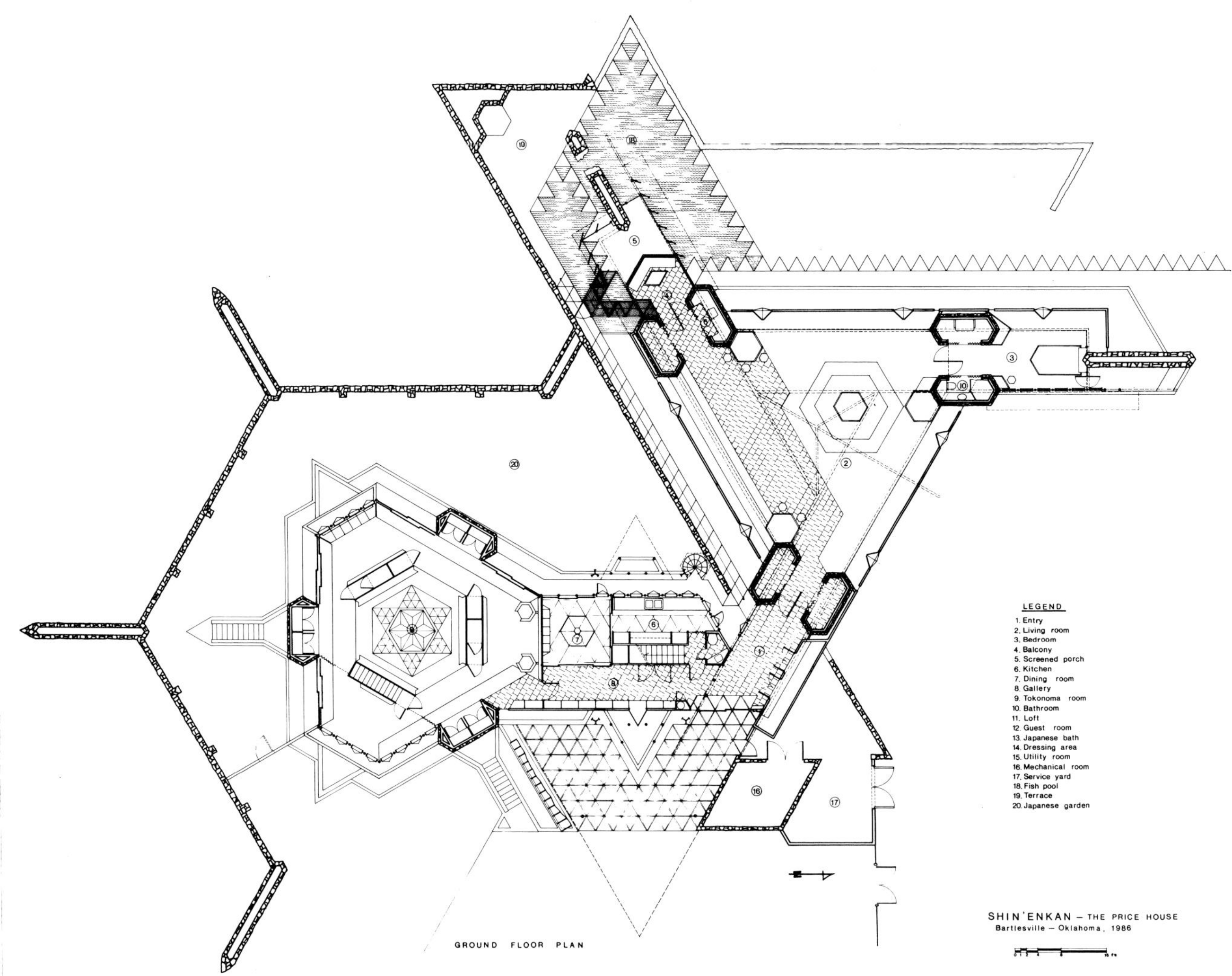

for Price and his Japanese wife, Etsuko.

The floor at the center of the inner space, defined by persimmon-colored carpet and a medallion of matching tile, held a large aquarium filled with multicolored Japanese *koi*. Hexagonal in shape, the glass walls of the aquarium extended into the space below to define an inverted pyramid on the vertical axis, reflected by a skylight above. Yet there was another component beneath the water: an ornamental collage of brilliant colors defining another space. Distorted by the motion of water, the space was perceived initially as fragments of color beyond the swimming goldfish. Only gradually was definition apparent as both walls and floor were covered with a continuous tile mural that obscured the juncture of horizontal and vertical planes. From the perspective below, the visual effect was equally astonishing, as the aquarium became a magnificent liquid skylight suspended in space and animated by goldfish harmonizing

Museum interior. Ryerson & Burnham Archives, Art Institute of Chicago.

Glass aquarium in Price House with visibility to space below. Photograph by Joe Price. Ryerson & Burnham Archives, Art Institute of Chicago.

with the colors of the mural-covered walls, ceiling, and floor. Fragments of the museum space, colorful paintings, and floating clouds seen through the skylight framed the view beyond.

Beneath this glass prism was a Japanese bath, with the walls, floor, and ceiling surfaced with a mosaic tile mural (see page 78). The glass aquarium, animated by the reflective fish and motion of water, established a transparent connection between the space below and the space above. It was, above all, an element of beauty, and approximates Goff's ideal of pure architecture existing only for the sake of aesthetics. It is also analogous to Bruno Taut's statement at the opening of the 1914 Glass Pavilion: "[It] has no other purpose than to be beautiful."[3] The presence of the ornament/bath provides clear interpretation of one of Goff's favorite expressions that also obliquely echoes Taut: "There's the reason, then there's the *real* reason."[4] With the Price House museum the reason for the space below was for bathing and the reason for the aquarium was to provide a humidified environment for the Japanese paintings, but the *real* reason for this ensemble was to create a beautiful artifact, a three-dimensional ornament. With the inclusion of an aquarium Goff also clearly communicates his posture on design: architecture embraces nature.

In 1974 Goff designed another addition. Developed as a tower to accommodate children on the second-floor and a private retreat for Price on the third floor, the exterior form fit seamlessly with the earlier work. Defined by a diamond-shaped plan, the tower rose through the flat-roofed carport on slender steel columns veneered with mirror tile and cast metal triangles.

On the second floor the acute angled corners were clipped, but on the floor above they were extended as cantilevered balconies. Sheltering the tower was a folded plane of gold-anodized aluminum with pronounced eaves that corresponded to the plan geometry. Goff covered the exterior walls of the tower with modular tile units made from the bark of African acacia trees. The textured surface of the bark harmonized with the garden walls of coal as a natural material. The interior of the retreat, accessed by a spiral stair encased in an embellished glass hexagon, was opulent with jewel-like murals adhered to the tower end walls of glass.

The visual effect of the tower, with its modulated scale, was one of a focal point as an exotic and abstract form rising upward from the Japanese garden. The tower, as the final addition, pleased Goff in terms of its overall effect on the totality of the design. "It needed," he said, "a vertical element to complete the composition."[5] The Price House with its two additions represented a major achievement for Goff. Over a period of nearly twenty years the house was expanded and modified to create a superb manifestation of his philosophy of architecture. It was a clear expression of the design ideals Goff characterized in the 273 studio, especially Theme, Variation, Development, and Modulation. It

Following spread

Left, Plan of Price House tower. Drawing by Irene Fatsea, OU College of Architecture, Design and Research Center. Courtesy College of Architecture, University of Oklahoma.

Center, Tower exterior and, *right,* interior door (and surrounding glass) to balcony. Photographs by author.

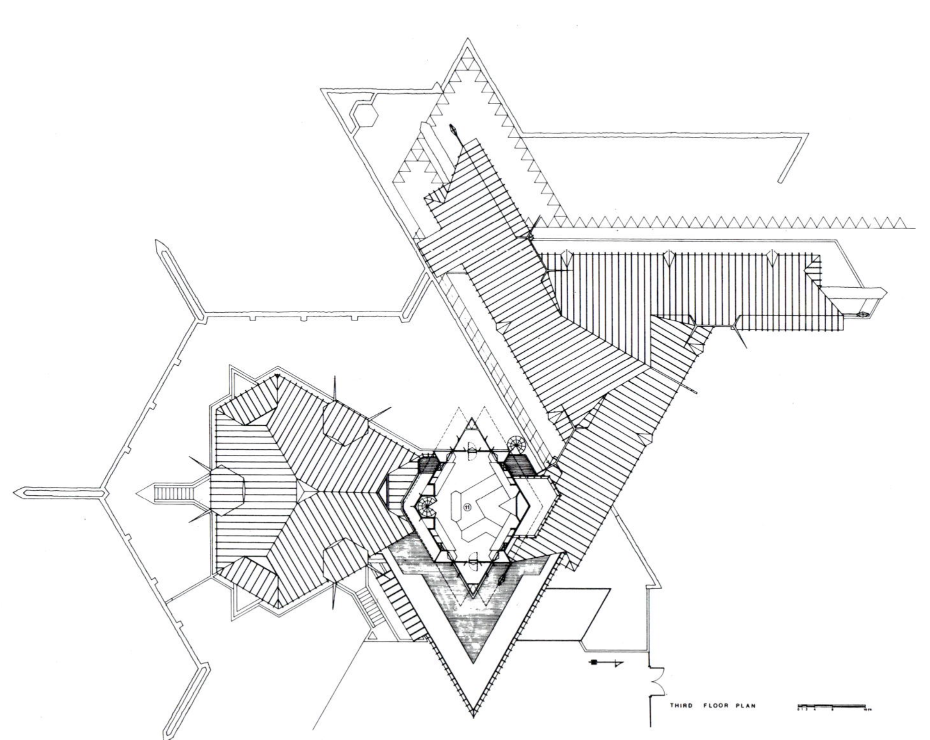
THIRD FLOOR PLAN

did not have the appearance of a house with multiple additions but a design that was developed at a single point in time. With the initial studio as a reflective prism poised lightly upon a green lawn, the crystalline geometry recalled the utopian ideals of German Expressionism as a source of inspiration. With pools of water on both the exterior, and interior as it was modified, the composition embraced elements of the natural world. The design was also an affirmation of Goff's commitment to the evolving aspirations and needs of his client. The three components—studio, museum, and tower—each served a different purpose and the differences were visualized by giving each its own expression.

There was also a great sense of continuity existing among the three components of the house with a seamless visual integration. The use of gold-anodized aluminum as an enclosing material established unity, yet the three components were linked together in other ways. All relied on variations of a triangular theme in the making of hexagonal and diamond-shaped forms to create symmetrical spaces in a larger asymmetrical composition. Although the completed design was so varied, the use of a module became less apparent. Two of the three components, studio and museum, were defined with a vertical axis as an ordering device. Even the third component, the retreat in the upper level of the tower, was defined by an axis but it was rotated horizontally and terminated by the art-glass murals at either end of the space. Cantilevers were abundant in all three components—roofs, beams, angled finials, decks, balconies—even

Facing page, Price House. Image of completed house. Photograph by author.

Below, Price House. Elevation drawings by Irene Fatsea, OU College of Architecture, Design and Research Center. Courtesy College of Architecture, University of Oklahoma.

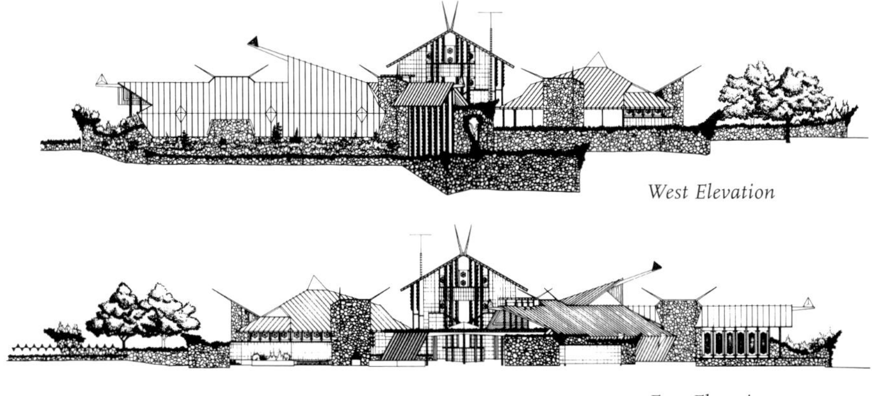

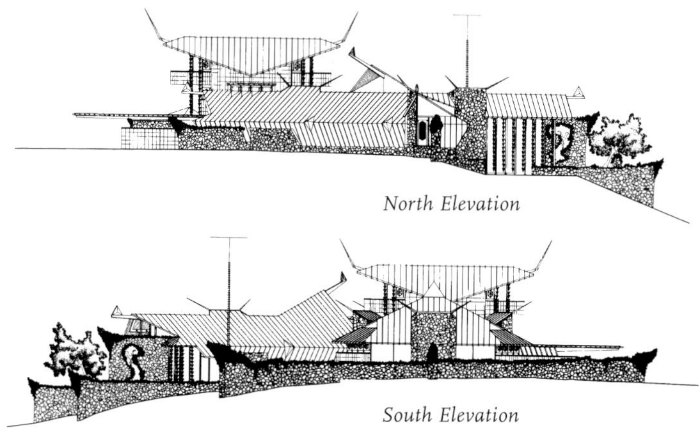

the bed in the original studio thrust dramatically into space. The few pieces of furniture were designed by Goff and much was built in. The floor plane in two of the components were modulated by recessed areas, one inviting entry for conversation and another with a transparent barrier of glass and water as an object to behold.

Goff had a masterful understanding of the play of opposites in design to create a dynamic tension of opposing forces. The interior of the initial studio, with its array of rich colors and textures, contrasted with the restraint of the museum interior. For the museum space Goff selected finishes and colors to create a space of repose that would not compete with the decorative paintings. Other parts of the total design also reveal, with equal clarity, the presence of visual dichotomies. This is particularly evident in the ensemble of elements associated with the screened porch and its continuum of a semitransparent volume, a plane of opaque coal, and a reflective pool of water. It was a design of contrasts. Elements of the composition were played against one another: frail elements contrasted with heavy elements; natural elements were juxtaposed with manmade elements; light colors contrasted with dark colors; and the pool of water magnified the design, giving depth by reflection.

Although the house was destroyed by arson with diesel fuel on a dark night in December 1996,[6] it represented a remarkable design of form and space that reflected a duality of design ideals in diversity and continuity. It was both a manifestation of Goff's endowment of a courage of convictions and a symbol of the persona of Joe Price and his wife, Etsuko, as they referred to the house as Shin'enkan, a Japanese word meaning "place of the faraway heart."

With the exception of the Price House, and another design of 1958, Goff did not pursue a typology of plan organization with centroidal geometry when he was in Bartlesville. Although he drew upon earlier conceptualizations for specific components of design he also experimented with varied compositions of diverse and freely arranged composite geometry. Forms tended to become bolder and more exaggerated. Designs of several houses were developed by combining rectilinear with angled geometry and there was a renewed interest

Al Dewlin House, project. Photograph in collection of author.

in curved geometry to create sinuous and fluid spaces.

Goff's 1956 house design for Al Dewlin, with curvilinear walls of coal and golden iron pyrites in the mortar, fell into this category. Never constructed, the design appears to emerge cicadalike from the High Plains of West Texas as an exotic creature of the earth. With its translucent, hornlike tubular forms defining ramps to secluded spaces at the flared ends, one would see the horizon set in motion by feather sculptures, as terminating elements, whirling in the wind. Yet the inclusion of feathered elements would have been problematic. It is unlikely they would have survived a season of intense West Texas winds.

Two houses illustrate variations of an expression of service components as a modulating element of façade design. Both the Motsenbocker House in Bartlesville and the Comer House in nearby Dewey, Oklahoma, have aspects of their presence conceptually derivative from an idea expressed earlier in both the Frank House and the Price House, one of placement of bathrooms and closets on a major elevation. Conceptually it allowed greater open interior space and the position of those functions offered opportunities to modulate the

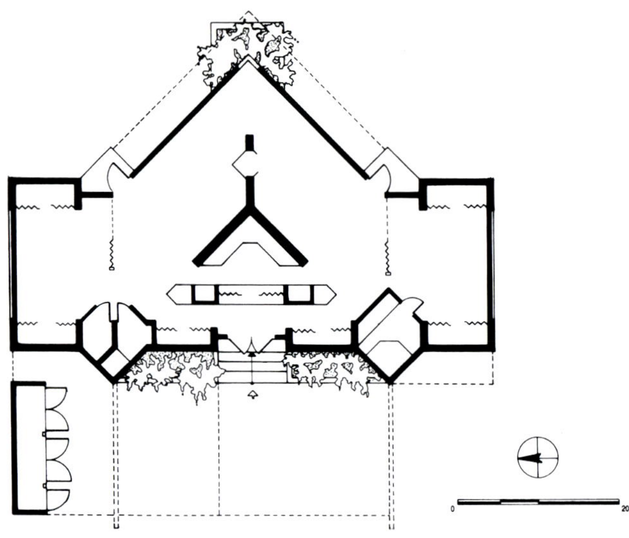

Left, C. A. Comer House, Dewey, Oklahoma. Plan drawing by OU College of Architecture, Design and Research Center. Courtesy College of Architecture, University of Oklahoma.

Right, Comer House, exterior. Photograph by author.

façade with contrasting scale, color, or textural hierarchies.

The modest C. A. Comer House, designed in 1957 for a small lot in an older neighborhood of Dewey, has a Y-shaped central fireplace dividing the space into three major zones with the kitchen located, at the client's request, nearest the entry. The configuration and position of the fireplace established a plan arrangement of composite geometry with projecting angled forms on both the front and back of the house. On the façade the angular bathrooms are visually small-scale painted wood-clad forms contrasting with projecting, rectangular brick-enclosed closets. To introduce natural light into the house the upper part of the façade is a large clerestory filling the gable. By recessing the glass to protect it from the west sun with a deep overhang, the shadow magnifies the thin edge of the roof. This quality of weightlessness is further amplified by the carport of translucent corrugated fiberglass panels supported on cantilevered wood beams twenty feet long. Structurally the cantilevers are actually double-cantilevered beams with diagonal cable-end supports balanced over decorated

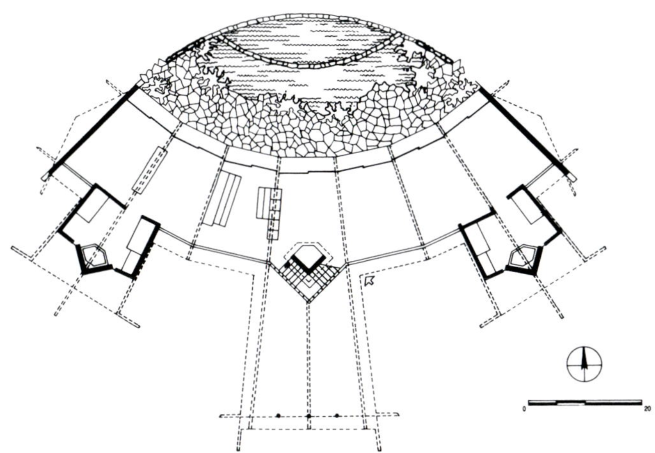

center posts rising above the cornice.

In the J. O. Motsenbocker House, Goff dramatically extended the concept of expression of service functions on the façade. The plan geometry of the 1957 design is derived from a segmented arc with two prominent bathroom towers of angled stone walls and extended cantilevered roofs thrusting upward into the sky. An ensemble of forms terminates the deep overhanging roofs with the fascia extended as outriggers, a notched cantilevered central beam and a vertical rod with a rhythm of ornamental red squares. Collectively this assemblage of lines pointing east, west, north, south, up, and down forms a visual magnet in the sky. A carport, at the center of the symmetrical plan, contrasts with the tower roofs by extension in the opposite direction to a point low to the ground. Penetrating the carport roof is another tower defining the fireplace chimney and stair. With this arrangement, Goff visualized the process of ascension from the entry at the lower level to the primary living area above by enclosing the stair with glass walls as it wrapped around the fireplace. Built into the side

Left, Motsenbocker House, exterior detail. Photograph by author.

Right, J. O. Motsenbocker House, Bartlesville, Oklahoma. Plan drawing by OU College of Architecture, Design and Research Center. Courtesy College of Architecture, University of Oklahoma.

of a hill, the design further suggests a play of opposites by distinctive treatment of the front and rear elevations. The articulated outer wall of the façade with high windows and clerestories offers privacy and evokes protection *from* the environment while the continuous glass wall at the back, overlooking a tranquil pool and garden, offers invitation and extension *to* the environment. This principle of duality, as a composition of both drama and repose, is ultimately the conceptual underpinning of the design.

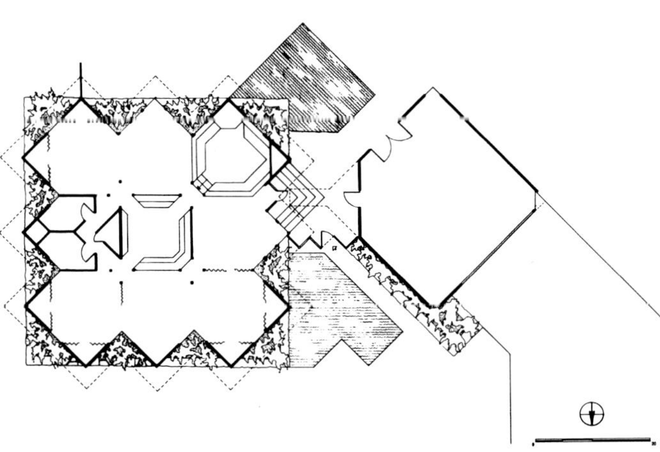

Above, Donald Pollock House, Oklahoma City, Oklahoma. Plan drawing by OU College of Architecture, Design and Research Center. Courtesy College of Architecture, University of Oklahoma.

Facing page, Pollock House, exterior. Photograph by author.

Another house of 1957 represents further exploration of design with modules developed in the 1950 Wilson House, discussed in the previous chapter. Although the earlier design had a sense of expansiveness with its interlocking modules arrayed in a linear composition, the house for Donald Pollock in Oklahoma City has nine modules grouped together in a square matrix on a corner suburban lot. In the plan the exterior walls of each of the perimeter modules are rotated at a forty-five-degree angle to overlap a square stone plinth and establish a sawtooth configuration. Each of the fourteen-foot-square modules has a hipped roof with a pyramidal skylight at its apex. Planes of the roofs at the perimeter are extended over the rotated walls toward the ground to mirror the form above. The visual effect of this configuration is one of a rhythm of independent diamond-shaped roofs that are connected at the corners.

The interior, which was modified by Goff after the house was purchased by Joe and Laura Warriner, has an open plan with the kitchen located in the center module. Only the bedrooms can be closed by accordion walls. It is an inward-looking design with a limited visual relationship to the exterior that was characterized by Laura Warriner as "like living in a jewel." Though the house appears small on the exterior, with an open plan and the ceiling of each module sloping to the skylight, Goff created a sense of spaciousness that belies the actual size.

Another component of the design is a detached studio, originally a garage, which is linked to the house visually by a covered walkway between reflecting pools on either side. Surmounted on the studio is a screened porch with a

sawtooth patterned roof of corrugated fiberglass as a variation of the geometric theme of the house with both blending and contrasting qualities.

The relationship of these two components is further magnified by color. The muted gray-green siding and stone plinth of the house harmonize with the blue-green roof panels of the screen porch, but contrast with the dark shingled roofs. The house is opaque and visually impenetrable, but the porch, repeating the rhythm of the diamond motif, is open with qualities of transparency and translucency as a manifestation of an ideal Goff articulated in his Architecture 273 lectures. The concept of natural light, openness, and flexibility of space led to client satisfaction. Laura Warriner commented that "every day I see some new wonderful idea that I had never seen before—especially the movement of light in the daytime and the total transition of the space at night."[7]

The only other prominent design constructed during the Bartlesville years with a centroidal-plan arrangement was the 1958 Emil Gutman House in Gulfport, Mississippi, which like the Price Studio, significantly extended Goff's vision of crystalline form. Built near a lake, and raised on clustered stilts above the ground to protect against the danger of flooding, the triangular plan was enclosed with a hipped roof with a form of the same profile repeated on the underside. Goff visually magnified the crystalline form of the house through enrichment of the surface. He had workmen dash bits of crushed glass and mirror into the wet plaster of the house's white stucco exterior so the prismatic surfaces would sparkle and reflect light. Built under the supervision of former OU student Robert Faust, the house exemplified an extraordinary level of craftsmanship and detailing. Faust commented, "It was just like building a big model." Faust also designed and built a machine that was used on the job site to crush the glass and mirror into shards applied to the exterior surfaces.

The expression of structure in the Gutman design was further amplified with the exterior walls of the triangular plan developed as deep, floor-to-cornice long-span steel trusses with the chords forming an X-shaped pattern. Trusses on two sides were fitted with screen wire to function as porches. Cantilevered

Facing page, Pollock House, exterior detail. Photograph by author.

Following spread

Left, Emil Gutman House, Gulfport, Mississippi. Plan drawing by OU College of Architecture, Design and Research Center. Courtesy College of Architecture, University of Oklahoma.

Right, Gutman House, exterior. Ryerson & Burnham Archives, Art Institute of Chicago.

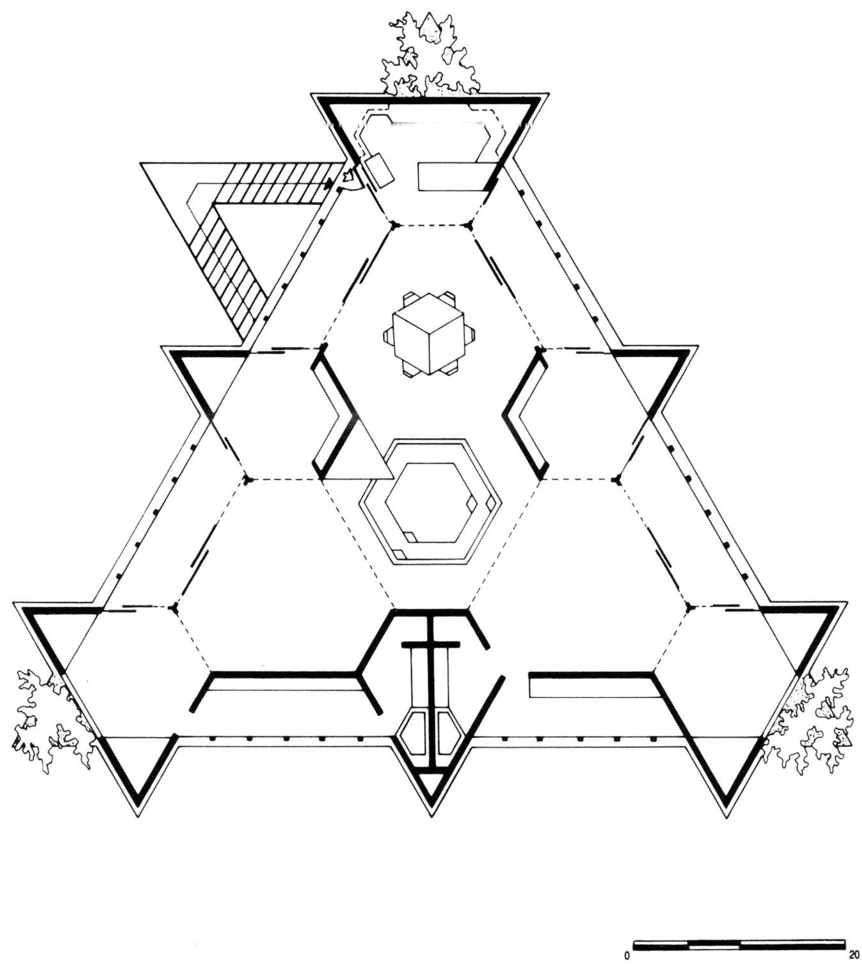
0
20

angular extensions from the corners and midpoints of the trussed walls served the private functions of bedrooms, baths, and kitchen, which repeated the triangular theme at a smaller scale.

The primary congregate space on the interior had a recessed conversation area with built-in seating in the shape of a hexagon with the hipped roof joining a pyramidal skylight directly above. The central interior element was adjacent to a dining area at one end and two subordinate living areas at the other end.

One of these spaces was for children and the other for their parents, and both could be closed to the central space with folding wood screens. All of the subordinate spaces had views to the exterior and access to the porches.

Unlike other designs with a rich palette of materials, the Gutman House was monochromatic. It was a pure crystal, poised above the earth, with cantilevered extensions at the perimeter suggesting growth. With exception of the structural components, painted blue as a didactic code, the exterior form of the white stucco shimmered and glistened from the shards of glass and mirror. The beautifully crafted Gutman House, destroyed by fire in the 1980s, represented for Goff a realization of visionary Expressionist imagery with design of a prism displayed on a pedestal of stilts as an objet d'art.

Two other houses of 1958 are significant as varied compositions of geometry arranged in asymmetrical patterns. The R. G. Durst House in Houston, Texas, has an association of both contrast and repose while the compact Jones House in Bartlesville is one of restraint and blending with the landscape. Apprentice Douglas Harris had joined Goff in the Bartlesville office following an introduction by Herb Greene.[8] As Goff prepared to design the Durst House, Harris suggested that he consider an asymmetrical design since his previous five designs, two of which were built, were symmetrical.

Goff responded to the wooded suburban site of the Durst House with a design defined by a segmented arc with wings projecting toward both the front and back.[9]

The curved façade is a wall of salmon-colored brick with alternating recessed courses and large circular windows with a partial dome extending above the cornice as terminating elements of the shed roof sloping toward the front. The dominant rhythm of windows imparts a startling and contrasting presence, but it assures privacy from the street and introduces a recurring circular motif in the design. A radial wing projecting toward the back of the property gives edge definition to an intimate outdoor area with views from within the house. Both the scale and composition of the architectural elements facing a secluded terrace are varied and contrast with the formality of the façade.

The circular theme is reaffirmed in an informal living area with a half-round opening for the fireplace facing a semicircular recessed hearth. On the wall opposite, a semicircular bay of glass with a high ceiling extends into the curved terrace. The visual effect is one of magnification with the centroid of the fireplace as the determining radius point of expansion outward into the landscape. Above the secondary living area is a bedroom with an apsed end contained by a cantilevered shed roof with a thin fascia and corners that curve outward, in a direction opposite to the wall below. A band of glass visually separates the roof from the dark-brown wall of shingles.

Over time the house became even more varied through a succession of owners. The second owner commissioned Goff to add another bedroom above the kitchen and Julia Gee, the third owner, had Goff add an upstairs playroom that later became a combined office/sewing room. Both of these later additions were modeled after the original upstairs bedroom. Interior modifications, at Gee's request, also included built-in seating, custom-designed furniture, and a fountain. Reflective mirror tile in varied colors, which had become Goff's favored material for ornament, was applied to the interior of the domed surfaces on the circular façade windows, around light fixtures, and in beam reveals and columns. Gee was also concerned about a problem of birds and raccoons nesting in the chimney. Goff responded with an effective ornamental design of painted concrete reinforcing bars and billiard balls. The house was ultimately transformed into an extraordinarily complex design with sixteen different floor

R. G. Durst House, Houston, Texas. Lower level plan and façade drawings by OU College of Architecture, Design and Research Center. Courtesy College of Architecture, University of Oklahoma.

Facing page, Durst House, façade. Photograph by author.

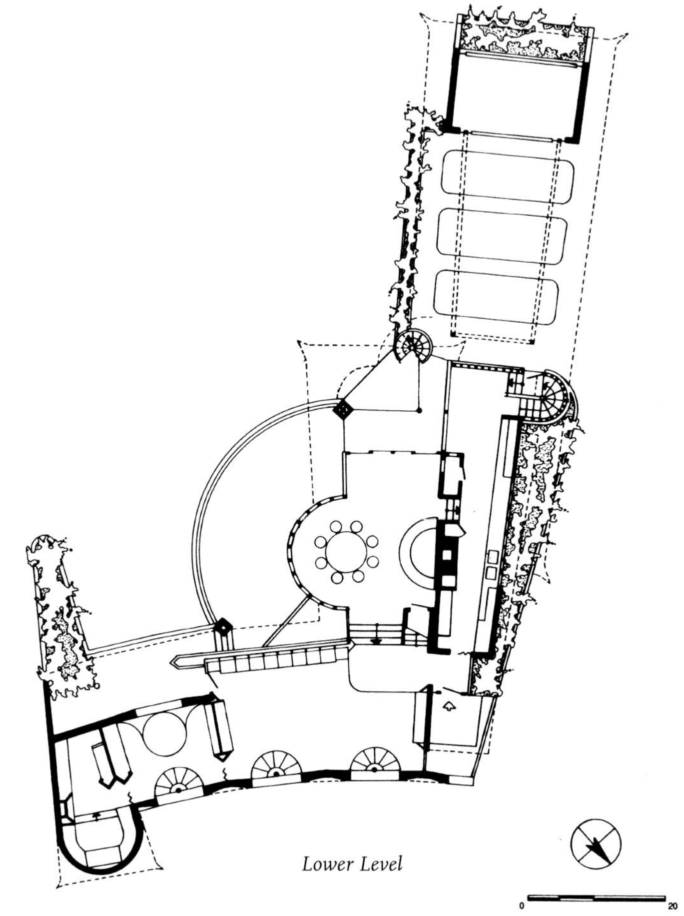

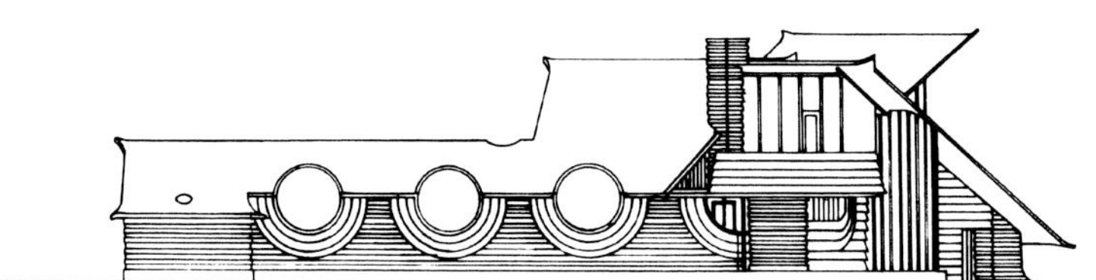

Façade

Durst House. Upper level plan and west elevation drawings by OU College of Architecture, Design and Research Center. Courtesy College of Architecture, University of Oklahoma.

Facing page, Durst House, exterior rear. Photograph by author.

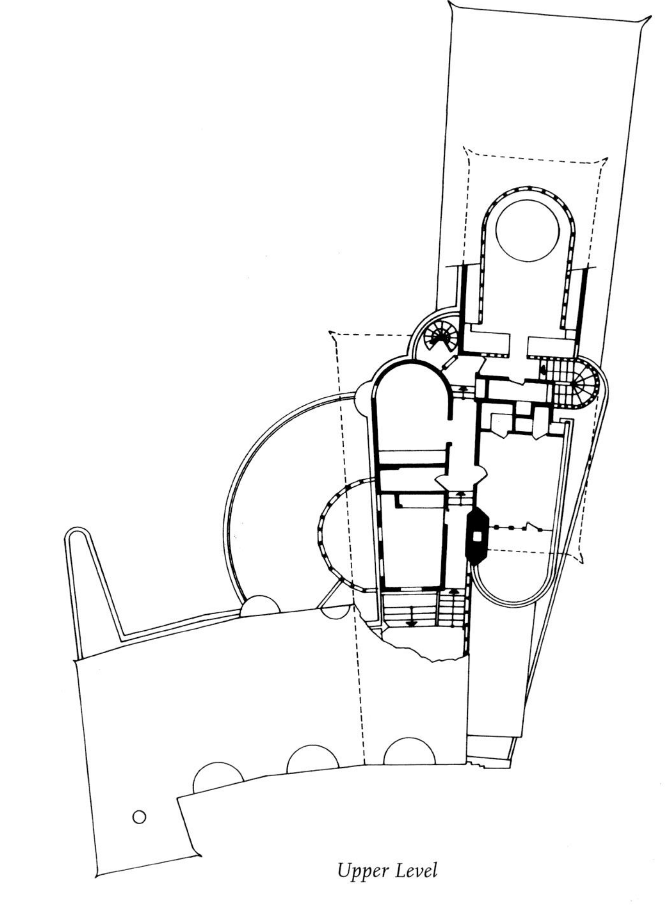

Upper Level

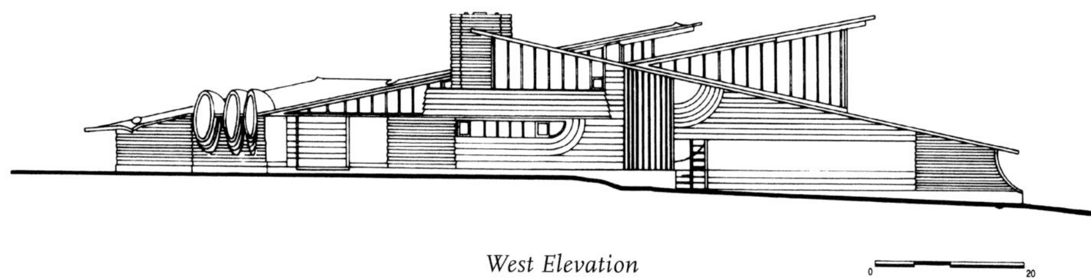

West Elevation

levels. Years later Gee poignantly commented on the relationship of shelter and the natural world. "I always feel as if I am on vacation when I am home. The flow, the natural feeling of openness, yet I have my privacy, that he blended my home with pine trees . . . living in any other house would be very boring."[10] Upon seeing completion of the final modifications Goff said to Gee, "The statement is complete."[11]

The split-level Howard Jones House has an irregular plan arrangement of octagonal forms interlocking with a rectangular form. The client's collection of antique hooked rugs determined the size and geometric configuration of the varied spaces.[12] The ensemble of forms is contained under a hipped roof that joins a massive octagonal chimney at the apex. Perimeter components include a two-story screened porch, a detached square carport connected to the entry by a covered walk, a triangular lily pool at the back of the house, and an elongated octagonal utility room projecting from another side. Although the plan is complex, Goff selected materials to visually delineate the differences of the two major geometries. The walls of the primary rectangular element are purple-brown brick with olive-green mortar and the angled forms are covered with shingles stained olive green. A defining feature of the design is an irregular rhythm of deep shelves projecting outward from the exterior walls. With an angled plate-glass covering, the feature served a dual purpose: the shelves were a place to display a prized collection of early American glassware that would sparkle in sunlight. And as a window, the glass allows views of the magnificent oak trees in the yard beyond. Windows at the upper level repeat the pattern below but they project upward and outward to join the soffit of the deep overhanging roof. Jones also wanted a fireplace in each room and Goff responded with design of a large octagonal fireplace at the lower level serving perimeter spaces. With four separate hearths contained within a single form the fireplace allowed sight lines from one space into another on the opposite side. The large central chimney also served two adjoining fireplaces in the bedrooms upstairs.

The compact Jones House does not have pronounced scale hierarchies often associated with Goff's buildings, yet it fulfilled client aspirations. The interplay of the two systems of geometry is subtle and the muted colors establish a harmonious relationship with the site. The color of the brick relates to the color of the trunks of the many trees and the olive-green shingles echo the color of leaves. It is a composition of restraint and repose as if Goff wanted the house to merge with nature.

One of Goff's few nonresidential commissions was the 1959 Bartlesville Redeemer Lutheran Church, which included design of the sanctuary with a detached education building that would be constructed first. The design Goff developed was one of extreme contrasts as a study in opacity and translucency. The sanctuary design had a long rectangular plan with rounded ends; Goff told Harvey Ferraro, one of his assistants, the geometry was derived from an unbuilt 1932 church design in Oklahoma City.[13] The similarities ended there as he proposed to build the walls of the sanctuary entirely of glass cullets and envisioned a gradation in thickness with the walls tapering and diminishing toward the top. The effect he wanted to achieve was one of a transition of light, dense and opaque at the bottom and translucent at the top. In this way one's eyes would be lifted heavenward. Although his design for the sanctuary was never built, the Education Building, completed in 1961, is an expression of tactile surface richness that was constructed on a limited budget. The flat-roofed, two-story rectilinear building has a raised center section defining a clerestory for the auditorium on the upper floor. Exterior walls of concrete block were veneered with an irregular pattern of gray-green limestone and studded with blue-green glass cullets clustered at the building corners. Square windows, rotated obliquely, form a static rhythm—with a counterpoint of daggerlike scuppers at the cornice—which magnifies the contrast with the random pattern of stone and cullets.

Two buildings of 1959 and 1960, the Gelbman House in Gainesville, Florida, and the Gryder House in Ocean Springs, Mississippi, reflect Goff's continued

Following spread

Left and center, Howard Jones House, Bartlesville, Oklahoma. Plan drawings by OU College of Architecture, Design and Research Center. Courtesy College of Architecture, University of Oklahoma.

Right, Jones House, exterior. Photograph by author.

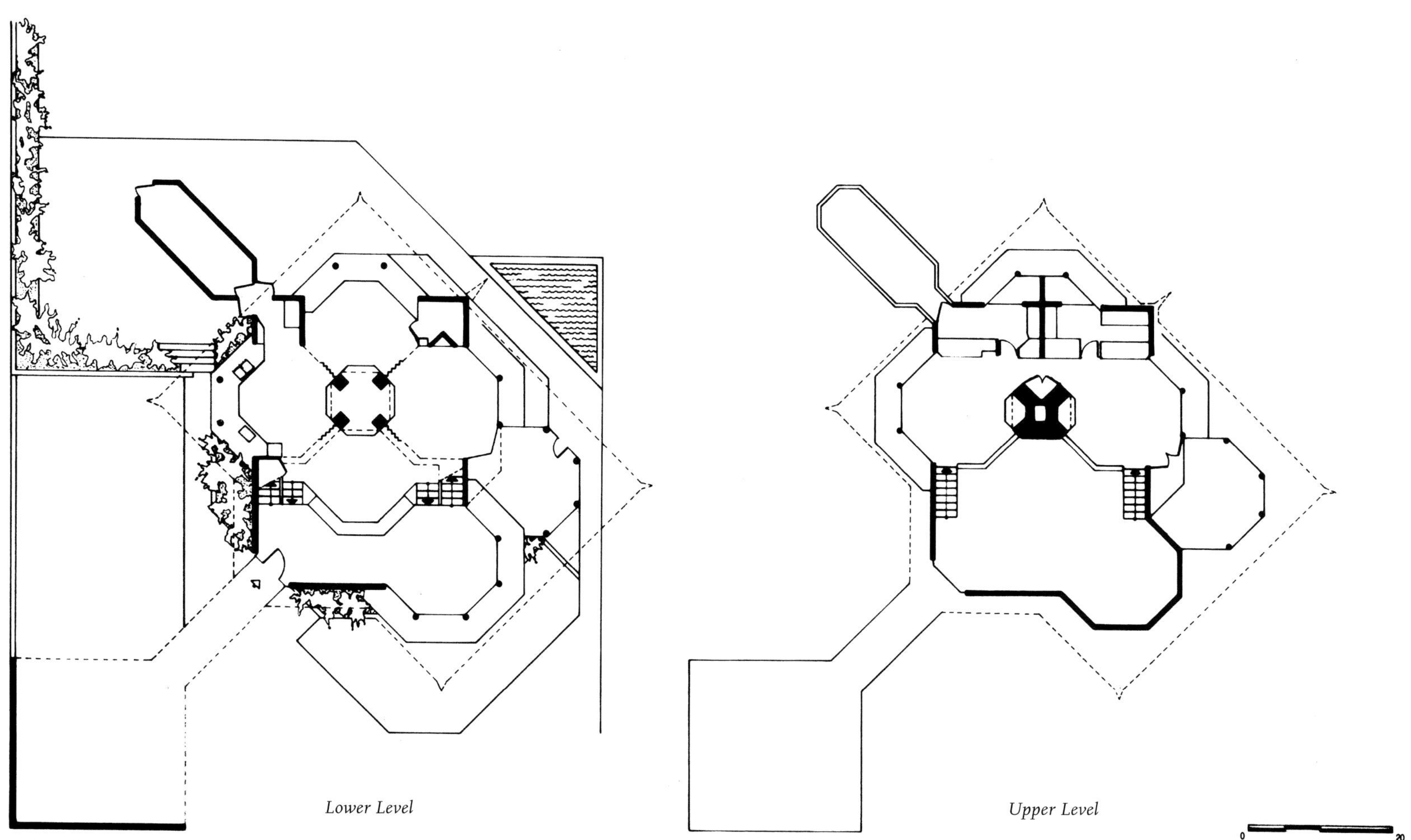
Lower Level
Upper Level
0
20

Redeemer Lutheran Church, Bartlesville, Oklahoma, façade. Photograph by author.

interest in circular and curved geometry with configurations of bilateral symmetry.

The plan of the Milton Gelbman House (1959) was developed as a two-story semicircular form with two radiating wings curved in the opposite direction. The sculptural presence of the curved forms on the façade was magnified with curved ramps, overlooking an exterior water garden. Converging to the center of the symmetrical design was an intermediate-level entry with interior stairs to a private upper zone or to congregate spaces below. The lower level had a living room in one wing, kitchen and dining area in the other with a family room in the two-story central area. The upper level was arranged with bedrooms overlooking the central space or opening onto terraces on the roofs of the carports.

The exterior walls of the lower level were veneered with a random pattern of multicolored marble. The upper level was defined by a projecting band of

closets clad with wood siding as a modulating element between the stone walls and a segmented clerestory of glass. The thin planes of the roofs, tilted upward, were cantilevered at the ends, which contrasted with the opaque forms of the curved walls below. The back elevation of the house was defined almost in its entirety by a glass wall.

With this composition of curved forms arranged on the site as a continuum of water garden, ramps, curved walls, and floating roof, Goff created a scale hierarchy of differentiated components by placing smaller forms in front of larger forms. The design also projected associations with the natural world with its plan of curved forms suggesting an undulating creature and the tilted, cantilevered symmetrical roofs evoking an image of a dragonfly about to gently alight on the water garden. The house was later demolished by a new owner who was more interested in the attributes of the site than the architecture.[14]

Above, Redeemer Lutheran Church, exterior corner detail. Photograph by author.

Following spread

Left and center, Milton Gelbman House, Gainesville, Florida, 1959. Plan drawings by OU College of Architecture, Design and Research Center. Drawings courtesy College of Architecture, University of Oklahoma.

Right, Milton Gelbman House façade. Photograph courtesy of Ryerson & Burnham Archives, Art Institute of Chicago.

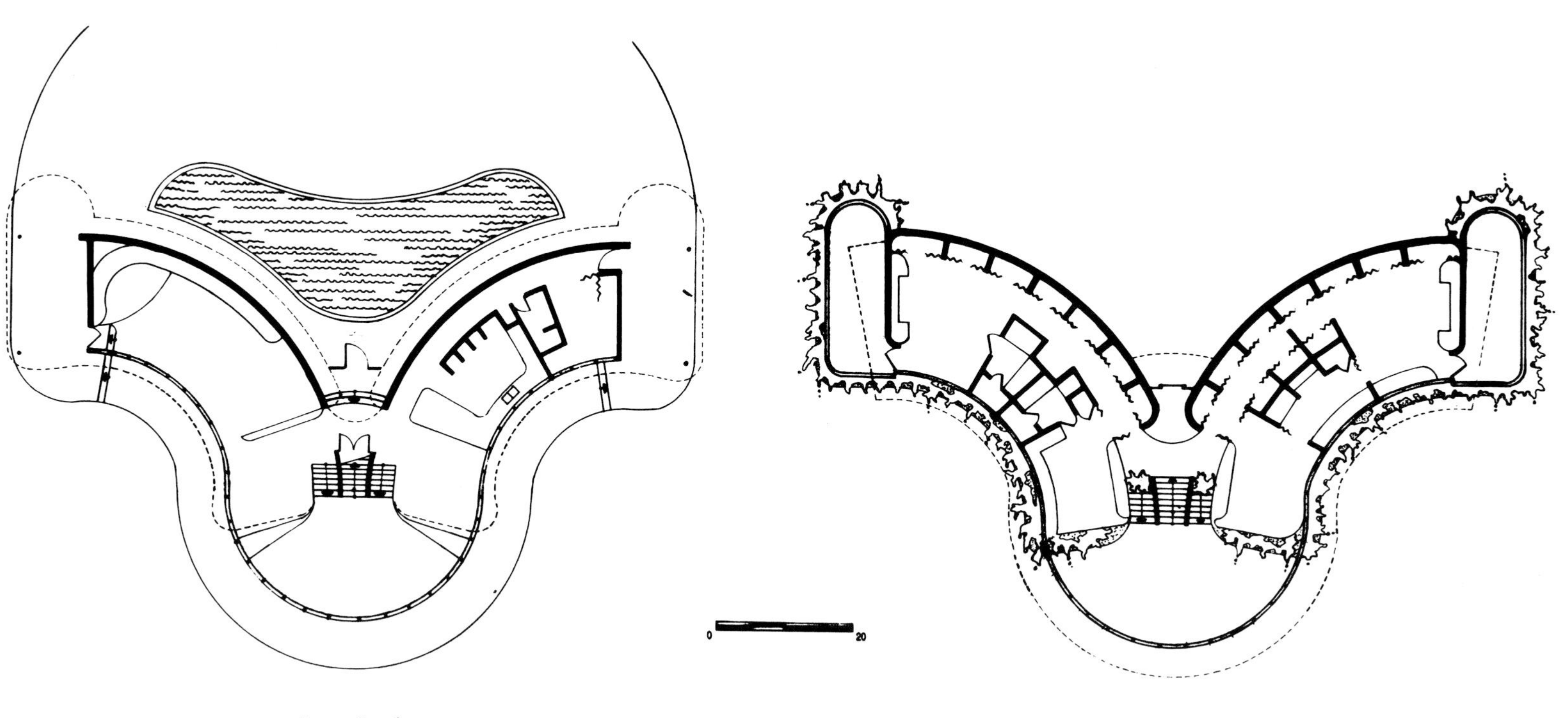

Lower Level

Upper Level

The split-level W. C. Gryder House, designed in 1960, continued Goff's exploration of the plasticity of curved geometry. Built at the edge of a bay in Ocean Springs, Mississippi, the house is set at the rear of a large circular lily pool. Access to the house is by a covered bridge crossing to the entry foyer at an intermediate level with bedrooms above and congregate spaces below. A two-story, centralized living room at the lower level has dual focal points aligned on an axis of symmetry with a fireplace below the entry and a projecting screen porch overlooking the ocean at the opposite end. On either side of the axis are pairs of glass-walled circular bays projecting through the curved exterior walls with those on one side defining a kitchen and dining alcove with built-in seating areas on the other side. In their initial meeting with Goff, Elaine Gryder requested that the kitchen not be isolated from the congregate living space. She also wanted a curved countertop in the kitchen. The geometry of the upper level has subtle differences from the lower level. The front and back walls are rectilinear to overhang the curved walls below and create a shadow line, which suggests an illusion of a hovering form above. At the outside corner of each bedroom is a cone-shaped cantilevered balcony with its shape inverted in the reflection of the lily pool.

Built by Robert Faust with meticulous craftsmanship, the building presents several points of reference to the source of the design. There is an affinity in the form of the saddle-shaped roof to the vernacular village architecture of Java. Goff also visualized elements of the natural world with inclusion of a water garden. The choice of color was another dimension of acknowledgment of nature: the muted lavender stucco walls harmonize with the surrounding dark-green pine and palmetto trees and the floating lily pads. There is a sense of tension in the curving spatial configuration of the geometry. Nothing is static. The dynamic roof both contrasts and blends simultaneously with the tubular canopy of the bridge. Both are curved planes but they exist in opposition in a state of delicate balance with one curving upward and the other curving downward. This association is amplified by the tile-covered balcony cones of the bedrooms, with the tips down, suggesting a fragile condition of balance. The curvilinear geometry of the façade is further magnified by the sinuous cat-eye windows in the bedroom walls.

A counterpoint of the design is the sculptural fireplace positioned near the entry with a round metal chimney extending high above and terminated with an ornament of curved metal flowerlike petals.

There is also an element of ambiguity to the façade design: it is one of Goff's most lyrical compositions, but it has a mysterious side. Collectively the façade suggests an anthropomorphic reference to a primitive mask with the canopy as nose, balconies as ears, and bedroom windows as eyes and with upturned beam ends as horns, suggesting a god of the underworld emerging from the water.

In the late 1950s Goff designed other houses but many remained unbuilt. As a new decade began, the number of commissions declined and his designs became more restrained. Goff's design of the James Fitchette House (1961) was both modest and restrained, a design decision also predicated on the accommodation of physical disabilities. The rectilinear house has a precise ordering of zoning and an abundance of natural light as an empathetic response to the visual impairment of his clients. A central corridor, defining the primary circulation path, has a continuous translucent skylight with concealed fluorescent lighting. The spine of light from above extends the length of the house demarking three zones: bedrooms on one side, kitchen and dining on the other, and living room at a lower level. Although the bedrooms are small Goff designed oversized pocket doors and omitted the upper part of the corridor wall to allow borrowed light from the linear skylight to both illuminate and enlarge the rooms visually.

KANSAS CITY, MISSOURI, 1964–1970

In 1964 Goff relocated his practice to Kansas City, Missouri. During his years of practice there, Goff designed six houses that are among his most notable work.

Following spread

Left, W. C. Gryder House, Ocean Springs, Mississippi, 1960. Plan drawings by OU College of Architecture, Design and Research Center. Courtesy College of Architecture, University of Oklahoma.

Center, Gryder House, interior detail of fireplace. Photograph courtesy of Ryerson & Burnham Archives, Art Institute of Chicago.

Right, Gryder House, façade detail. Photograph by author.

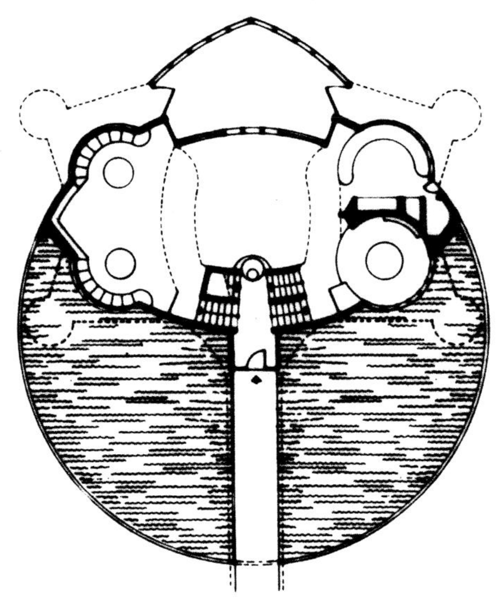

Lower Level

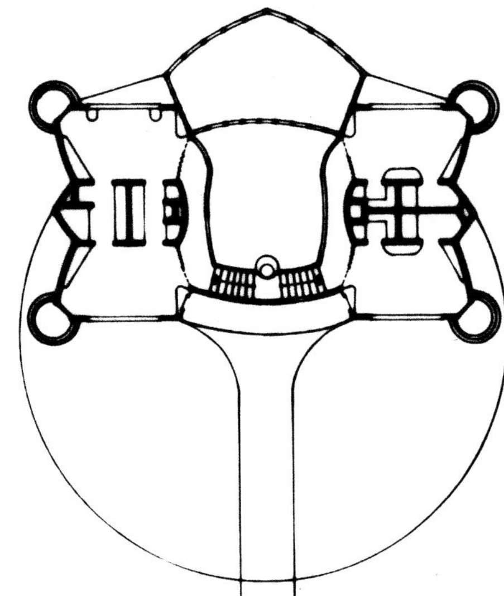

Upper Level

Facing page, James Fitchette House, Bartlesville, Oklahoma, 1961. Photograph by author.

The floor plan geometry of these houses suggests a continuation of themes established earlier, but each design is distinctively different. The dominant motifs include a reliance on symmetrical configurations of centroidal plan geometry or linear compositions. Yet there were also changes in his expression. Four of these houses have a limited palette of materials. They are, with minor exceptions, monochromatic, built of a single material with color dominating the exterior form.

Goff designed the William Dace House in the small Oklahoma Panhandle town of Beaver in 1964 soon after he moved his office to Kansas City. It is a design of interplay of rhythmic, abstract geometric forms of stucco painted deep red. The primary form of the symmetrical design, rising two and one-half stories, is a tall rectangular element with apsed ends and projecting opaque cylinders attached to the sides. The planar walls at the upper level originally had white-painted wood siding with angular glazed openings.[15]

The interior volume of the end bays opens full height to a living room "platform" above, suspended by cable supports from the roof structure. The living room overlooks a studio below with views of the High Plains rangelands at the west end with a dining area and stair on the opposite end. The plan of the lower level has six rooms of equal size, three on either side of a central service core of bathrooms and a utility room. Five of these rooms are bedrooms and the sixth, next to the dining area, is a kitchen. The walls of all these rooms are adjacent to the service core corridors with wood accordion partitions and can be either open or closed. Attached to each room is a cylindrical lazy-Susan closet with cone-shaped extensions that create a dominant rhythm and echo the geometry of the circular end bays of the larger central form.

Sheltering this continuum of smooth-surfaced forms are several planar, cantilevered roofs tapered to a thin edge at the fascia with each of the independent roofs giving further definition to the form it encloses. The dominant central form has a rectangular roof with a pronounced overhang as it cantilevers over the circular ends. A smaller secondary roof, positioned above the primary roof,

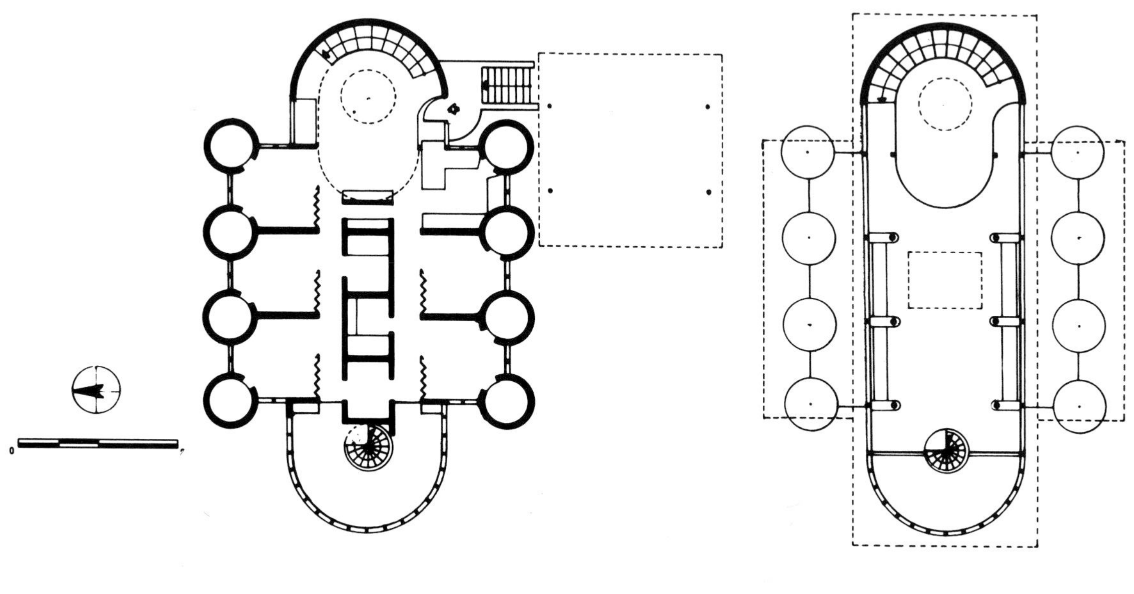

William Dace House, Beaver, Oklahoma, 1964. Plan drawings by OU College of Architecture, Design and Research Center. Courtesy College of Architecture, University of Oklahoma.

has a continuous clerestory to provide natural light from all directions into the living room. A half level below the primary roof are smaller roofs projecting from the side walls to embrace the rows of cylindrical closets on either side. The visual effect is one of a rhythm of abstract forms that lightly touches its tip to the horizontal planes above and below. Even the carport, as an incidental element of the design, is a minimalist abstraction. It too is simply a floating plane supported by four slender columns inset from the perimeter.

The Dace House is a design of circular and planar geometric motifs defined by a limited palette of materials and color with a logical clarity of internal zoning for different activities that corresponds to the hierarchy of form. The design is an expression of dualities: of opacity and transparency; of intense color contrasting yet harmonizing with the green shortgrass of the landscape; of solid geometric forms played against light, hovering horizontal planes with the thinnest of edges; and of delicacy and monumentality, for it is indeed a

Dace House, exterior. Photograph by author.

large house. The Dace House also reveals the importance of client and site as essential determinants of an expression of individuality. It was red because that was the favored color of the client. The cylindrical closets, forming an articulated rhythm, further suggest a subliminal reference to the many circular bins and elevators associated with dry-land grain farming. They are common elements throughout the rural landscape of western Oklahoma.

The year 1965 was extraordinarily productive for Goff. He designed thirteen houses, two apartment buildings, a fraternity house, two office buildings, and alterations to three existing buildings.[16] Five of the houses and a realty office were built. One of his most inspired designs of that year was a linear composition of interlocking stone cylinders rising from a forested wilderness as a poetic praise of nature. It was built on a large rural acreage near Cobden, Illinois, for Hugh Duncan, a professor of sociology at Southern Illinois University in Carbondale. Duncan was Goff's most knowledgeable client with his research on the social implications of buildings. In his book *Culture and Democracy*, Duncan advanced the thesis that buildings affect behavior and must express the needs of people. His interest in architecture was more than academic as he also collected artifacts and ornament from demolished buildings, especially those of Sullivan and Prairie School architects. He also embraced Sullivan's view that nature was the primary source of emotional stimulation and inspiration. The circular, linear theme Goff developed for the remote site was appealing to Duncan as it expressed, he believed, the interdependency of man and nature.

The house was built in a dense hardwood forest of oak, walnut, hickory, and maple with an animal kingdom of wild turkeys, golden eagles, coyotes, and many deer. Goff walked the entire acreage in search of the best location for the house.[17] The site he selected was adjacent to a bluff of striated stone outcroppings that were weathered gray and covered with lichen. One of the outcroppings intersects the house, creating the illusion the house is an extension of the landscape.

Facing page, Dace House, exterior side. Photograph by author.

In the context of this intense expression of primal nature Goff developed a design of three tall stone cylinders with a continuous serpentine one-story element woven around the towers with the roof pitched in the opposite direction. The serpentine form, with a ribbon skylight at the juncture of the towers, defined a sequence of living spaces, bedrooms, and library. Two smaller detached cylinders, as a study and guesthouse, terminated both ends of the symmetrical composition.[18] Six hundred tons of dark- and light-brown sandstone were collected from nearby creek beds for double-wythe construction with stone on both the exterior and interior of the curved walls.

The theme established in the symmetrical plan geometry is amplified by a circular motif in elevation. A large circular opening at the front of the house terminates the serpentine wall as it overlaps the terrace from the living room. Circular glazed openings also provide views of the wooded landscape from bedrooms. Within the house, at the tangent points where the serpentine wall changes from one side of a tower to the other, circular openings provide access to other major spaces. The undulating circulation path through the house pro-

Above, Hugh Duncan House, Cobden, Illinois, 1965. Plan drawing by OU College of Architecture, Design and Research Center. Courtesy College of Architecture, University of Oklahoma.

Facing page, Duncan House, exterior. Photograph by author.

vides a rich visual experience that is highly varied spatially with a pronounced chiaroscuro effect. With its linear theme of circular forms the design recalls Goff's 273 lecture on "Modulation."

Goff incorporated the collection of Duncan's architectural ornament into the masonry walls, and the house's stone floors were salvaged from Civil War–era sidewalks from the nearby town of Anna. Goff made another reference to both client and regional heritage by utilization of Duncan's collection of antique iron barrel hoops as railings for the terrace. The design is suggestively rich with subliminal associations: it is a place of enchantment and wonder with a fairy-tale echo of lost children discovering a palace in the forest.

Two houses of 1965, both built in Kansas City, were organized spatially as centroidal designs. The Lawrence Hyde House in Kansas City, Kansas, has a cruciform floor plan recalling the configuration of some of Wright's early designs in Chicago. Contrasting with the canted exterior walls of the house, clad with dark-gray shingles with light- and dark-green trim, is a square brick garage positioned at an angle and finished with a light-green glaze and green-tinted weeping mortar joints. Green was the favored color of the client.[19]

The two components are joined by an entry foyer defining the major node of circulation. It serves both the front and back yards and vertical circulation for the split-level design of primary living space above a multipurpose space

Lawrence Hyde House, Kansas City, Kansas, 1965. Plan drawing by OU College of Architecture, Design and Research Center. Courtesy College of Architecture, University of Oklahoma.

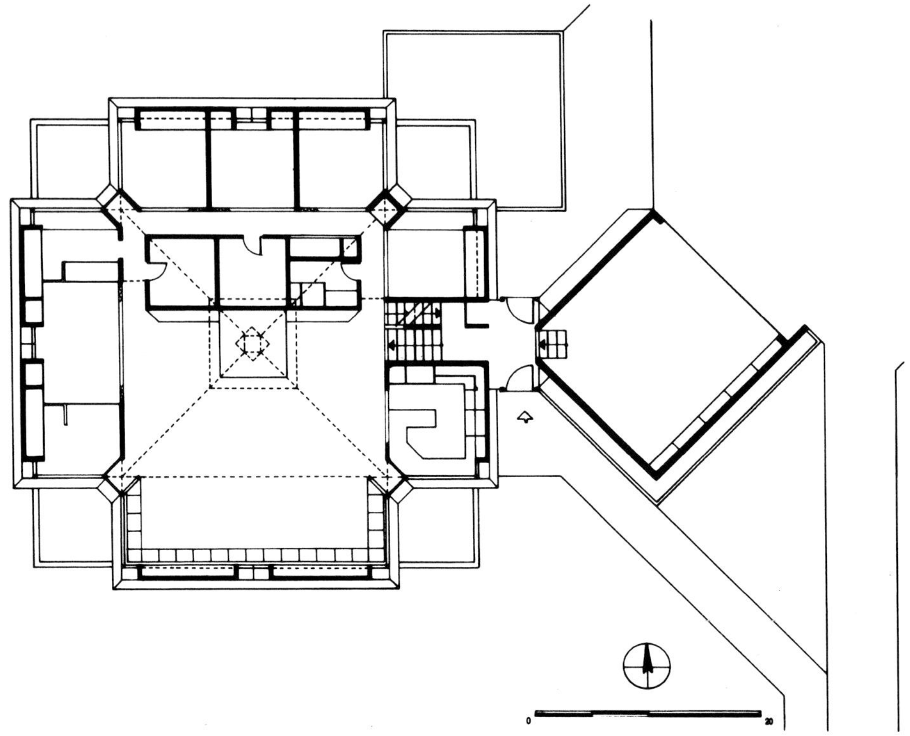

below. The plan of the house is symmetrical with a hipped roof over the central part with flat roofs with deep projections defining the side extensions. The extended sides of the square central space accommodate bedrooms, kitchen, work, and study areas, and a large alcove with built-in seating for the living room. Structurally the house is post-and-beam construction with laminated wood beams decorated with a rhythm of painted light-green, gray-green, and dark-green rectangles alternating with copper bands. The connecting foyer is also supported by paired beams that cantilever into both the living room and above an exterior deck atop the garage. Terminating the cantilevered beams at both ends are ornamental octagonal armatures studded with a cluster of glass ashtrays.

The exterior walls of the house are visually separated from the cantilevered flat roofs by a continuous band of fixed glass without mullions. The effect is one of the roof as an autonomous component that is floating above. Similarly,

Hyde House, exterior. Photograph by author.

the cantilevered floor joists of the canted walls are fitted with an angled skirt that hovers above the ground to impart a sense of lightness.

The primary living space, defined by the hipped roof, is a variation of a centroidal plan with a vertical axis. A rectangular block of bathrooms with a low, independent ceiling intrudes into the central living room under the pyramidal roof. Although it provides privacy for the bedrooms, its presence disrupts the symmetry of the prismatic volume. Yet Goff used the back wall of the service block facing the living room to great advantage by creating a backdrop for an array of elements defining the vertical axis. A fireplace, recessed into a platform hearth of light-green glazed brick, has a suspended metal hood and chimney penetrating the large pyramidal skylight above. Hanging from the rim of the skylight are planes of iridescent, curled plastic rain. The service block wall is enriched with an angled mural of pale-violet mirror tile banded with gold, red tile, and exterior shingles. With a burning fire, one experiences dual images

Following spread

Left, Hyde House, façade detail. Photograph by Alex E. Toye.

Right, Hyde House, interior. Photograph by Robert Bowlby.

of both yellow-orange flame and a distorted reflection from the violet-colored mirror tile. At times one can also see the sun or moon through the large skylight above, but it too is transformed into shimmering fragments by the translucent plastic rain.

The 1965 James Nicol House in Kansas City, Missouri, is another composition of centroidal geometry determining functional and spatial organization. It was the third of three designs by Goff. The symmetrical split-level house, with a detached carport and storage area, has a centralized octagonal living space at the upper level. Like the Hyde House, the bedrooms, kitchen, dining area, and entry are all defined as smaller modules at the perimeter with a guest bedroom and multipurpose room at the lower level. The one-acre site had dozens of hardwood trees and Goff, when he was designing the house, would come from his nearby office "during day or night and sit here under the trees to study the site."[20] Only one tree had to be removed.

Both the exterior walls, with angled windows, and octagonal hipped roof are clad with fancy-butt shingles stained a muted gray-green with black trim. The front door is inset with a pattern of purple glass ashtrays and the cornice incorporates a band of mirror tile that would "sparkle in late afternoon sun and in the headlights of approaching cars and moonlight reflecting from the lily pool."[21]

On the interior, the walls of the smaller, flat-roofed octagonal spaces at the perimeter are painted in colors of an intense hue—blue, purple, red-orange, avocado, and fuchsia—to contrast with the muted shade of green in the central living area. The defining element of the monumental but serene central space is a continuum of components that animate a vertical axis. The patterned ceiling of light-green shingles converges to an octagonal skylight. Suspended below the skylight is an octagonal tube that dripped water down strands of copper wire attached below the surface of a circular basin of water.[22] Constructed from the end section of a steel boiler tank, the basin is raised at the perimeter so it appears to float above the floor. Within the pool a circular ring of gas jets, raised slightly above water level, could be operated simultaneously with the falling water. A large, octagonal ring of built-in seating recessed into the floor and covered with light-green carpet surrounds this mysterious composition, creating a space of restrained grandeur around the axis. With this array Goff created an environment celebrating the phenomena of nature—of sky, water, fire, and earth.

In 1969, with few commissions, Goff accepted Joe Price's invitation to travel to Asia and for nearly two months in the spring of that year they toured Japan, Bali, Thailand, and Singapore. Upon return to Kansas City he worked sporadically on two book manuscripts, lectured, and accepted short teaching assignments at several universities. In the fall of 1969 he had opportunities to travel in Europe for a series of lectures and exhibits. On that trip he visited some of his favorite buildings, including the Palais Stoclet in Brussels, the Maison de Verre in Paris, and buildings by Gaudí in Barcelona.[23]

Two beautifully crafted houses in the early 1970s designed for a father and son in the corn belt of southern Minnesota illustrate major differences in appearance while revealing similar sources of conceptualization. The notion of specificity, in response to the individuality of clients and building sites with tangible characteristics, was central to Goff's ideas about architecture. For the Glen and Luetta Harder family, turkey farmers near the town of Mountain Lake, he developed a linear scheme with a rectangular floor plan of multiple levels projecting from a gently sloping hill. It was a design that accommodated a large family and reflected the expansiveness of the landscape. For Glen Harder's parents, Jacob and Anna Harder, a retired couple, he designed a compact, circular house with a central atrium that related to the scale of the neighborhood in the small town of Mountain Lake.

Glen Harder discovered Goff through an article in *Friends*, a magazine publication of General Motors. Attracted to his philosophy of architecture, and wanting a house different from others, Harder contacted Goff—with difficulty—in February 1970. "He was living in a dilapidated house with an

Following spread

Left, James Nicol House, Kansas City, Missouri, 1965. Plan drawing by OU College of Architecture, Design and Research Center. Courtesy College of Architecture, University of Oklahoma.

Right, Nicol House, exterior. Photograph by author.

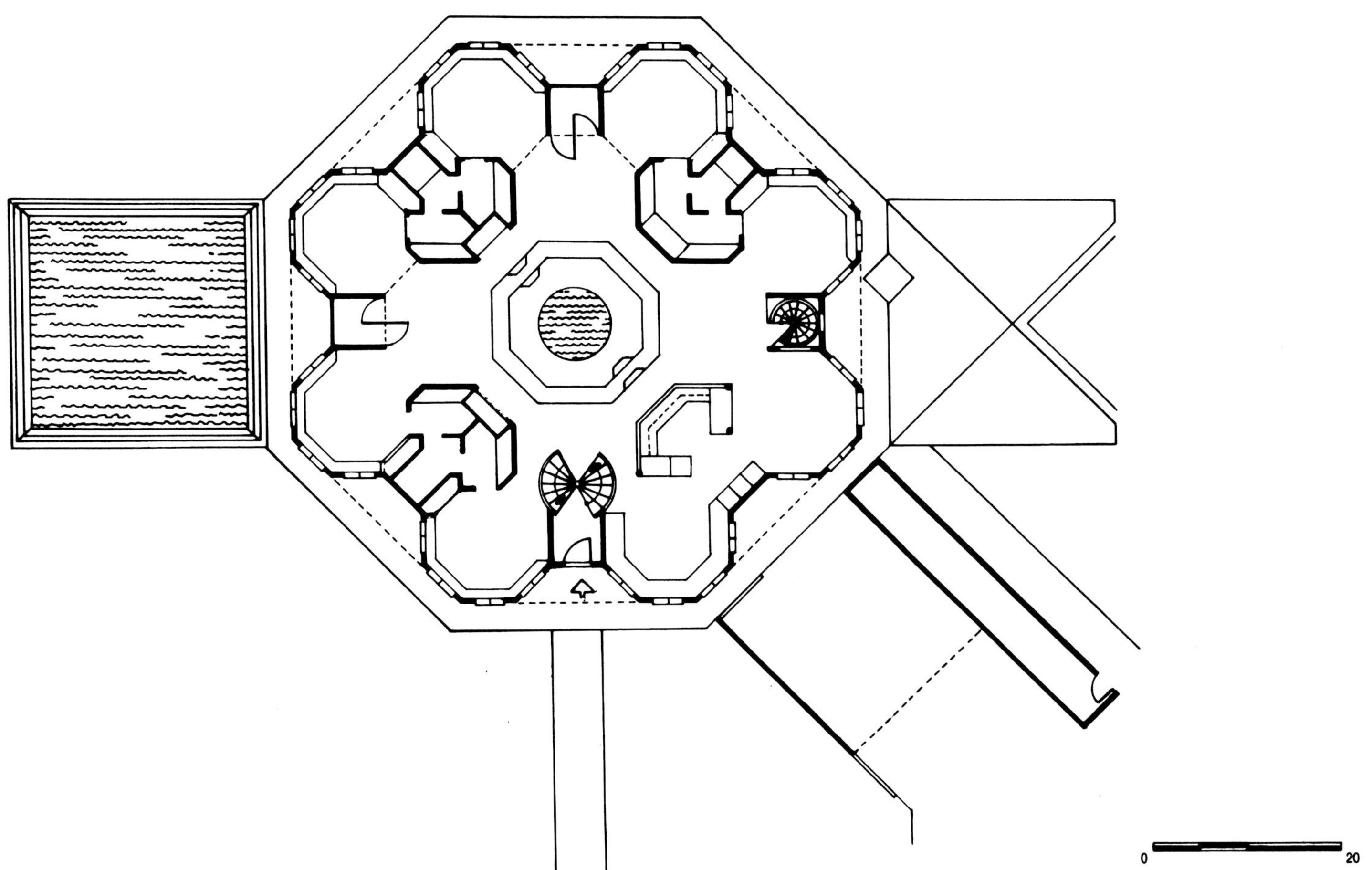
0
20

Left and right, Nicol House interior. Skylight above, water basin below. Photographs by author.

unlisted phone number and preparing to leave Kansas City and move to Texas," Harder said.[24] Luetta and Glen Harder told Goff of their desire for a house as a retreat from their work environment but with an "illusive line between outside and inside."[25] They wanted a design that would project warmth and portray truthfulness in structure and materials with no pretense.

The symmetrical split-level linear plan of the ninety-by-twenty-foot house was organized on two floors with ancillary spaces at the juncture of the entry. The centralized living room, positioned one-half level up from the entry, dominated the upper floor with kitchen and dining area at one end and two bedrooms at the other end. The lower floor featured another bedroom, a children's playroom, office, sewing room, and utility room. Goff again utilized an open plan with accordion wood walls serving as partitions. A secondary congregate space, a half level up from the living room, overlooked the space below and provided access to the screened porch surmounted on the three-car garage.

All of the major spaces were oriented toward the west to take advantage of the prevailing breeze and view of the landscape falling away from the house. With immense fields of corn stretching to the horizon, it was a design of remarkable appropriateness. Goff located the house by simply cutting a wide swath through one of the cornfields and seeding it with prairie grass at the suggestion of Luetta Harder. The house seemed to arise from an ocean of corn when seen from a distance. Goff made references to the landscape in other ways, with a balcony cantilevered the entire length of the upper floor to provide outdoor access and shade the spaces below. The balcony was enclosed with a continuous spandrel clad in taffy-colored shingles and curved outward and downward at the ends. The balcony created a strong shadow line and appeared to float. The curved ends and color of the balcony emulated the form and color of the tassels of the growing corn plants. Goff magnified the illusion of light, hovering forms with a modified hipped roof with deep overhanging eaves elaborated by tapering the roof plane to a knife edge to meet the soffit. The profile of the roof edge also had a distinct scalloping rhythm with projecting ends that allude to an association of a birdlike form suspended in space. Goff wrapped the entire roof, including the soffit, in bright orange Astroturf.[26] The choice of color was significant: it was the favored color of Luetta Harder and it established a harmonious relationship with the dark green leaves of the corn plant. With inclusion of wood shingles on most of the interior fixed walls, and orange carpet, the interior harmonized with exterior materials.

Three massive chimneys, serving multiple fireplaces, built of glaciated boulders and terminated with a curved metal rain cap contrasted with the linear ensemble of roof and balcony. Tapering from a broad base at the bottom as they curved upward, they appeared to have been heaved up from the earth by some primordial force. The multicolored boulders of the chimneys made further reference to a specific place as they are so common in the area, having been pushed to the surface by freeze-thaw cycles, that local farmers joke that

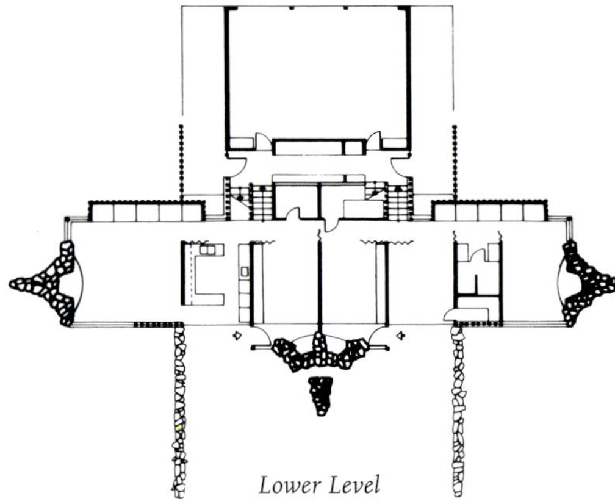

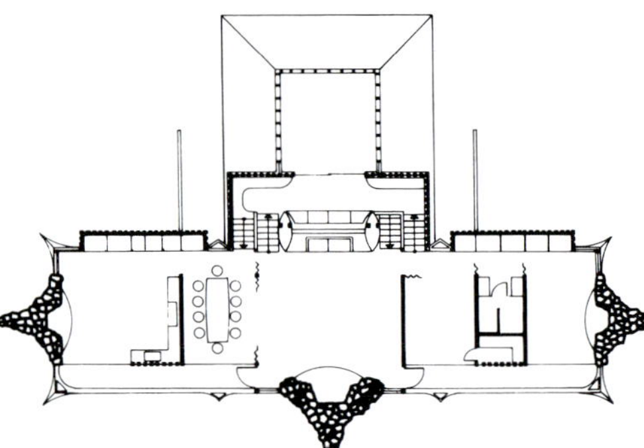

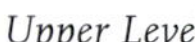

Left, Glen Harder House, Mountain Lake, Minnesota, 1970. Plan drawings by OU College of Architecture, Design and Research Center. Courtesy College of Architecture, University of Oklahoma.

Right, Glen Harder House, façade. Photograph by author.

Facing page, Glen Harder House, exterior side. Photograph by author.

their first crop were rocks. On the interior, the presence of boulders defining the chimneys as a planar element was dramatized by a skylight above. Goff magnified their compositional importance as focal points with the inclusion of geometric mosaic murals. Each of the three fireplaces had a different design that was personally installed by Goff.

The Harders commented on the spatial flexibility of their house. It was comfortable for just the two of them but would also accommodate their many children and grandchildren. Luetta Harder expanded on her satisfaction: "It was and continues to be a new experience every day. The longer we live here the more we realize we truly inhabit a work of art."[27] The house was destroyed by fire in 1994.

Prior to completion of the house Goff designed a house for Glen Harder's retired Mennonite parents, Jacob and Anna, in the village of Mountain Lake. In their initial interview with Goff, Anna Harder requested that the design include "a circular stair, bay windows and flower boxes."[28] The split-level design has a circular form, a half level up from the entry, juxtaposed over a smaller square

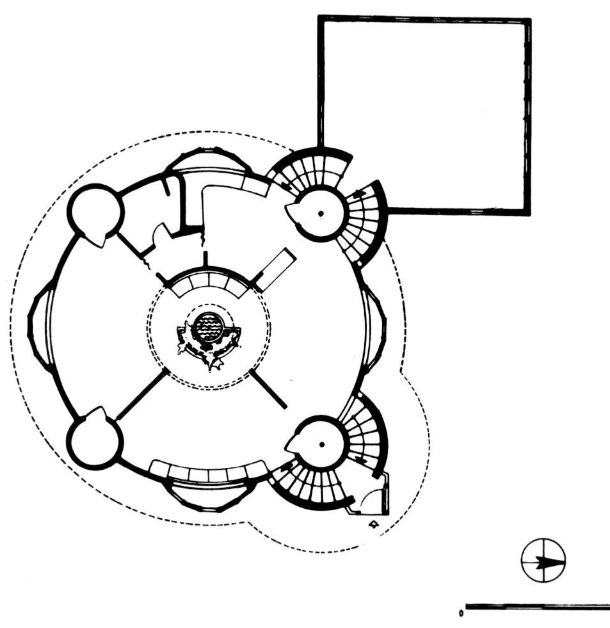

Above, Jacob Harder House, Mountain Lake, Minnesota, 1970. Plan drawing by OU College of Architecture, Design and Research Center. Courtesy College of Architecture, University of Oklahoma.

Facing page, Jacob Harder House, exterior. Photograph by author.

component below. The circular form is organized internally into distinct zones of activity much like the second design of the Garvey House. The living room is at the center with a bedroom, dining room, kitchen, and bathroom defined by an outer ring within the circle. Radial fixed partitions separate these peripheral functions one from the other. The curved walls defining the central living room, with the exception of the kitchen/bathroom core, are accordion panels, which could be closed for privacy or opened to expand the volume spatially.

The radial partitions, defining four quadrants, are terminated by cylindrical, lazy-Susan closets that are expressed on the exterior. Goff created a second axis of projecting circular bay windows with flower boxes framed into the perimeter wall below. The modulated exterior surface with its rhythm of alternating curved forms engaged to a circular wall cantilevered over the square form below to create a strong shadow line. All of these surfaces—roof, fascia, soffit, closet cylinders, bay windows, and walls—are clad in fish-scale wood shingles painted light green. The rounded ends of the shingles echo the primary circular theme and suggest a sense of softness to the composition. The configuration of all the components and materials is a clear statement of a design principle of "Theme, Variation and Development" Goff discussed in his 273 studio lectures.

Contrasting with the shingled surfaces, Goff enclosed two of the closet cylinders with a larger half circle that contain stairs connecting the upper level to the lower level of office, informal living area, and guest bedroom. The exterior material for both stairs is a dark maroon-colored brick in a stacked-bond pattern. The cylinder on the façade also serves as entry and the taller one at the back connects both levels with a 1981 garage addition with a sewing room above.

The integration of structure with the geometric configuration of the house is seamless and, like many of Goff's houses, the presence of structure serves more than one function. A compression ring, defining the skylight at the center of the primary living space, connects the roof joists to a tension ring at

the exterior wall to resist the horizontal thrust of the conical roof. Goff also fastened the ends of the interior radial walls with an intermediate circular tie ring. All of the tie rings are laminated wood painted a muted dark red. The intermediate tie ring, suspended overhead, serves other purposes. It provides a track for the white pearlescent accordion walls to close off the bedroom and dining room; it also provides an armature for a rhythm of exposed-bulb light fixtures; it defines a wall for the kitchen/bathroom quadrant with a space for built-in seating in the living room and a surface for a mosaic tile mural; and it gives visual definition to the atriumlike space with its central vertical axis.

The convergence of the conical roof, with its ceiling surface of scalloped shingles and the presence of a fountain aligned beneath the skylight, magnify the vertical axis of the centroidal design. The fountain, with red, orange, and blue lights beneath the surface of the water, glows and flickers at night through the skylight. "When we first moved into the house some of our neighbors were alarmed . . . they thought some kind of satanic ritual was going on here," Jacob Harder said.[29]

Facing page, Jacob Harder House, interior. Photograph by author.

TYLER, TEXAS, 1970–1982

In late 1970 Goff moved to Tyler, Texas, at the invitation of Bruce Plunkett. Plunkett had studied architecture with Goff at OU during the early 1950s and later became a successful developer. He wanted Goff to design both houses and community facilities for a new residential venture located at a nearby lake. Plunkett, who had been a loyal friend for three decades, thus became a patron much like Joe Price. Plunkett commissioned Goff to do a painting of *La Mer* in 1965, which Goff completed over a two-year period in Kansas City. The idea of the painting developed in 1950 during an evening music session that concluded with Debussy's *La Mer,* when Goff mentioned he would like to do a painting as a visual interpretation of his favorite music composition.

Goff talked again of this idea on the return trip from a 1952 lecture tour at the University of Toronto, McGill University, and Harvard. Upon conclusion of the lectures Goff and Plunkett, as driver of the car, went to New York City to visit the composer Edgar Varèse. One evening they talked about Debussy and Varèse showed Goff the manuscript of *La Mer.* Varèse and Debussy had been friends since 1908 and Debussy had given the original score to Varèse. On the long trip back to Oklahoma Goff again spoke to Plunkett of his desire to do a painting of *La Mer.*[30]

The painting originally hung at one end of a large rectangular room in the Plunkett house. At the opposite end of the room was a glass wall overlooking an exterior pool of water. On evening visits, after locating his office in Tyler, Goff would sit on the far side of the pool looking at the reflection of the painting in the water while listening to Debussy's composition.[31]

Much of the architectural work Goff did for Plunkett was speculative and the designs tended to be restrained. An exception was the house for Plunkett's family designed before Goff left Kansas City. The plan of the two-story house combined two rectilinear wings at right angles inset with a quarter circle that functioned as a recreation room on the lower floor and a large screened porch on the floor above. The curved theme was extended by scalloped roof eaves and a rhythm of circular elements defining the primary elevations. The lower part of the façade is brick with semicircular high windows terminated at the spring line by an overhanging second floor with a wall of glass and wood shingles. The upper floor of the façade is an inversion of the pattern below: the wood shingles, in the context of the glass wall, are laid in a semicircular pattern to complete the geometric motif. Goff magnified the dominance of the circular theme by placing an exterior light fixture at the center. The fixtures—large, plastic globes with a yellow neon corkscrew-shaped filament—are the primary ornament, like a bull's-eye in a target, which amplifies the façade rhythm. The design also included an onion dome belvedere with a band of circular windows but it was not built.[32]

Facing page, Detail of *La Mer* painting by Goff, 1965–67. Courtesy of OU College of Architecture.

While Goff continued his work for Plunkett he also had other clients. In 1974 he designed a second house for Celestine Barby in Tucson, Arizona.[33] With a linear plan twenty feet wide that was bent at an oblique angle, the split-level design was developed with a central open space with circulation by ramps adjacent to the exterior walls. The intermediate level defines the entry, kitchen, and a dining area overlooking the lower-level living room that features a raised fireplace with water dripping from the lip of the hood into a basin beneath. The upper level, stepped back from the central space, has a studio in one wing and small study and bedroom in the other wing. Both overlook the interior below and connect to an exterior balcony at either end.

The Barby House represents Goff's affirmation of the importance of client and site as primary design determinants. Dust-colored concrete masonry units, on both the exterior and interior, give the house an immediate presence of visual relatedness as an extension of the desert landscape. The stepped-wall motif at both ends of the linear form has multiple associations that amplify its meaning to both place and client: with its battered forms it has a reference to the ancient architectural heritage of regional Native American cultures; it visualizes the importance of southwestern Indian art to Celestine Barby as both artist and collector; and the emblematic character of the ensemble anticipates the ornamental stepped motif stenciled on the exposed wood roof joists on the interior. The configuration of these elements also illustrates a fundamental principle of design embraced by Goff—that of visual termination. By ending the linear exterior forms with angled cantilevered roof corners, cantilevered balcony and planter boxes, and by extending and stepping the walls at the lower level to correspond, by inversion, to the reverse batter of the wall above, he created a composition of dynamic termination. As a principle of design he discussed in his 273 lectures, visual termination was an imperative learned from Wright and undoubtedly magnified by his understanding of music composition.

The 1979 Al Struckus House in Woodland Hills, California, was the last residential design of Goff's to be built. Struckus, a retired engineer, had seen Goff's work in *Vogue* magazine and contacted him to commission a painting.

Struckus later asked Goff to design a house in a wooded canyon on a sloping lot fifty by one hundred feet. As the property was small, Goff developed a vertical scheme of a four-story cylindrical tower twenty-four feet in diameter. With a ground-floor entry and guest quarters, second-floor kitchen and dining with access to an exterior terrace, third-floor bedroom, and fourth-floor living room, all of the three upper floors are linked together visually by an asymmetrical interior open space. From the living room one has a view down into the dining room two floors below. Attached at the perimeter of the tower are four engaged cylinders, at the quarter points, six feet in diameter, which serve a variety of functions. Some are exclusively utilitarian and provide space for lazy-Susan closets, a utility room, shower/tub, pantry, circular bookshelves, and a secondary fire exit. One of the cylinders, adjacent to the interior open space, provides alcoves for aesthetic enrichment. On the second floor is a fish pool, on the third floor a *tokonoma* for display of art, and on the fourth-floor a fireplace in the living room.

A larger half cylinder, twelve feet in diameter, is also attached to the façade to define a spiral stair forty-eight-feet tall. An intermediate landing between each floor provides space for a window seat with a view through a Plexiglas dome. The spiral stair also serves as a gallery for display of a collection of ceramics. Each tread has a small radial partition extending from the perimeter wall to join the identical tread above. With glass shelving at eye level the stair also became a continuous helical gallery. It was a way of enriching the journey along the vertical path, one of providing a varied and stimulating experience with artifacts that had specific meaning for Struckus.

The primary exterior materials are redwood and ivory-colored stucco with a shallow-pitched conical roof with deep overhangs and exposed rafter tails. A large domed skylight at the center of the tower floods the interior with natural light. The dominant element of the façade is the vertical array of hemispherical domes lighting the landings of the spiral stair. With their stucco, telescoping fish-mouth surrounds, the rhythm of domes, with the top dome rising above

Following spread

Left and center, Bruce Plunkett House, Tyler, Texas. Plan drawings by OU College of Architecture, Design and Research Center. Courtesy College of Architecture, University of Oklahoma.

Right, Plunkett House, exterior. Photograph by author.

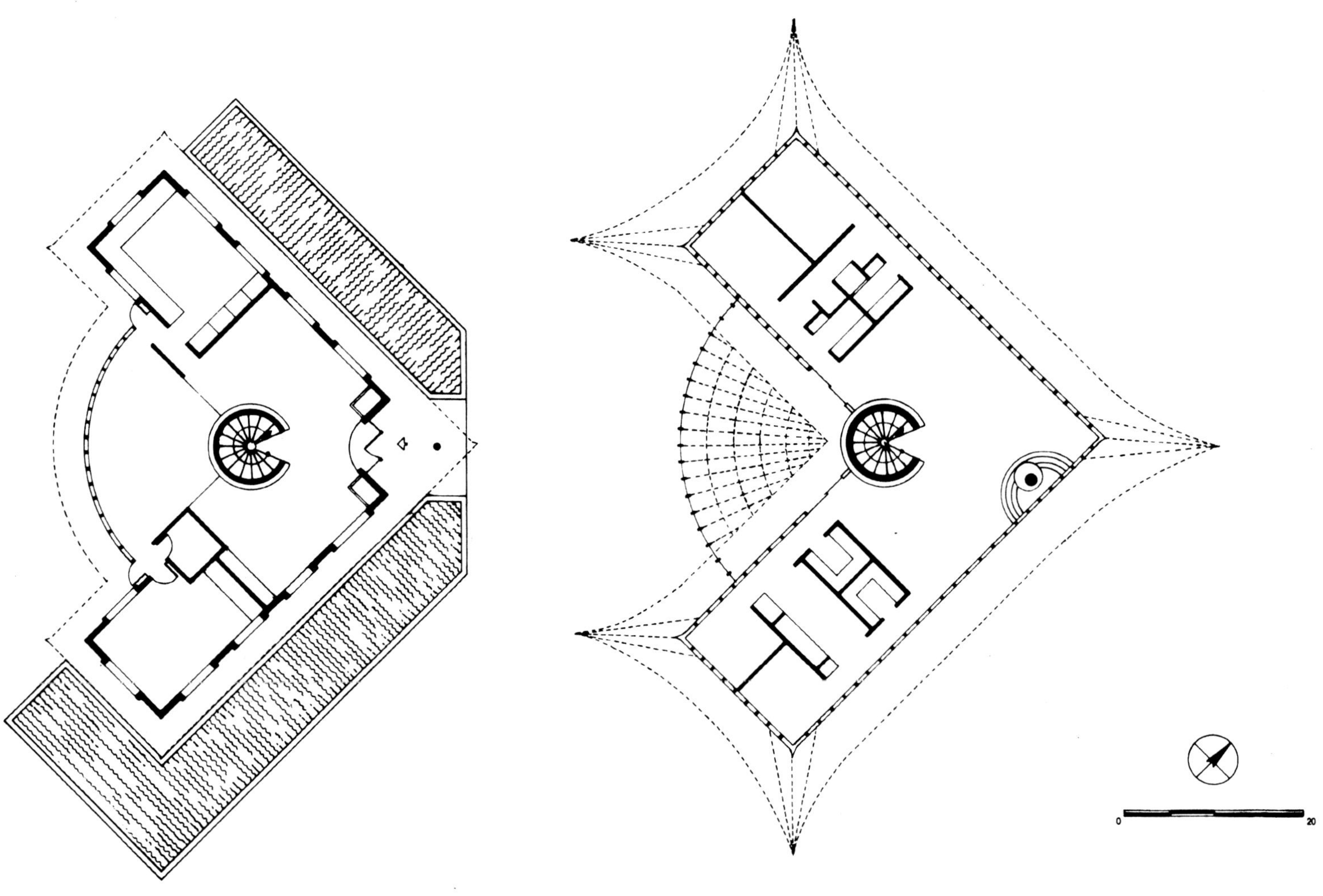

Lower Level

Upper Level

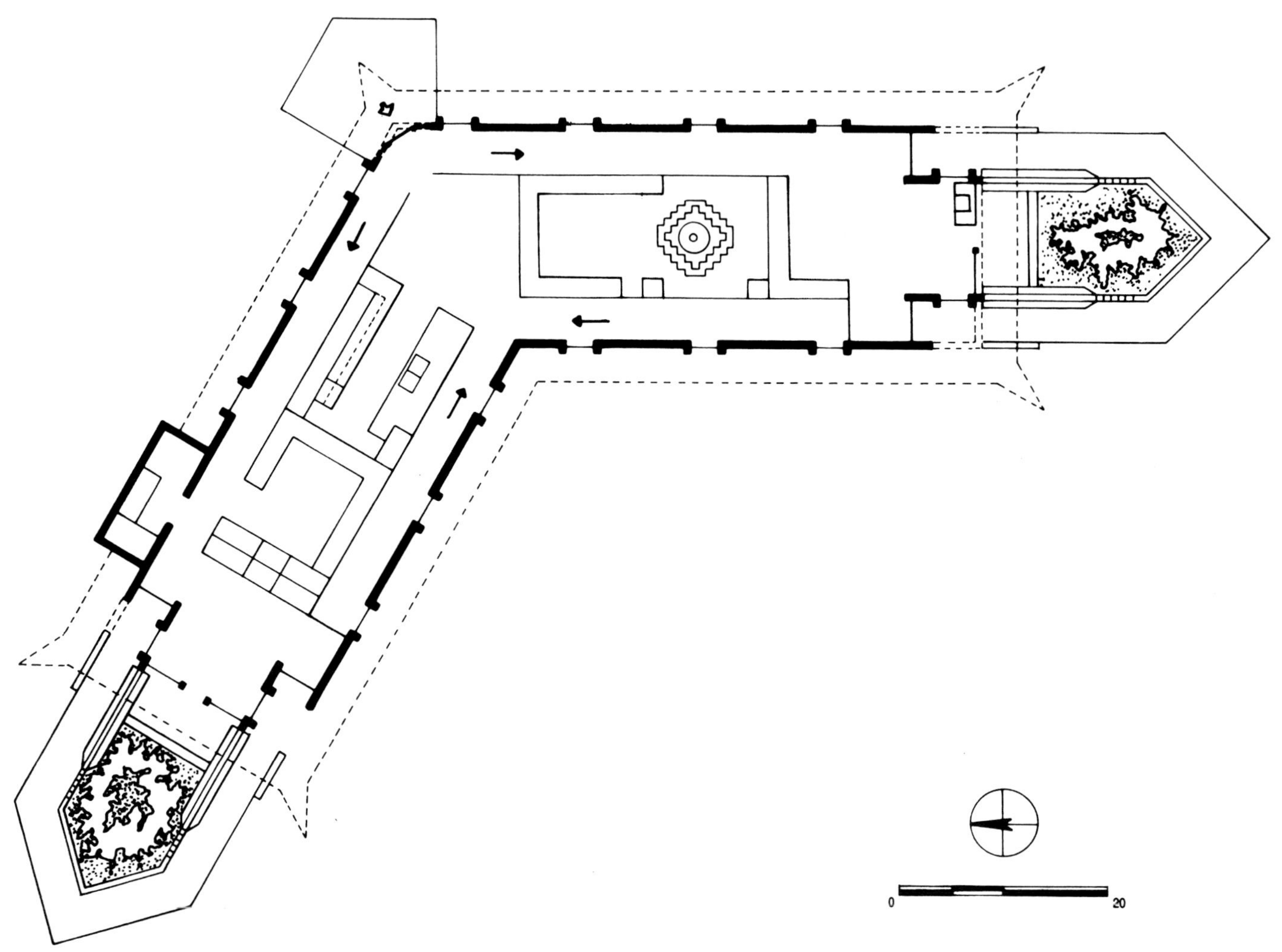

Above, Celestine Barby House, Tucson, Arizona, 1974. Plan drawing by OU College of Architecture, Design and Research Center. Courtesy College of Architecture, University of Oklahoma.

Facing page, Barby House, exterior. Photograph by author.

Painting by Goff, commissioned by Al Struckus. Courtesy of Struckus.

the cornice, extends the verticality of the tower. The form of the surrounds also relates to the pattern of the curved exterior walls with alternating panels of fixed glass and redwood. The pattern of the panels is varied by the positioning of wood framing members attached to the two-by-six-inch studs to form segmental arches that alternate in their direction of curvature. The visual effect is a pattern of curved elements forming a rhythm of geometric shapes similar to the stucco window surrounds on the façade. While one is a rhythm of vertical elements, the other is a series of horizontal rhythms. Although the pattern of alternating transparent and opaque panels is visually rich, its presence also is a logical response to site conditions. Built on a very small lot with close neighbors, it was a way of fragmenting views of the roofs of nearby houses and providing privacy.

Struckus never had a contract for architectural services, only a verbal agreement, and said Goff talked to him "like he's a friend rather than your architect. I felt like I had known him a long time—we clicked right from the start—whatever I brought up he had a positive solution."[34] Goff was appreciative of Struckus's commitment and said to him, "Where would I be if I didn't have clients like you."[35]

Goff's last major building was a museum to house Joe Price's expanding collection of Japanese paintings. The concept of a private museum was explored initially through adaptive reuse of a large barn on the Starview Farm acreage in Bartlesville but soon evolved into design of a free-standing public building. As the project developed, several sites were considered, but it was only months before Goff's death that a final decision was made: the museum would become the Japanese Pavilion of the Los Angeles County Museum of Art.

The concept underpinning the design was the premise that the art was the client. Joe Price articulated the design parameters when he said: "It had to have natural changing light, to allow the art to be seen in shadows and in sunlight. You had to see each painting up close and from a distance. You had to see only

Following spread

Left, Al Struckus House, Woodland Hills, California, 1979. Plan drawings by OU College of Architecture, Design and Research Center. Courtesy College of Architecture, University of Oklahoma.

Right, Struckus House, façade. Photograph by author.

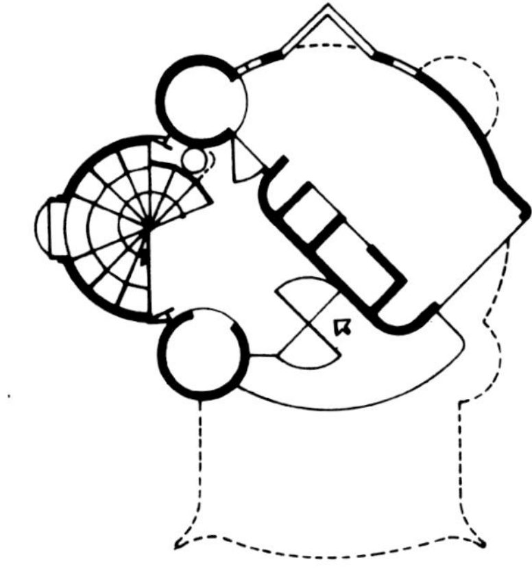

First Level

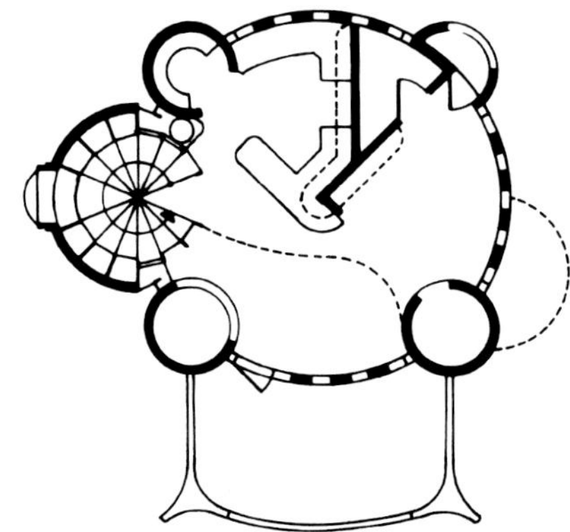

Second Level

Third Level

Fourth Level

Los Angeles County Museum of Art, structural detail.

one painting at a time. It couldn't have glass but it must be safe."[36]

The museum is defined by two adjoining galleries that appear nearly identical in form but not in size. The smaller gallery has several floors to house the existing museum collection of Japanese sculpture and scrolls, and a study space for scholars. The larger gallery is devoted exclusively to exhibition of Joe Price's collection. The indeterminate plan of both galleries approximates a triangular shape, except the exterior walls extend outward to form curved surfaces. The theme of geometric configuration is sustained by inclusion of curvilinear ramps and circular stair towers, which modulate the scale of the composition.

Major building materials include rock-faced gray-green stone at the base with a section of gray plaster above and pleated panels of translucent, insulated plastic to diffuse the light within, like Japanese *shoji* screens. Columns are recessed from exterior walls to rise above the planar roof and are joined together with curving, steel box-beams for attachment of cable supports for the deep overhanging roof.

Within the primary exhibition gallery, a curvilinear ramp weaves through the space around large tokonomas for the display of art. The tokonomas, rising totemlike from black, ceramic-tiled basins of water, are positioned adjacent to intermittent viewing platforms at different levels as extensions of the curving ramp. One can see the art close up, without reflective glass, but cannot touch it.

Major features of the design were established long before the site was known. Bart Prince assisted Goff in construction of a full-scale plywood model of a tokonoma in the loft of the barn at Starview Farm. After Goff's death, Joe Price designated Prince as the architect-of-record with responsibilities for design development, preparation of the technical documents, and weekly meetings during the construction phase. The problems were formidable. A primary concern was development of an underground ventilation system for the accumulation of seeping methane gas from the adjacent Las Brea Tar Pits. And there were frequent meetings with both the museum board of directors and Los Angeles code enforcement officials. Even during the construction phase, the multitude of compound concave and convex curves required improvised plastering tools. Because conventional tools would not work, Prince and the plastering subcontractor utilized rubber balls and curved pieces of plastic buckets as screeds to form the plaster surfaces.[37]

The Pavilion of Japanese Art is significant in Goff's oeuvre in several respects. Its imagery is a clear manifestation of continuing inspiration drawn from nature. The pavilion has an animalistic presence with its pleated, translucent panels evoking an association of an exotic flying creature with its wings folded over its body and the tusked, curved beams suggesting a weapon for survival. The expression of the building and specific location—next to the Las Brea Tar Pits—was fortuitous as the design resonates with the prehistoric creatures buried beneath its black, reflective surface. The basins of water within the principal gallery, black and reflective as the Tar Pit, provide further reference to specific phenomena of the natural world. The cable-supported roof reflects

Following spread

Left, Japanese Pavilion of the Los Angeles County Museum of Art. Plan drawing by OU College of Architecture, Design and Research Center with review by Bart Prince, architect. Courtesy College of Architecture, University of Oklahoma.

Right, Japanese Pavilion, exterior. Photograph by author.

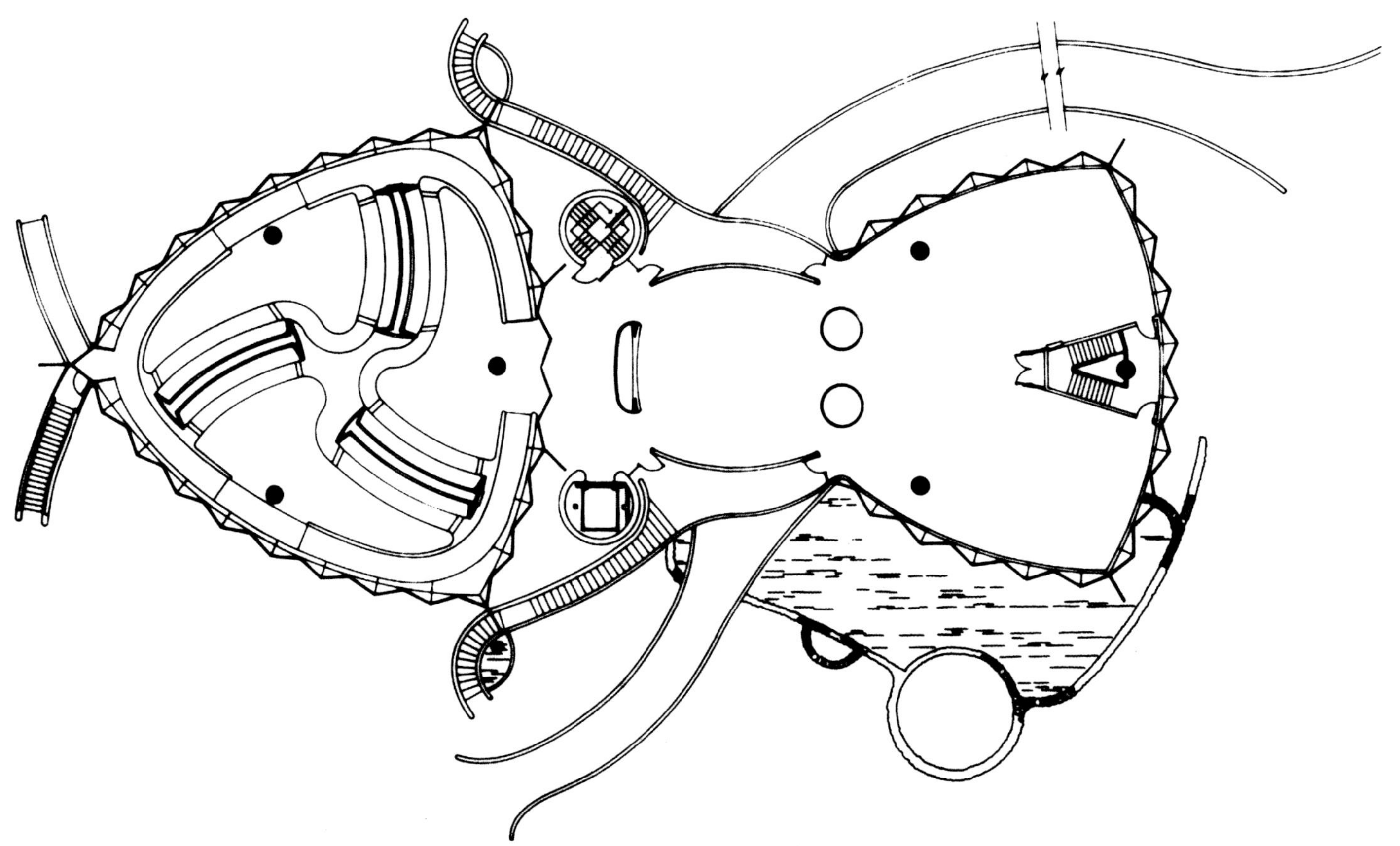

Left, Japanese Pavilion, translucent wall. Photograph by author.

Right, Japanese Pavilion, interior, tokonoma. Photograph by Robert Bowlby.

Facing page, Japanese Pavilion, exterior detail.

fulfillment of a major motif of forms floating in space.

The building also reflects Goff's commitment to addressing the needs of the client—the art—as a major determinant. To a great extent the building is the way it is because of his logical response to the art. In this sense the museum reflects an integrated expression of a continuum of original thinking and feeling. Goff trusted his intuition in pursuit of visions rich with meaning for both his clients and himself. The Japanese Pavilion represents a masterful summation of a life predicated on his convictions of fusing artistry with empathy.

It has to be something that improves
human life, with some spirit,
some feeling, some real ideas
contributing to human welfare:
joyful, with light, air, free spaces:
things that are alive, that are art.

JOHN LAUTNER

Only those who will risk
going too far can possibly find
out how far they can go.

T. S. ELIOT

CODA

The University of Oklahoma honored Bruce Goff during the last year of his life with a Distinguished Visiting Professorship to teach a seminar similar to his earlier 273 studio.[1] The following summer his health declined, and he died on August 4, 1982. On June 8, 1983—his birth date—a memorial celebration was held at OU, with hundreds of people attending. The guests included former students, apprentices, clients, friends, and faculty colleagues. Jack Golden, a former student, announced the formation of a new architectural organization called Friends of Kebyar, whose publications and meetings would nurture the quest for creative growth. "Kebyar," a Balinese word meaning "flowering," was the chosen name for a private design school Goff had hoped to develop. W. H. Raymond Yeh, dean of the College of Architecture, also announced the intention to establish the Bruce Goff Professorship of Creative Architecture to bring distinguished architects to the university as participants in the teaching program. Dr. George L. Cross, president of the university from 1944 to 1968, endorsed the professorship in memory of the "greatest creative genius I have

Gravestone of Bruce Goff in Graceland Cemetery, Chicago. Design by Grant Gustafson, photograph by author.

known and a gentle man whose friendship I have treasured. . . . I consider the addition of Bruce Goff to our faculty as one of the most fortunate things that has happened to the university during my tenure as president."[2]

In retrospect it is likely that Bruce Goff's visions, in both professional practice and teaching, drew upon the self-reliant ethos of the American West, which nurtured development of his individualism and the ennobling courage to act on his ideals and convictions. Like Wright, he often quoted the writings of Thomas Carlyle with his mandate that the ideal is within us. Carlyle believed that history is a biography of men of conviction and the "heroic mantle was bestowed not upon those who followed, but those who took the lead."[3] Bruce Goff, living quietly in Middle America, was one of the pioneering leaders of twentieth-century building.

Peacock on cantilevered beam at Joe Price House. Photograph by author.

On October 7, 2000, his ashes were interred in Chicago's Graceland Cemetery in a Frankhoma pottery urn not far from the graves of Louis Sullivan and Mies van der Rohe. The triangular granite and bronze monument inscribed with Goff's stylized typography and a blue-green glass cullet was designed by former apprentice Grant Gustafson. A statue of Goff, sculpted by OU School of Art faculty member Sohail Shehada, was then placed in a niche at the entry of the campus's Visitors Center on the historic North Oval.

Notes

1. FOUNDATIONS

1. David G. De Long, *The Architecture of Bruce Goff: Buildings and Projects, 1916–1974*, 2 vols. (New York: Garland, 1977), 5.
2. De Long, *Bruce Goff: Toward Absolute Architecture* (New York: Architectural History Foundation, 1988), 6–7.
3. Frank Lloyd Wright, "In the Cause of Architecture," *Architectural Record* 23 (March 1908): 157.
4. De Long, *Bruce Goff*, 8.
5. Ibid., 9.
6. Robert Bowlby, interview with author, Denver, Colo., January 1989. Bowlby, a University of Oklahoma graduate, was an apprentice to Goff.
7. Louis Sullivan, *The Autobiography of an Idea* (New York: W. W. Norton, 1926), 245–55.
8. Donald D. Egbert, "The Idea of Organic Expression and American Architecture," in *Evolutionary Thought in America*, ed. Stow Persons (New Haven: Yale University Press, 1950), 365.
9. Louis Sullivan, *Kindergarten Chats* (New York: Wittenborn, Shultz, 1947), 169.
10. Ibid., 174.
11. Frank Lloyd Wright, *An Organic Architecture: The Architecture of Democracy* (London: Land Humphries, 1939), 4.
12. Robert McCarter, "The Integrated Ideal: Ordering Principles in the Architecture of Frank Lloyd Wright," in *Frank Lloyd Wright: A Primer in Architectural Principles*, ed. Robert McCarter (New York: Princeton Architectural Press, 1991), 272.
13. Ibid., 261–65.
14. Ibid., 274.
15. Sullivan, *Kindergarten Chats*, 114.
16. Egbert, "Idea of Organic Expression," 353.
17. Bruce Goff, "About Absolute Art" (unpublished prose poem, August 1932), 2. Witt Collection, College of Architecture, University of Oklahoma; hereafter cited as Witt Collection.
18. Bruce Goff, "Of Beauty and Architecture" (unpublished paper, 13 pp., June 1961), 2. Witt Collection.
19. Bruce Goff, "Notes on Architecture" (unpublished paper, 13 pp., June 1957), 1. Witt Collection.
20. Egbert, "Idea of Organic Expression," 95.
21. Sullivan, *Kindergarten Chats*, 198.
22. Ibid., 114.
23. Goff, "Notes on Architecture," 1.
24. Goff, "Beauty and Architecture," 3.
25. Goff, "About Absolute Art," 2.
26. Philip B. Welch, ed., *Goff on Goff: Conversations and Lectures* (Norman: University of Oklahoma Press, 1996), 227–31.
27. Edmund Wilson, *Axel's Castle: A Study in the Imaginative Literature of 1870–1930* (New York: Charles Scribner's Sons, 1931), 2.
28. Ibid., 21.
29. Ibid., 20.
30. A. G. Lehmann, *The Symbolist Aesthetic in France, 1885–1932* (Oxford, England: Blackwell, 1968), 116–18.
31. Arthur Symons, *The Symbolist Movement in Literature* (New York: Dutton, 1958), 19.
32. Ibid., 3.
33. Lehmann, *Symbolist Aesthetic*, 54.
34. Ibid., 58.
35. Claude Debussy, "Monsieur Croche the Dilettante Hater," in *Three Classics in the Aesthetic of Music* (New York: Dover, 1962), 12.
36. Welch, *Goff on Goff*, 135.
37. Debussy, "Monsieur Croche the Dilettante Hater," 3.

38. Welch, *Goff on Goff*, 277. Goff's statement has a parallel with Ralph Waldo Emerson's characterization of the artist as the "mouthpiece of the soul," as F. O. Matthiessen put it in *American Renaissance* (1941).
39. Victor Ilyitch Seroff, *Debussy: Musician of France* (New York: Putman, 1956), 293–94.
40. Gertrude Stein, "Composition as Explanation," *Dial* 81 (October 1926): 327–36.
41. "Pride of the Prairie," *Architectural Forum* 88 (March 1948): 99.
42. Takenobu Mohri, *Bruce Goff in Architecture* (Tokyo: Kenchiku Planning Center, 1970), 205–6.
43. Frank Lloyd Wright, *An American Architecture*, ed. Edgar Kaufmann (New York: Barnes & Noble Books, 1998), 45.
44. Bruce Goff, "Goff on Goff," *Progressive Architecture* (December 1962): 102.
45. Iain Boyd Whyte, "The Expressionist Sublime," in *Expressionist Utopias: Paradise, Metropolis, Architectural Fantasy*, ed. Timothy O. Benson (Berkeley: University of California Press, 2001), 128. The ideals and intellectual history of German architects of this era are revealed by the "Utopian Circular Letters" in Ulrich Conrad and Hans G. Sperlich, *The Architecture of Fantasy* (New York: Frederick A. Praeger, 1962), 128–56.
46. Whyte, "The Expressionist Sublime," 132. Also see Rosemarie Haag Bletter, "Paul Scheerbart's Architectural Fantasies," *Journal of the Society of Architectural Historians* 34, no. 2 (May 1975): 83–97. Toller's proclamation resonates with the writings of Paul Scheerbart, author of *Glass Architecture* and friend of Bruno Taut. His mantra, "Without a glass palace life is a burden," was inscribed on Taut's Glass Pavilion at the Cologne, Germany, Werkbund Exhibition.
47. David Frisby, "Social Theory, the Metropolis, and Expressionism," in *Expressionist Utopias: Paradise, Metropolis, Architectural Fantasy*, ed. Timothy O. Benson (Berkeley: University of California Press, 2001), 88.
48. Ibid., 88.
49. Whyte, "The Expressionist Sublime," 121–26.
50. James Gresham, letter to author, December 7, 2009.
51. Bowlby, interview, January 1989. Goff seldom talked about his abstract paintings and would usually refer to them as exercises for relaxation. It was not uncommon for him to produce ten or twelve consecutive paintings at a time. He would often submerge a partially completed painting in a bathtub to create a wash of color through serendipitous chance and indeterminacy. He also believed the paintings might be displayed with any orientation. For Goff, there was no top or bottom.
52. De Long, *Architecture of Bruce Goff*, 223. Goff's familiarity with designs by the German Expressionist architects is revealed in the class notes of Rolland Ristine, an OU student in the early 1950s.
53. De Long, *Bruce Goff*, 13–15.
54. Ibid. Goff also discovered the work of Antoni Gaudí in 1922, the year he graduated from high school.
55. Charles Cabot, *The Architecture of Bruce Goff* (BBC, 1976), TV.
56. De Long, *Bruce Goff*, 12–13. Goff admired the writings of Bragdon on the necessity for beauty in architecture through "numerically based patterns" of ornament and the use of "joyous color."
57. Claude Bragdon, *The Beautiful Necessity: Seven Essays on Theosophy and Architecture*, 2nd ed. (New York: Alfred A. Knopf, 1927), 101. The origins of the metaphor of architecture as "frozen music" are also discussed in a paper by Steven Grabow titled "Frozen Music: The Bridge Between Art and Science" and an essay by Daniel F. MacGilvray, "The Proper Education of Musicians and Architects." Both refer to Johann W. Goethe who defined architecture as "petrified music" (1829), and Friedrich von Schelling in *The Philosophy of Art* (1859) posited architecture as "the music of the plastic arts . . . in a sense solidified music."
58. Bart Prince, interview with author, Norman, Okla., October 1992. Prince was an apprentice to Goff.
59. Welch, *Goff on Goff*, 239.
60. Jeffrey Cook, *The Architecture of Bruce Goff* (New York: Harper and Row, 1978), foreword.
61. Jack Golden, discussions about architecture and music with author, Norman, Okla., September 1956–May 1957.
62. Bruce Goff letter to Elizabeth M. Kassler (née Mock), February 9, 1952. Witt Collection.
63. Sidney K. Robinson, "Bruce Goff and Music," in *The Architecture of Bruce Goff, 1904–1982: Design for the Continuous Present*, ed., Pauline Saliga and Mary Woolever (Chicago: Art Institute of Chicago, 1995), 35–36.

64. Golden, discussions with author, September 1956–May 1957.
65. Seroff, *Debussy*, 293.

2. FIRST DESIGNS

1. De Long, *Bruce Goff*, 8–11.
2. Ibid., 9.
3. Angie Debo, *Tulsa: From Creek Town to Oil Capital* (Norman: University of Oklahoma Press, 1943), 97.
4. De Long, *Bruce Goff*, 22.
5. De Long, *Architecture of Bruce Goff*, 57.
6. Sally Kitt Chappell and Ann Van Zanten, *Barry Byrne, John Lloyd Wright: Architecture and Design* (Chicago: Chicago Historical Society, 1982), 24.
7. Goff had previously designed a house at the corner of 11th Place and Owasso in Tulsa for Adah Robinson in 1923. The design of interlocking white stucco forms suggests an influence of European modernism.
8. "A Twentieth Century Church: Boston Avenue Methodist Church" (dedicatory booklet) (Tulsa, Okla.: Boston Avenue Methodist Episcopal Church, 1929).
9. De Long, *Architecture of Bruce Goff*, 67.
10. Sheldon Cheney, *The New World Architecture* (New York: Longmans, Green, 1930), 341–43.
11. De Long, *Architecture of Bruce Goff*, 64.
12. De Long, *Bruce Goff*, 30–32.
13. Ibid.
14. Ibid., 34–38.
15. Mark Andrew White, *Oklahoma Moderne: The Art and Design of Olinka Hrdy* (Norman: Fred Jones Jr. Museum of Art, University of Oklahoma, 2007), 28–36. Bill E. Peavler's essay on Riverside Studio in *Of the Earth: Oklahoma Architectural History* (1980), with interviews of Goff and Hrdy, includes personal interactions with both client and colleague. Shriner and Hrdy had conflicting views over the murals and Goff had to serve as the mediator. The murals have disappeared but the OU Art Museum has the original watercolor designs on paper.
16. De Long, *Bruce Goff*, 42.
17. Bruce Goff, "A Declaration of Independence," *Western Architect* 39 (January 1930): 17–18.
18. Oklahoma Architects Registration Board, telephone interview with author, March 2003. There is some confusion over the exact date of Goff's license. Their records show he was licensed in 1931. On a personnel form for the University of Oklahoma, dated October 25, 1946, Goff stated he was licensed in 1929, the same year of his advancement to partnership in the firm.

3. A LANGUAGE OF CONCEPTUALIZATION

1. Robert Harbison, *The Built, the Unbuilt, and the Unbuildable: In Pursuit of Architectural Meaning* (Cambridge, Mass.: MIT Press, 1991), 172.
2. Goff, "About Absolute Art," 2.
3. Frank Lloyd Wright, "Modern Architecture, Being the Kahn Lectures," in *Frank Lloyd Wright Collected Writings*, ed., Bruce Brooks Pfeiffer (New York: Rizzoli International, 1992), 32.
4. Egbert, "The Idea of Organic Expression and American Architecture," 369–72.
5. Ibid. 365.
6. Ibid., 366.
7. Ibid., 365.
8. Sullivan, *Autobiography of an Idea*, 245–55.
9. Egbert, "The Idea of Organic Expression and American Architecture," 361–63.
10. Debussy, "Monsieur Croche, the Dilettante Hater," 8.
11. "Pride of the Prairie," *Architectural Forum* 88 (March 1948): 94–101.
12. Phillip B. Welch, ed., *Goff on Goff: Conversations and Lectures* (Norman: University of Oklahoma Press, 1996), 281.
13. Ibid., 201–2.
14. Ibid., 67.
15. Ibid., 99–100.
16. Ibid., 62.
17. Ibid., 212
18. Wallace Stevens, *Collected Poetry and Prose* (New York: Library of America, 1997), 50.
19. De Long, *Bruce Goff*, 61–62. In my August 1989 interview with architect Robert Deme, then current owner, he mentioned that the stair landing/alcove originally opened to a porch that was later enclosed to enlarge the alcove.
20. Ibid., 64–66.
21. Interview with Ed Hansen, Pensacola, Fla., June 1987. Hansen, an OU classmate, apprenticed with Goff in 1961, the year of our graduation.
22. Interview with Bart Prince, Norman, Okla., October, 1992.
23. "Pride of the Prairie," 190.
24. Charles Jencks and Nathan Silver, "Towards an Articulate Environment," chap. 5 in *Adhocism: The Case for Improvisation* (Garden City, N.Y.: Anchor Press, 1973), 84–85.
25. De Long, *Bruce Goff*, 73.
26. Stephen Mooring, "Buildings and Projects by Bruce Goff," *Architectural Design* 48, no. 10 (1978): 35.

27. Bruce Goff, letter to Eleanor Bittermann, June 19, 1951. Witt Collection.
28. Interview with Robert A. Bowlby, Denver, Colo., January, 1989.
29. Interview with Harvey Ferrero, Lincoln, Neb., April 1993.
30. Rosemary M. Nielsen and Robert H. Solomon, "The Clash of the Lasting and the Catastrophic in the *Odes* of Horace," in *Climate and Literature: Reflections of Environment*, ed. Janet Perez and Wendell Aycock (Lubbock: Texas Tech University Press, 1995), 7–17.
31. Wendell McClendon, "Zola's Uses of Climate in *The Land*," in *Climate and Literature: Reflections of Environment*, ed. Janet Perez and Wendell Aycock (Lubbock: Texas Tech University Press, 1995), 43–54.
32. Robert Kostka, "Bruce Goff and the New Tradition," *The Prairie School Review* 7, no. 2 (1970): 331.
33. Bruce Goff, "Notes on Architecture" (June 1957), 9–10. Witt Collection.
34. Interview with Robert A. Bowlby, Denver, Colo., January, 1989. Two painters worked two days gluing feathers to the interior surfaces of the hood.
35. Iain Boyd Whyte, "The Expressionist Sublime," in *Expressionist Utopias: Paradise, Metropolis, Architectural Fantasy*, ed. Timothy O. Benson (Berkeley: University of California Press, 2001), 127.
36. The feature of water as an element of composition also appears in the 1930 proposal for the Phi Beta Delta fraternity house, Colmorgan House (1939), Bartman House (1941), Ledbetter House (1947), Wilson House (1950), proposed Crystal Chapel (1950), Bavinger House (1950), initial Garvey design (1952), Frank House (1955), Price Studio (1956), Pollock House (1957), Jones House (1958), Gelbman House (1959), Gryder House (1960), Nicol House (1965), both the Glen and Jacob Harder Houses (1970), Plunkett House (1970), and Struckus House (1979).
37. De Long, *Bruce Goff*, 82–85.

4. TEACHING ORGANIC ARCHITECTURE

1. Henry Kamphoefner (professor of architecture), letters to Goff, August 5, 1946, and August 23, 1946, and to George L. Cross (University of Oklahoma president), August 5, 1946, and September 3, 1946. Witt Collection. In the August 23, 1946, letter, Kamphoefner cautioned Goff that his salary expectations should be within the "general pattern the University is able to pay." He mentioned that Jens Rud Nielsen, a physics research professor and famous authority on spectroscopy, received $5,000 for a nine-month appointment. In the September 3 letter Kamphoefner refers to Goff as the "best candidate for the directorship that we have so far considered."
2. Goff, letter to Cross, August 22, 1946. Witt Collection.
3. Royden Dangerfield, letter to Cross, November 2, 1946. Witt Collection.
4. Fred Langhorst, letter to Richard N. Kuhlman (chairman of the School of Architecture), November 6, 1946. Witt Collection.
5. Kuhlman, letter to Cross, November 5, 1946. Witt Collection.
6. Frank Lloyd Wright, letter "To Whom It May Concern," November 12, 1946. Witt Collection.
7. Cross, telegram to Goff, November 5, 1946. Witt Collection.
8. George L. Cross, "Bruce Goff," n.d., 3 p. Witt Collection. Goff was appointed chairman of the School of Architecture by the OU Board of Regents, See OU Board of Regents, "Minutes of June 11, 1947." The appointment, which was unanimous by the faculty, was effective beginning September 1.
9. Appointments to the faculty by Goff are primarily drawn from pages 10 and 11 of an unpublished manuscript on the history of the OU College of Engineering by Professor Thomas Love. Synopses of faculty during Goff's tenure are also included in *Sooner Shamrock* 13, no. 3 (March 1953): 40–60, and 15, no. 2 (December 1954–January 1955): 10. Other sources include correspondence from Goff to Sidney Abraham, a former student, October 18, 1949, and Mendel Glickman, November 16, 1955. Witt Collection.
10. Goff, letter to John Leineweber, November 7, 1950. Witt Collection.
11. Goff, memo to student body, n.d. Witt Collection.
12. Goff's disdain of the International Style was a common theme in both his lectures and informal discussions.
13. Goff, letter to Leineweber, November 7, 1950. Witt Collection.
14. Goff, letter to Jan Reiner, April 13, 1949. Witt Collection.
15. Goff, letter to Douglas Haskell, March 29, 1951. Witt Collection.
16. Herb Greene, telephone interview with author, January 2010.
17. Frank L. Faust, letter to Goff, July 21, 1952. Witt Collection.

18. Goff, letter to Frank Faust, July 30, 1952. Witt Collection.
19. Vincent Carrera Loor, letter to Goff, July 1, 1951. Witt Collection.
20. Goff, letter to Loor, August 15, 1951. Witt Collection.
21. Jack Golden, discussion with author, Norman, Okla., 1956–57.
22. Ibid.
23. Delon Howell (National Architectural Accrediting Board [NAAB]), telephone interview with author, March 2003.
24. Goff, letter to Mendel Glickman, November 16, 1955. Witt Collection.
25. Robert Faust, interview with author, Auburn, Ala., June 1987.
26. Goff, letters to Mary Mix (executive director of Division of Pan-American Affairs at the American Institute of Architects), six letters, August 1, 1949–November 28, 1949. Witt Collection.
27. Mary Mix, letter to Goff, November 3, 1949. Included was a copy of the catalogue "Contemporary Architecture in the United States, 1947–1949." Witt Collection.
28. Goff, letter to Blaine Imel, June 15, 1950. Witt Collection.
29. Charles Jencks, "Philip Johnson and the Smile of Medusa," in *Philip Johnson: The Constancy of Change*, ed. Emmanuel Petit (New Haven, Conn.: Yale University Press, 2009), 142.
30. Goff, letter to Elizabeth Kassler (née Mock), February 9, 1952. Witt Collection.
31. Goff, letter to Kassler, February 9, 1952. Witt Collection.
32. De Long, *Bruce Goff*, 307.
33. *Sooner Shamrock* 15, no.2 (December 1954–January 1955): 10.
34. Philip Welch, letter to Goff. The date of the letter is incomplete but the context suggests it was written in 1954, the year following Welch's completion of the graduate program at OU. Witt Collection.
35. Bart Prince, discussion with author, Norman, Okla., October, 1992.
36. Jack Golden, discussion with author, spring 1957.
37. Comment to author, May 1961.
38. *Sooner Shamrock* 15, no. 2 (December 1954–January 1955): 10.
39. John J. Schultz, telegram to Goff, May 15, 1952. Witt Collection.
40. John Hurtig, telephone interview with author, June 2003.
41. James A. Gresham, "Revisiting Mies and Goff," 2001. Witt Collection.
42. Siegfried Giedion, *Space, Time and Architecture*, 4th ed. (Cambridge, Mass.: Harvard University Press 1965).
43. Ibid., 482.
44. Bruce Goff, "Aesthetic Food for Architects," n.d., 4 pp. Witt Collection.
45. Herb Greene, telephone interview with author, January 2006.
46. Welch, *Goff on Goff*, 232.
47. Jerri Bonebrake, interview with author, Norman, Okla., January 2009.
48. Goff, "Aesthetic Food for Architects."
49. Bonebrake, interview with author, Norman, Okla., April 1993.
50. Robert A. Bowlby, interview with author, Denver, Colo., January 1989.
51. James Gresham, letter to author, November 22, 2009. Goff also taught a history course on pre-Columbian and Asian architecture, which were completely ignored by most American architecture schools.
52. Ibid.
53. Robert A. Bowlby, interview with author, Norman, Okla., March 2004. The student who received the winter coat was Jack Golden.
54. Robert A. Bowlby, discussion with author, 1989, identified the primary reading assignments. Later I had access to audiotapes from Jerri Bonebrake of Goff's Architecture 273 lectures recorded by Shizuo Oka in 1951. I transcribed and edited the recordings. The sequence of lectures presented here may not correspond exactly to Goff's sequence of presentation as the numbering of some of the tapes were duplicated. I also had access to 273 class notes of Bill Peavler in 1951 and Ernest Jacks in 1955. Illustrations of student design projects date from the early 1950s.
55. Jack Golden, discussion with author, Norman, Okla., 1956–1957.
56. Nelson Brackin, telephone interview with author, August 1992.

5. PROFESSIONAL PRACTICE AT OU

1. Architecture 273 lectures, tape-recorded by Shizuo Oka, 1951, at OU. Jerri Bonebrake Collection.
2. Bruce Goff, interview with author, Norman, Okla., January 1982.
3. Lois Ledbetter, telephone interview with author, January 1982.
4. The institute was later named the Cerebral Palsy Institute.
5. Goff, letter to Douglas Haskell, October 2, 1954. Witt Collection.
6. Goff, letter to Philip Welch, September 22, 1954. Witt Collection.
7. Robert Overstreet (OU alumnus and former Goff apprentice), interview with

author, Corte Madera, Calif., July 1988.
8. Ibid.
9. Ibid.
10. Cabot, *Architecture of Bruce Goff.*
11. Jeffrey Cook, *The Architecture of Bruce Goff* (New York: Harper and Row, 1978), 41.
12. Julius Cox, interview with author, Boise City, Okla., August 1988.
13. Robert A. Bowlby, interview with author, Denver, Colo., January 1989.
14. Rex Slack (OU alumnus and former Goff apprentice), interview with author, Muskogee, Okla., February, 1995.
15. Robert Overstreet (OU alumnus and former Goff apprentice), interview with author, Corte Madera, Calif., July 1988.
16. "Crystal Chapel," *Architectural Forum* 93, no. 1 (July 1950): 88.
17. George Lynn Cross, "Appendix N," *The Seeds of Excellence* (Norman: University of Oklahoma Press, 1986), 248–51.
18. De Long, *Bruce Goff,* 104. Other architects who wrote in support of the Crystal Chapel included Carl Koch, George Nelson, Pietro Belluschi, Walter Gropius, John Lloyd Wright, Alden Dow, John Lautner, Alfonso Iannelli, Barry Byrne, Gregory Ain, and Robert Anshen.
19. Questions on "campus location" of the Crystal Chapel by visiting architects were often directed to senior faculty members by office staff.
20. Goff, letter to Olga Gueft, November 15, 1951. Witt Collection.
21. Gene Bavinger's studio was initially located at the top of the spatial continuum of the house, which limited the size of his paintings. He later constructed an independent studio on the site that would accommodate larger works.
22. De Long, *Architecture of Bruce Goff,* 272–73. The twenty-eight participating students who worked on the Bavinger House are identified in a footnote.
23. As related by Jack Golden, Norman, Okla., 1956–57.
24. Paul Heyer, *Architects on Architecture* (New York: Walker & Company, 1966), 71.
25. Goff, letter to Jesse J. Siegel, editor of *Authenticated News,* September 30, 1955. Witt Collection.
26. Harrison Kerr, letter to *LIFE* magazine, September 21, 1955. Witt Collection. Goff admired Kerr as both a composer and effective teacher. In an interview with Herb Greene, Kerr mentioned that Goff encouraged Greene and James Gresham to take Kerr's introductory lecture course on contemporary music, November, 2009.
27. Welch, *Goff on Goff,* 293.
28. Cited in David Michael Hertz, *Angels of Reality: Emersonian Unfoldings in Wright, Stevens and Ives* (Carbondale: University of Southern Illinois Press, 1993).
29. Jerri Bonebrake, interview with author, Norman, Okla., July 2004.
30. Goff was gay. In an interview with President Emeritus George L. Cross in August 1992, Cross mentioned there had been a complaint made in the early 1950s about Goff's homosexuality. This was brought to the attention of both President Cross and the Board of Regents. Cross talked to Goff about it and Goff assured him he was not involved with students. In 1955 Goff was forced to leave the city of Norman because of an inappropriate relationship. The circumstances of this event, which involved entrapment, are discussed in William H. Wilson's unpublished manuscript "Bruce Goff, We Love You," Norman, Okla., 1986, 135 p. Witt Collection.
31. Goff, letter to Colly and Paolo Soleri, December 12, 1955. Witt Collection.

6. A CONTINUING PRESENCE

1. De Long, *Bruce Goff,* 126.
2. Goff, interview with author, Norman, Okla., 1982.
3. Dennis Sharp, *Modern Architecture and Expressionism* (New York: George Braziller, 1966), 87.
4. In a 1956 discussion with Jack Golden, he mentioned that this expression was one Goff frequently used to explain a duality of purpose through transformation of a functional element into an artifact of beauty.
5. Bart Prince, interview with author, Norman, Okla., October, 1992. Goff made this observation to Prince shortly after completion of the second addition to the Price House in Bartlesville.
6. The cause of the fire was attributed to arson.
7. Elizabeth Mitchell, "Bruce Goff and His Clients: A Collaborative Relationship" (Ph.D. diss., Birmingham [England] School of Architecture, 1990), 89. Mitchell was an exchange student at OU in 1990. Witt Collection.
8. Herb Greene, telephone interview with author, June 2009.
9. Herb Greene, telephone interview with author, November 2009. The asymmetry of the design was at the suggestion of Douglas Harris, an apprentice and later associate with Goff.
10. Mitchell, "Bruce Goff and His Clients," 89.

11. Julia Gee, interview with author, Houston, Texas, July 1990.
12. Greene, telephone interview with author, November 2009.
13. Harvey Ferrero (former Goff apprentice), interview with author, Lincoln, Neb., April 1993.
14. The animalistic presence of the house is akin to the design for Al Dewlin.
15. In the 1990s the owner of the house replaced the painted siding with faux stone. The loss of visual integrity precluded its listing on the National Register of Historic Places.
16. De Long, *Bruce Goff*, 355–56. Buildings constructed include a ski lodge in Crested Butte, Colorado; the Hugh Duncan House near Cobden, Illinois; Ben Fitzgerald Realty Office in Tyler, Texas; the Lawrence Hyde House in Overland Park, Kansas; the Roland Jacquart House in Sublette, Kansas; and the James Nicol House in Kansas City, Missouri.
17. Richard Helstrom, telephone interview with author, October 2000.
18. The study was not built as Goff had designed.
19. Lawrence Hyde, interview with author, Kansas City, Kan., August 1989.
20. James Nicol, interview with author, Kansas City, Mo., August 1989.
21. Nicol interview, 1989.
22. Ibid. Goff had originally proposed a glass fishbowl set into the floor of the primary volume, but Nicol did not accept his suggestion. The concept reappeared in the 1966 addition to the Joe Price house.
23. De Long, *Bruce Goff*, 248–49. Goff gave lectures in Berlin, Frankfurt, Stuttgart, Brussels, Liege, and Paris.
24. Glen Harder, interview with author, in rural Mountain Lake, Minn., August 1989.
25. Glen Harder also mentioned that the construction cost ultimately exceeded his budget by 100 percent.
26. Luetta Harder, interview with author, 1989. The Astroturf deteriorated and the roof was later clad with a plasticized material of the same color.
27. Mitchell, "Bruce Goff and His Clients," 88.
28. Jacob and Anna Harder, interview with author, Mountain Lake, Minn., August 1989.
29. Ibid.
30. *La Mer* Portfolio. A portfolio of Goff's painting titled *La Mer* was prepared in the early 1980s by the OU College of Architecture as a fund-raising gift for donors to the Bruce Goff Professorship of Creative Architecture.
31. *Friends of Kebyar*, no. 40 (1988): 20. It is also included in the prologue of the *La Mer* Portfolio.
32. David G. De Long, "Bruce Goff and the Evolution of an Architectural Ideal," in *In Search of Modern Architecture: A Tribute to Henry-Russell Hitchcock*, ed. Helen Searing (New York: Architectural History Foundation; Cambridge, Mass.: MIT Press, 1982), 348.
33. In 1962 Goff designed a house for Celestine Barby in Beaver, Oklahoma.
34. Mitchell, "Bruce Goff and his Clients," 9.
35. Al Struckus, interview with author, Woodland Hills, Calif., July 1988.
36. "Japanese Art Finds a Home in LA," *Tulsa Daily World*, March 20, 1989.
37. Bart Prince, interview with author, October 1992. Prince and Goff had a strong bond of friendship and they worked together on several projects during the last decade of Goff's career. They also traveled to Japan in 1974 for a series of exhibitions and lectures. In 1978 they traveled to Europe and visited architectural schools in England and Scotland. Prince's insights into Goff's life and work are discussed in his essay "Bruce Goff, Friend and Teacher" in *triglyph* no.1 (Fall 1984): 33–37.

CODA

1. William S. Banowsky (OU president), letter to Goff, September 18, 1981. Witt Collection.
2. George L. Cross, "Excerpts from Statements at the Celebration of the Life of Bruce Goff," in "The Legacy of Bruce Alonzo Goff," special edition, *Friends of Kebyar* 6.4, no. 40 (1988): 14.
3. Sam W. Haynes, *Soldiers of Misfortune* (Austin: University of Texas Press, 1990), 211.

Bibliography

ARCHIVAL SOURCES

Bruce Goff Personnel File, Office of the Provost, University of Oklahoma.
Correspondence: various letters, memos, and telegrams.

OU Board of Regents. "Minutes." May 25, 1948, 2,722 pp.

Witt Collection, College of Architecture, University of Oklahoma.

"Contemporary Architecture in the United States, 1947–1949: An Exhibit by the American Institute of Architects for the VII Congreso Panamericano de Architectos and for loan to the Department of State for international circulation." 4-page catalog, October 28, 1949.

Correspondence: various letters and telegrams.

Cross, George L., President Emeritus. "Bruce Goff," n.d., 3 pp.

Fatsea, Irene D. "The Architecture of Bruce Goff During the Years 1946–1956: An Exploration of Design Determinants Through Selected Analysis of Selected Buildings." Master's thesis, University of Oklahoma, 1987.

Ferrero, Harvey. Sketch with notations of the proposed dining room table for the second design of the Robert G. Allen House (1959), Bartlesville, Oklahoma, 1993.

Goff, Bruce. "About Absolute Art." Prose poem, August 1932, 2 pp.

———. "Aesthetic Food for Architects," n.d., 4 pp. Location in Goff's university correspondence file suggests this was written in January 1952.

———. Forty-Four Architectural Realizations," manuscript, 140 pp.

———. "Notes on Architecture." Paper, June 1957, 13 pp.

———. "Of Beauty and Architecture." Paper, June 1961, 13 pp.

———. "Of Debussy: Music and Architecture," ca. 1962, 9 pp.

———. *A Portfolio of Photographs of Paintings.*

———. "Protest for Architecture," n.d., 16 pp.

———. "The School of Architecture at the University of Oklahoma, 1947–1956," n.d., 1 p.

Grabow, Steven. "Frozen Music: The Bridge Between Art and Science." Paper presented at the Centennial Design Symposium on Organic Pluralism at the University of Oklahoma, Norman, March 1990.

Gresham, James A. "Revisiting Mies and Goff," 2001, 20 pp.

Hurtig, John. "Memoir," 2012, 104 pp.

Jacks, Ernest. Architecture 273 class notes, 1955.

Love, Thomas. "History of The University of Oklahoma College of Engineering: Chapter V, World War II and Post War Recovery, 1940–1950," March 1992, 47 pp.

Mitchell, Elizabeth. "Bruce Goff and his Clients: A Collaborative Relationship." Ph.D. diss., Birmingham, England, School of Architecture (with research at OU as an exchange student), 1990.

Peavler, Bill. Architecture 273 class notes, 1951.

Wilson, William H. "Bruce Goff, We Love You," Norman, Oklahoma, 1986, 135 pp.

INTERVIEWS WITH THE AUTHOR

Barby, Celestine. Tucson, Ariz., July 1988.

Bavinger, Eugene. Norman, Okla., multiple interviews, 1960–1990s.

Bonebrake (née Hodges), Jerri. Oklahoma City, Okla., multiple interviews, late 1980s–2009.

Bowlby, Robert. Denver, Colo., January 1989; and multiple telephone interviews to 2010.
Brackin, Nelson. Telephone interview, August 1992.
Cross, George L. (University of Oklahoma president emeritus). Norman, Okla., August 1992.
Cox, Julius. Boise City, Okla., August 1988.
Dace, Mrs. William. Beaver, Okla., July 1978.
Deme, Robert. Colmorgan House, Glenview, Ill., August 1989.
Faust, Robert. Auburn, Ala., June 1987.
Ferrero, Harvey. Lincoln, Neb., April 1993.
Frank, Mrs. John. Sapulpa, Okla., July 1978 and July 1990.
Gee, Julia. Durst House, Houston, Texas, July 1990.
Goff, Bruce. Bartlesville, Okla., March 1959; Norman, Okla., 1975; and Norman, Okla., multiple interviews, 1981–1982.
Golden, Jack. Norman, Okla., multiple discussions on Goff, September 1956–May 1957 and September 1989.
Greene, Herb. Norman, Okla., multiple discussions on Goff, September 1957–May 1961; and Berkeley, Calif., July 1988; and multiple telephone interviews to 2010.
Gresham, James. Tucson, Ariz., July 1988; Norman, Okla., 2004; and multiple telephone interviews to 2010.
Gryder, Elaine. Ocean Springs, Miss., June 1987.
Hansen, Edward. Pensacola, Fla., June 1987.
Harder, Glen, and Luetta Harder. Mountain Lake, Minn., August 1989.
Harder, Jacob, and Anna Harder. Mountain Lake, Minn., August, 1989.
Howell, Delon. Washington, D.C., National Architectural Accreditation Board (NAAB), telephone interview, March 2003.
Hurtig, John. Pueblo, Colo., multiple telephone interviews, June 2003–2010.
Hyde, Lawrence. Kansas City, Kan., August 1989.
Jewell, Opal. Bartman House, Fern Creek, Ky., August 1989.
Jones, E. Fay. Telephone interview, March 2001.
Jones, Lucille. Bartlesville, Okla., July 1991, October 1992, and June 1995.
Kuhlman, Richard N. Norman, Okla., March 1992.
Ledbetter, Lois. Norman, Okla., telephone interview, March 1989.
Nicol, James, and Betty Nicol. Kansas City, Mo., August 1989.
Oklahoma Architects Registration Board. Telephone interview, March 2003.
Overstreet, Robert. Corte Madera, Calif., July 1988.
Price, Joe. Bartlesville, Okla., July 1978; Corona del Mar, Calif., June 1988.
Prince, Bart. Albuquerque, N.M., March 1990; Norman, Okla., October, 1992.
Robinson, Sidney. Ford House, Aurora, Ill., August 1989.
Slack, Rex. Muskogee, Okla., February 1995.
Stefan, Herb. Unseth House, Park Ridge, Ill., August 1989.
Struckus, Al. Woodland Hills, Calif., July 1988.
Walden, Marjorie. Comer House, Dewey, Okla., June 1988.
Ward, John. Edmond, Okla., December 2001.
Warriner, Laura. Pollock House, Oklahoma City, Okla., February 1991.

BOOKS, ARTICLES, THESES, AND PAPERS

Adams, David. "Rudolf Steiner's First Goetheanum as an Illustration of Organic Functionalism." *Journal of the Society of Architectural Historians* 51, no. 2 (June 1992): 182–204.
"A Twentieth Century Church: Boston Avenue Methodist Episcopal Church." Dedicatory booklet. Tulsa, Okla.: Boston Avenue Methodist Episcopal Church, 1929.
Balakian, Anna E. *Surrealism: The Road to the Absolute.* New York: Dutton, 1970.
Banham, Reyner. *Theory and Design in the First Machine Age.* New York: Fredrick A. Praeger, 1960.
"Bauten und Entwurfe von Bruce Goff, 1935–1957." *Bauwelt* 4 (January 27, 1958).
"Biographical Notes on Bruce Goff." *Architectural Design* 48, no. 10 (1978): 6.
Bletter, Rosemarie Haag. "Paul Scheerbart's Architectural Fantasies." *Journal of the Society of Architectural Historians* 34, no. 2 (May 1975): 83–97.
"The Boston Avenue Methodist Episcopal Church, South, Tulsa, Oklahoma." *Architectural Record* 66 (December 1929): 519–26.
Bragdon, Claude. *The Beautiful Necessity: Seven Essays on Theosophy and* Architecture. 2nd ed. New York: Alfred A. Knopf, 1927.
———. "Letters from Louis Sullivan." *Architecture* 64 (July 1931): 7–10.
Brooks, H. Allen. *The Prairie School: Frank Lloyd Wright and his Contemporaries.* Toronto: University of Toronto Press, 1972.
"Bruce Goff: OU's Practical Architect." *Sooner Magazine* 20, no. 11 (1948): 10–11.
"Bruce Goff's Working Drawings: Pollock House, Gutman House, Gryder House, Hyde House, Duncan House, and Price House." *Architectural Design* 48, no. 10 (1978): 81–96.
Burden, Ernest. *Visionary Architecture: Unbuilt Works of the Imagination.* New York: McGraw-Hill, 2000.

Cahill, James. "The Collectors: Eccentric Visions of Nature." *Architectural Digest* (December 1983): 150–55.

Chadwick, Charles. *Symbolism*. London: Methuen, 1971.

Chappell, Sally Kitt, and Ann Van Zanten. *Barry Byrne, John Lloyd Wright: Architecture and Design*. Chicago: Chicago Historical Society, 1982.

Cheney, Sheldon. *The New World Architecture*. New York: Longmans, Green, 1930.

Conrads, Ulrich, and Hans G. Sperlich. *The Architecture of Fantasy*. New York: Frederick A. Praeger, 1962.

Cook, Jeffrey. *The Architecture of Bruce Goff*. New York: Harper and Row, 1978

———. "Bruce Goff's Influence on American Architecture." *Architectural Design* 48, no. 10 (1978): 75–80.

———. "The Idiosyncratic Skins of Bruce Goff." *AIA Journal* (October 1981): 69–72.

Cross, George Lynn. "Appendix N," *The Seeds of Excellence*. Norman, Okla.: Transcript Press, 1986. 248–251.

———. "Excerpts from Statements at the Celebration of the Life of Bruce Goff." *Friends of Kebyar*, no. 40 (1988): 14.

"Crystal Chapel." *Architectural Forum* 93, no. 1 (July 1950): 86–89.

Debo, Angie. *Tulsa: From Creek Town to Oil Capital*. Norman: University of Oklahoma Press, 1943.

Debussy, Claude. "Monsieur Croche, the Dilettante Hater." In *Three Classics in the Aesthetic of Music*. New York: Dover, 1962.

De Long, David G. *The Architecture of Bruce Goff: Buildings and Projects, 1916–1974*. 2 vols. New York: Garland, 1977.

———. "Bruce Goff and the Continuation of the Continuous Present," *Architectural Design* 48, no. 10 (1978): 67–74.

———. "Bruce Goff and the Evolution of an Architectural Ideal." In *In Search of Modern Architecture: A Tribute to Henry-Russell Hitchcock*, edited by Helen Searing. New York: Architectural History Foundation; Cambridge, Mass.: MIT Press. 1982.

———. "Bruce Goff Reconsidered." In *The Architecture of Bruce Goff, 1904–1982: Design for the Continuous Present*, edited by Pauline Saliga and Mary Woolever. Chicago: Art Institute of Chicago, 1995.

———. *Bruce Goff: Toward Absolute Architecture*. New York: Architectural History Foundation, 1988.

———. "The Shape of Pragmatic Invention: Work by Bruce Goff." *L'architecture d'aujourd'hui*, no. 227 (June 1983): 56–57.

———. "A Tower Expressive of Unique Interiors." *Journal of the American Institute of Architects* 71 (July 1982): 78–83.

Dewlin, Al. "Architecture's Unpredictable Artist." *Coronet* 43, no. 5 (March 1958): 40–45.

Egbert, Donald D. "The Idea of Organic Expression and American Architecture." In *Evolutionary Thought in America*, edited by Stow Persons. New Haven, Conn.: Yale University Press, 1950.

Fatsea, Irene D. "The Architecture of Bruce Goff during the Years 1946–1956: An Exploration of Design Determinants Through Selected Analysis of Selected Buildings." Master's thesis, University of Oklahoma, 1987.

Frisby, David. "Social Theory, the Metropolis, and Expressionism." In *Expressionist Utopias: Paradise, Metropolis, Architectural Fantasy*, edited by Timothy O. Benson. Berkeley: University of California Press, 2001.

Genova, Pamela A. *Symbolist Journals: A Culture of Correspondence*. Burlington, Vt.: Ashgate, 2002.

Giedion, Sigfried. *Space, Time and Architecture*. 4th ed. Cambridge, Mass.: Harvard University Press, 1965.

Gimeno, Harold. "Department of Architecture, University of Oklahoma." *Art in Architecture* 1, no. 1 (April 1928): 18.

Glickman, Mendel. "Teaching Structural Engineering to Students of Architecture." Conference paper, April 1961, 4 pp.

Goff, Bruce. "Bruce Goff: As an Architect." *Architectural Design* 48, no. 10 (1978): 2.

———. "A Declaration of Independence." *Western Architect* 39 (January 1930): 17–18.

———. "Goff on Goff." *Progressive Architecture*. December 1962.

———. "Projects and Buildings." *L'architecture d'aujourd'hui*, no. 227 (June 1983): 1–79.

———. "Riverside Hall, Tulsa, Oklahoma." *Western Architect* 38 (December 1929): 220.

Golden, Jack. Introduction to *The Architecture of Bruce Goff, 1904–1982: Design for the Continuous Present*, edited by Pauline Saliga and Mary Woolever. Chicago: Art Institute of Chicago, 1995.

Goodner, Bill. "No Warmed Over Ideas." *Sooner Magazine* 24, no. 3 (November 1951): 7–10.

Greene, Herb. *Mind and Image: An Essay on Art and Architecture*. Lexington: University of Kentucky Press, 1976.

———. "Recollections of Bruce Goff as Teacher." *Architectural Design* 48, no. 10 (1978): 52–54.

Harbison, Robert. *The Built, the Unbuilt, and the Unbuildable: In Pursuit of Architectural Meaning*. Cambridge, Mass.: MIT Press, 1991.

Haynes, Sam W. *Soldiers of Misfortune*. Austin: University of Texas Press, 1990.

Heinz, Thomas A. "Architecture: Bruce Goff." *Architectural Digest* (April 1981): 124–29.

Henderson, Arn. "Bruce Goff: An Interpretation of Organic Theory," presented at the annual meeting of the Southeast Society of Architectural Historians, University of Arkansas, November, 1998, 13 pp.

———. "The Buildings of Bruce Goff," presented at the Centennial Design Symposium on Organic Pluralism at the University of Oklahoma, Norman, March, 1990, 12 pp.

———. "The Buildings of Bruce Goff: A Compositional Pattern," presented at the annual meeting of the Southeast Society of Architectural Historians, Georgia Tech University, October 1997, 13 pp.

———. "Preservation of a Modern Masterpiece: The Price House by Bruce Goff," with D. Hardy, J. Haggard, and I. Fatsea, presented at the Association of Collegiate Schools of Architecture meeting, Arizona State University, October, 1986, 16 pp.

Hertz, David Michael. *Angels of Reality: Emersonian Unfoldings in Wright, Stevens and Ives*. Carbondale: Southern Illinois University Press, 1993.

Heyer, Paul. *Architects on Architecture*. New York: Walker, 1966.

Hickman, Money L., and Yasuhiro Sato. *The Paintings of Jakuchu*. New York: Asia Society Galleries; Harry N. Abrams, 1989.

Hitchcock, Henry-Russell. *In the Nature of Materials*. New York: Duell, Sloan and Pearce, 1942.

"The House That Gene Built." *Sooner Magazine* 28, no. 1 (September 1955): 5–9.

"Houses of Bruce Goff." *Architecture and Urbanism*, 134 (November 1981)

Iannelli, Alfonso. "The Boston Avenue Methodist Episcopal Church of Tulsa, Oklahoma." *Western Architect* 38, no. 10 (1929): 173–74.

Inland Architect. "Special Issue: Bruce Goff: An Architectural Original" 23, no. 8. (December 1979).

Ives, Charles E. "Essays Before a Sonata." In *Three Classics in the Aesthetic of Music*. New York: Dover, 1962.

Jencks, Charles. "Philip Johnson and the Smile of Medusa." In *Philip Johnson: The Constancy of Change*. Edited by Emmanuel Petit. New Haven, Conn.: Yale University Press, 2009.

Jencks, Charles, and Nathan Silver. "Towards an Articulate Environment." Chap. 5 in *Adhocism: The Case for Improvisation*. Garden City, N.Y.: Anchor Press, 1973.

Kostka, Robert. "Bruce Goff and the New Tradition." *The Prairie School Review* 7, no. 2 (1970).

Le Coultre, Martijn F. *Wendingen: A Journal for the Arts, 1918–1932*. New York: Princeton Architectural Press, 2001.

"The Legacy of Bruce Alonzo Goff." Special edition, *Friends of Kebyar* 6.4, no. 40 (October/November 1988).

Lehmann, A. G. *The Symbolist Aesthetic in France, 1885–1895*. Oxford, England: Blackwell, 1968.

Lesure, Francois, and Roger Nichols, eds. *Debussy Letters*. Cambridge: Harvard University Press, 1987.

Levine, Neil. *The Architecture of Frank Lloyd Wright*. Princeton, N.J.: Princeton University Press, 1996.

Lockspeiser, Edward. *Debussy*. London: J. M. Dent and Sons, 1980.

Loving, Jerome. *Emerson, Whitman and the American Muse*. Chapel Hill: University of North Carolina Press, 1982.

MacGilvray, Daniel F. "The Proper Education of Musicians and Architects." *Journal of Architectural Education* (November 1992): 87–94.

Maher, George W. "A Plea for Indigenous Art." *Architectural Record* 21 (June 1907): 429–33.

March, Lionel. "Bruce Goff and 'The Architecture of Happiness'." *Architectural Design* 48, no. 10 (1978): 7–9.

Matthiessen, Francis Otto. *American Renaissance: Art and Expression in the Age of Emerson and Whitman*. New York: Oxford University Press, 1941.

McCarter, Robert. "The Integrated Ideal: Ordering Principles in the Architecture of Frank Lloyd Wright." In *Frank Lloyd Wright: A Primer in Architectural Principles*, edited by Robert McCarter. New York: Princeton Architectural Press, 1991.

McClendon, Wendell. "Zola's Uses of Climate in *The Land*." In *Climate and Literature: Reflections of Environment*. Edited by Janet Perez and Wendell Aycock. Lubbock: Texas Tech University Press, 1995.

McCoy, Esther. "Bruce Goff." *Arts and Architecture* 2, no. 3 (1983): 44–47.

Mead, Christopher. *Houses by Bart Prince: An American Architecture for the Continuous Present*. Albuquerque: University of New Mexico Press, 1991.

Mohri, Takenobu. *Bruce Goff in Architecture*. Tokyo: Kenchiku Planning Center, 1970.

Mooring, Stephen. "Buildings and Projects by Bruce Goff." *Architectural Design* 48, no. 10 (1978): 16–49.

———. "A Starting Point: Bruce Goff and His Clients." *Architectural Design* 48, no. 10 (1978): 15.

Nielsen, Rosemary M., and Robert H. Solomon. "Writing the Bodies of Water: The Clash of the Lasting and the Catastrophic in the *Odes* of Horace." In *Climate and Literature: Reflections of Environment*, edited by Janet Perez and Wendell Aycock. Lubbock:

Texas Tech University Press, 1995.
Park, Ben A. "The Architecture of Bruce Goff." *Architectural Design* 27 (May 1957): 151–74.
Peavler, Bill E. "Bruce Goff's Riverside Music Studio." In *Of the Earth: Oklahoma Architectural History*, edited by Howard L. Meredith and Mary Ellen Meredith. Oklahoma City: Oklahoma Historical Society, 1980.
Pehnt, Wolfgang. *Expressionist Architecture*. New York: Praeger, 1973.
Peter, John. *The Oral History of Modern Architecture*. New York: Harry N. Abrams, 1994
Peyre, Henri. *What is Symbolism?* Tuscaloosa: University of Alabama Press, 1980.
Pillet, Michel. "L'insolite Monsieur Bruce Goff." *L'architecture d'aujourd'hui* no. 102 (June–July 1962): 50–57.
Price, Joe. "A Client's View of Bruce Goff." *Architectural Design* 48, no. 10 (1978): 50–51.
Price, Joe D. "A Personal Recollection of Bruce Goff." In *The Architecture of Bruce Goff, 1904–1982: Design for the Continuous Present*, edited by Pauline Saliga and Mary Woolever. Chicago: Art Institute of Chicago, 1995.
"Pride of the Prairie." *Architectural Forum* 88 (March 1948): 94–101.
Prince, Bart. "Bruce Goff, Architect: A Personal Memoir." *L'architecture d'aujourd'hui*, no. 227 (June 1983): 50–52.
———. "Bruce Goff, Friend and Teacher." *Triglyph* 1 (Fall 1984): 33–37.
Robinson, Sidney K. "Bruce Goff and Music." In *The Architecture of Bruce Goff, 1904–1982: Design for the Continuous Present*, edited by Pauline Saliga and Mary Woolever. Chicago: Art Institute of Chicago, 1995.
Rosenblum, Robert. *Modern Painting and the Northern Romantic Tradition: Friedrich to Rothko*. New York: Harper and Row, 1975.
Saliga, Pauline, and Mary Woolever, eds. *The Architecture of Bruce Goff, 1904–1982: Design for the Continuous Present*. Chicago: Art Institute of Chicago, 1995.
Samuelson, Timothy. "Bruce Goff in Chicago." In *The Architecture of Bruce Goff, 1904–1982: Design for the Continuous Present*, edited by Pauline Saliga and Mary Woolever. Chicago: Art Institute of Chicago, 1995.
Scully, Vincent, Jr. *Frank Lloyd Wright*. New York: Braziller, 1960.
Sergeant, John. "Bruce Goff, the Strict Geometrist." *Architectural Design* 48, no. 10 (1978): 55–62.
———. "An Introduction to Bruce Goff." *Architectural Design* 48, no. 10 (1978): 3–5.
Seroff, Victor Ilyitch. *Debussy, Musician of France*. New York: Putman, 1956.
Seznec, Jean. "Odilon Redon and Literature." In *French 19th Century Painting and Literature*, edited by Ulrich Finke. New York: Harper and Row, 1972.
Sharp, Dennis. *Modern Architecture and Expressionism*. New York: George Braziller, 1966.
Sooner Shamrock 13, no. 3 (March 1953): 40–50.
———. 15, no. 2 (December–January 1954–55): 10.
Stein, Gertrude. "Composition as Explanation." *Dial* 81 (October 1926). 327–36.
Stevens, Wallace. *Collected Poetry and Prose*. New York: The Library of America, 1997.
"St. Paul's Methodist Episcopal Church." *Western Architect* 20 (August 1914): 87–88.
Sullivan, Louis H. *The Autobiography of an Idea*. New York: W. W. Norton, 1926.
———. "The Chicago Tribune Competition." *Architectural Record* 53 (February 1923): 151–57.
———. *Kindergarten Chats*. New York: Wittenborn, Shultz, 1947.
Symons, Arthur. *The Symbolist Movement in Literature*. New York: Dutton, 1958.
Szarkowski, John. *The Idea of Louis Sullivan*. Minneapolis: University of Minnesota Press, 1956.
Tallmadge, Thomas E. "The Chicago School." *Architectural Review* 15 (April 1908): 69–74.
"The H. C. Price Company." *Sooner Shamrock* 13, no. 4 (May 1953): 11–13.
Van Deventer, M. J. "Architectural Sculpture, Artist Preserves a Bruce Goff Original." *Oklahoma Home-Garden* 10, no. 12 (July–August 1986): 18–22.
Van Zanten, David, William Jordy, Wim De Witt, and Rochelle Berger Elstein. *Louis Sullivan: The Function of Ornament*. New York: W. W. Norton, 1986.
Welch, Philip B. "Bruce Goff, Teacher and Mentor." In *The Architecture of Bruce Goff, 1904–1982: Design for the Continuous Present*, edited by Pauline Saliga and Mary Woolever. Chicago: Art Institute of Chicago, 1995.
———, ed. *Goff on Goff: Conversations and Lectures*. Norman: University of Oklahoma Press, 1996.
White, Mark Andrew. *Oklahoma Moderne: The Art and Design of Olinka Hrdy*. Norman: Fred Jones Jr. Museum of Art, University of Oklahoma, 2007.
Whyte, Iain Boyd. "The Expressionist Sublime." In *Expressionist Utopias: Paradise, Metropolis, Architectural Fantasy*, edited by Timothy O. Benson. Berkeley: University of California Press, 2001.

Wichmann, Siegfried. *Japonisme: The Japanese Influence on Western Art in the 19th and 20th Centuries*. New York: Harmony Books, 1981.

Wilson, Edmund. *Axel's Castle: A Study in the Imaginative Literature of 1870–1930*. New York: Charles Scribner's Sons, 1931.

Wright, Frank Lloyd. *An American Architecture*, edited by Edgar Kaufmann. New York: Barnes & Noble Books, 1998.

———. *An Autobiography*. New York: Duell, Sloan and Pearce, 1943.

———. *Genius and the Mobocracy*. New York: Horizon, 1971.

———. "In the Cause of Architecture." *Architectural Record* 23 (March 1908): 155–221.

———. "In the Cause of Architecture, Second Paper." *Architectural Record* 35 (May 1914): 405–13.

———. "The Language of Organic Architecture." *Architectural Forum* 98 (May 1953): 106–7.

———. "Modern Architecture, Being the Kahn Lectures." In *Frank Lloyd Wright Collected Writings*, edited by Bruce Brooks Pfeiffer. New York: Rizzoli International, 1992.

———. "Notes on the Harold Price Company, Bartlesville, Oklahoma." *Sooner Shamrock* 13, no. 4 (May 1953): 37–42.

———. *An Organic Architecture: The Architecture of Democracy*. London: Land Humphries, 1939.

———. "Organic Architecture Looks at Modern Architecture." *Architecture Record* 111 (May 1952): 148–52.

———. *The Story of the Tower: The Tree That Escaped the Crowded Forest*. New York: Horizon, 1956.

NATIONAL REGISTER OF HISTORIC PLACES NOMINATIONS IN YEAR ORDER

Everett, Diana. "Boston Avenue Methodist Church," National Historic Landmark Nomination, Bruce Goff, Architect, Tulsa, Okla., 1999, 27 pp.

Henderson, Arn. "Donald Pollock House," Bruce Goff, Architect, Okla. City, Okla., 2001, 18 pp.

———. "Eugene Bavinger House," Bruce Goff, Architect, Norman, Okla., 2001, 19 pp.

———. "H. E. Ledbetter House," Bruce Goff, Architect, Norman, Okla., 2001, 19 pp.

———. "Hopewell Baptist Church," Bruce Goff, Architect, Edmond, Okla., 2002, 23 pp.

———. "John Frank House," Bruce Goff, Architect, Sapulpa, Okla., 2002, 17 pp.

———. "Multiple Property Nomination for Resources in Oklahoma Designed by Bruce Goff," 2000, 88 pp.

———. "Riverside Studio," Bruce Goff, Architect, Tulsa, Okla., 2001, 14 pp.

Spencer, Brenda R. "Wallace McGregor House," Bruce Goff, Architect, Tulsa, Okla., 2014, 32 pp.

FILM, CATALOGS, RECORDING, AND PORTFOLIOS

Cabot, Charles, dir. *The Architecture of Bruce Goff*. BBC TV. In association with Shin'enkan Foundation, 1976.

Goff, Bruce. *Architecture by Bruce Goff*. Portfolio. Billings, Mont.: Yellowstone Art Center.

———. *La Mer* Portfolio. A portfolio of Goff's painting titled *La Mer* prepared by OU College of Architecture as fund-raising gift for donors to the Bruce Goff Professorship of Creative Architecture, early 1980s.

Henderson, Arn. "Bruce Goff: A Pattern of Composition." Videotape lecture, *Bruce Goff Symposium*, Price Tower Arts Center. Bartlesville, Okla., November 9, 2003.

Murphy, William, and Louis Muller. *A Portfolio of the Work of Bruce Goff*. New York: Architectural League of New York and the American Federation of the Arts.

Oka, Shizuo. Architecture 273 lectures, OU School of Architecture. Tape recordings, early 1950s. Topics include: Rhythm; Opacity, Translucency and Transparency; Modulation; Balance; Theme, Variation and Development; Incident, Terminal, Climax; Site Relationships; Orchestration of Materials; Ornament; and Scale. Jerri Bonebrake Collection.

Index

Page numbers in italic type indicate illustrations. Structures and designs listed without the name of the architect provided in parentheses were designed by Bruce Goff.

"About Absolute Art" (Goff), 15, 52
"absolute" architecture, 53. *See also* organic architecture
adaptation and progress, 12, 55, 56
African culture, influence of, 26, 121–22
Alan, Howard, *109*
Alton, Kansas, 4
ambiguity, intentional, 18, 223
American culture and architectural style, 4, 13, 54–55, 270. *See also* cultural identity/spirit in design
American Institute of Architects (AIA), 95–96, 166
American Scholar, 54–55
Amsterdam School, 45
anchoring/floating element contrast, 131, 135, 164
angular geometry, examples of, 47, 48, 58, 62, 63, *67*, 71, 226
Architectural Forum, 73, 74, 93, 142, 148, 158
Architecture 273 studio topics (design principles): balance, 113, *114*; incident, terminal, and climax, 115–17, *118*, 252; modulation, 66, 110, *112*, 115, 158, 193, 232; opacity, translucency, and transparency, 108–9, *111*, 168–69, 205; orchestration of materials, 119–21, *123*; ornament, 121–22; overviews of, 5–6, 105–7, 124; rhythm, 107–8, *109*; scale, 122–24; site relationships, 117–19; theme, variation, and development, 113–15, *116*, 158, 193, 246
Architecture of Bridges, The (Mock), 91
Arcosanti (community), 178
Art Nouveau, 27, 110
arts and crafts movement, 24–25
arts and music as inspiration, 4, 27–30, 99–100. *See also* Japanese art; music
ashlar patterns, 130, 143
Asia, Goff's trip to, 239
Asian music, 26
Astroturf, 243, *244*
asymmetry: Bavinger House, 159; Boston Avenue Methodist-Episcopal Church, 40; design principles of, 59, 62, 63, 179; Durst House, 208; Garvey House, 168; Riverside Studio, 45; Taliesin West, 14. *See also* balance, design principle; symmetry
Ausgeführte Bauten und Entwürfe von Frank Lloyd Wright, 9
Austrian Secession, 24
Autobiography of an Idea, The (Sullivan), 12, 55
avant-garde style, 23, 25, 45

balance, design principle, 113, *114*. *See also* asymmetry; symmetry
Barby (Celestine) House, 252, *256–57*
Barcelona Pavilion (Mies van der Rohe), 92
Bartlesville, Oklahoma years, 179, 180–223
Bartlesville Redeemer Lutheran Church, 215, *218, 219*
Bartman (Irma) House, 62–63, *64–65*
Bartning, Otto, 24
Bartók, Béla, 26, 107
Basic Design Studio (course), 101
Baudelaire, Charles, 18
Bavinger (Gene) House, 81, 159–66, *167*, 168–69
Beardsley, Aubrey, 27
beauty and philosophy of design, 17, 54, 192–93
"begin again and again," 16, 165. *See also* "continuous present" concept

Behrens, Peter, 24
Belluschi, Pietro, 96
Boggs, J. Palmer, 91
Boléro (Ravel), 107, 116
Bonebreak, Jerri Hodges, 100, 178
Boston Avenue Methodist-Episcopal Church, 40–45
Boulez, Pierre, 26
Brackin, Nelson L., 124
Bragdon, Claude F., 24–25
Brooks, Ernest, 17
Broom (magazine), 25
Bruce Goff Professorship of Creative Architecture, 269–70
built-in furniture. *See* furniture, built-in
Built in the U.S.A. (Mock), 91
Burden, Ernest, *118*
Burgett, William S., 90
Burmese architecture, 121
Byrd, Norman L., 91
Byrne, Barry, 39–40, 43

Cabinet of Dr. Caligari, The (film), 103
cables, structural, 70, 85–86, *167*, 200, 226, *262*, 263, *267*
Camp Parks (California), 73–74, *75–77*
cantilever techniques, examples of, 197; balconies, 222, *225*, 243, 252; beams, 184–85, 200, 201, 234; floors, 143; furniture, 181; pavilion-based structures, 86; roofs, 71, 82, 149, 152, 181, 201, 219, 226, 252; signs, 74; split-level designs, 66
Carlyle, Thomas, 270
centroidal geometry, examples of, 59–60, 63, 82, 226, 238
change, concepts of, 12–13, 19–20, 22, 55–56. *See also* evolution
Cheney, Sheldon, 44
Chicago, Ill., 40, 49
Chicago Academy of Fine Arts, 49
Christ the King Catholic Church, 40, 43
churches: Bartlesville Redeemer Lutheran Church, 215, *218*, *219*; Boston Avenue Methodist-Episcopal Church, 40–45; Camp Parks Chapel, 74, *76–77*; Christ the King Catholic Church, 39–40, 43; Crystal Chapel (OU), 96, 153–59; Hopewell Baptist Church, 136–42; MIT Chapel, 110
circular elements/designs: Bavinger House, 159–66; Duncan House, 230; Durst House, 208–9; Ford House, 142–43; Frank House, 171; Garvey House, 168–70; Gelbman House, 218; Jacob Harder House, 246; Ledbetter House, 130; Leidig House, 84–86; Plunkett House, 250; windows, 208–9, 230. *See also* curved elements/designs; cylindrical elements
Clarke, Harry, 27
classical music, 4, 17–18. *See also* Debussy, Claude
classicism in architecture, 11, 12, 16, 54. *See also* traditional design, disdain for
clerestories, examples of: Bartman House, 62; Comer House, 200; Dace House, 228; Gelbmen House, 219; Hyde House, 234–35; and natural light, 81–83
client-centric design: art as client, 259, 262, 266; Barby House, 252; and color choices, 142, 174, 229, 232, 243; disability accommodations, 223; Goff's adoption of, 37; importance of, 4, 25; Riverside Studio, 47
climax, design principle, 115–17, *118*, 252
coal elements, 81, 143, *146*, 184, 187
Cobb, Ray, 153
Cole, Mrs. C. C., 44
collage composition, 73, 78, *79*
Colmorgan (Paul) House, 59, *60–61*
color: and client-centric design, 142, 174, 229, 232, 243; Crystal Chapel, 156; and mitigation of mass, 108–9; and modernist movements, 23–25; monochromatic themes, 226; and nature, balance with, 222, 228; and ornament, 78, 122; and site-centric design, 15, 215, 222, 243, 252, *257*
Comer (C. A.) House, 199–200
common objects in design: balloons, 74; billiard balls, 209; feathers, 83; Goff's philosophy on, 73; kitchen objects, 137; notions, 78. *See also* re-purposed objects in design
composite geometry, examples of, 62, 63, 171, 200. *See also* geometric techniques, examples of
composition: and "continuous present" concept, 21–22, 105, 165; Goff's commitment to, 13, 57–58, 93, 99–104; Goff's view of his paintings, 27–28; and music, influence of, 10, 17–21, 26–27; novel juxtapositions, 73; thematic, 62–63
"Composition as Explanation" (Stein), 21, 105
conceptualization, Goff's premises of, 51
Concerto no. 2 (Bartók), 108
Congreso Panamericano de Arquitectos (Pan-American Congress of Architects), 95–96
continuity in design principles, 13, 66, 68, 71
"continuous present" concept, 21–22, 105, 165
contrast in design, 71, 119, 174, 178, 198, 201–2, 228–29
Coonley House (Wright), 122
counterpoint concept, 71, 84, 107, 108, 124, 215
Cox (Julius) House, 149–52
Cross, George L., 89, 90, 153, 269–70
Crystal Chapel (OU), 96, 153–59
crystalline imagery/elements: Bartman House, 59; Boston Avenue Methodist-Episcopal Church, 44; Crystal Chapel (OU), 153, 157–59; Expressionist symbology, 23, 24; Gutman House, 205; Price House, 197
cullets, glass, 165, *183*, 184, 187, 215, *218*, *270*, 271
cultural identity/spirit in design, 54–55, 87,

122. *See also* American culture and architectural style
Culture and Democracy (Duncan), 230
curved elements/designs: Gelbman House, 218–19; geometry, 62, 63; Gryder House, 222–23; Plunkett House, 250. *See also* circular elements/designs; cylindrical elements/designs
cylindrical elements/designs: Bavinger House, 159; Dace House, 226, 228; Duncan House, 230; Garvey House, 168; Harder House, 246; Struckus House, 253

Dace (William) House, 226, 228, *231*
Dalí, Salvador, 103
Dana House (Wright), 120
Darwin, Charles, 12, 53, 55
Davis, John, *125*
Debussy, Claude, *10*; and "discipline in freedom," 56–57; Goff's discovery of, 9–10, 17–18; in Goff's teaching, 105, 107, 116, 119, 124; parallels to design composition, 71; traditional structure, rejection of, 17, 19–21. *See also La Mer* (Debussy)
"Declaration of Independence, A" (Goff), 48
De Long, David G., 84
democracy and architectural philosophy, 15, 55, 94. *See also* cultural identity/spirit in design; self-expression, freedom of
"desert crete," 110
design principles. *See* Architecture 273 studio topics
development, design principle, 115, *116*, 193, 246
Dewlin (Al) House, 199
Dial (magazine), 25
diamond-shaped elements/spaces: Crystal Chapel, 153, 156; Phi Beta Delta House, 47; Pollock House, 202, 205; Price House, 78, 185, 193, 197
dichotomies/dualities: and contrast in design, 71, 118–19, 174, 178, 198, 201–2, 228–29; opacity, translucency, and transparency, 169, 205; textural, 73
"discipline in freedom" concept, 4, 10, 56–58, 94, 124
diversity in architecture and Goff's philosophy, 3–4, 87
dodecahedrons, 136
"Drunken Boat, The" (Rimbaud), 30
dualities in design. *See* dichotomies/dualities
Duchamp, Marcel, 73
Dudok, Willem, 117
Duncan (Hugh) House, 81, 229–30, 232, *233*
Durst (R. G.) House, 208–14

Einstein Tower (Mendelsohn), 99
elements (classical) in design, 80–83, 152–53, 169, 239, 252
"Elements of Design" course. *See* Architecture 273 studio
Ellington, Duke, 26
Emerson, Ralph Waldo, 53, 54–55
emotion. *See* feelings and emotion in design philosophy
"Emperor of Ice Cream, The," 57–58
environment-based design, 14–15. *See also* organic architecture; site-centric design
Ernst, Max, 24
erotic themes, 24, 30
Erté (Romain de Tirtoff), 25
Europe, Goff's trip to, 239
European architecture, 1920s and '30s, 45
evolution, 12–13, 14, 15, 54. *See also* change, concepts of
exhibits of OU student work, 95–98
experience *vs*. knowledge, 23
Expressionism, 23–24, 44, 98–99. *See also* German Expressionism
exterior views, design strategies, 82, 259

Fallingwater (Wright), 113
Farnsworth House (Mies van der Rohe), 106, 148
Faust, Robert, 93, 95, 98, *112*, *123*, *126*, 205, 222
feelings and emotion in design philosophy, 18–19, 20–21, 57
Fern Creek, Kentucky, 62
Ferraro, Harvey, 215
film series at OU, 103–4
Fini, Leonor, 24
fireplaces, techniques for: as design element, 209, 222, 223, 235, 243–44; as divider, 200; elemental force symbology, 83, 238, 239, 252; shared chimneys, 214; and water features, 153
Fitchette (James) House, 223, *227*
"Flexicore," 152
floating design elements: anchoring element contrast, 131, 135, 164; balconies, 243; carports, 228; functional zones/spaces, 81, 86, 160; hovering illusion, 222, 235; roofs, 62, 86, 134, 235, 266; water features, 238–39. *See also* cantilever techniques
"floating world" art, 28
floor plan geometry, overviews, 58, 63
Flowers of Evil (Baudelaire), 23, *24*
"Flutex" glass, 75
Ford, Ruth, 89, 142, 147
Ford (Ruth and Albert) House, 69, 81, 87, 142–49, *149*
formal balance, 113, *114*
form and surface, orchestration of, 70–80
"form follows function," 14
found object in design. *See* re-purposed objects in design
Fountain, The (Ravel), 17–18
Frank (John) House, 171–78
Frankoma Pottery, 174, 271
fraternity house design, 47–48, *50*
Friends (magazine), 239

Friends of Kebyar, 269
"frozen music," 25, 100
Fuchs, Ernst, 24
Fuller, Buckminster, 105
functionalism, structural, 12, 53, 55
functional/spatial definition, 38, 66
furniture, built-in: beds, 38; Goff's philosophy on, 81; seating, 171, 185, 208, 209, 222, 234, 239, 249

Gardner, James H., 120
Garrison, Robert, 40
Garvey (John) House, 68, 166, 168–71
Gaudí, Antoni, 98, 107, 117, 122
Gee, Julia, 209, 214
Gelbman (Milton) House, 215, 218–21
"Gemmeaux," 156
geometric techniques, examples of: angular, 47, 48, 58, 62; Bartlesville years, 198; centroidal, 59–60, 63, 82, 226, 238; composite, 62, 63, 171, 200; curved, 62, 63; floor plan typologies, overviews, 58, 63; radial, 63, 159, 168, 171, 209, 246, 249; rectilinear, 59, 82, 148–49, 152. *See also* crystalline imagery/elements; *individual shape names*
German Expressionism, 23–25, 44, 153, 163, 197. *See also* crystalline imagery/elements
German Romantic philosophy, 53
Giedion, Siegfried, 98–99
Glasgow tearooms (Mackintosh), 122
glass, techniques in: collage/mural, 78, 79, 185, *188*, 193, *195*, 197; crushed, 205; cullets, 165, *183*, 184, 187, 215, *218*, *270*, 271; "Flutex," 75; mirror tile, 74; opacity, translucency, and transparency, 108–9; plate glass, polished, 75; pleated, 40; Vitrolite, 49. *See also* crystalline imagery/elements; windows
Glass Architecture (Scheerbert), 274n46
"glass boxes" in International Style, 92
Glass Pavilion (Taut, B.), 192
Glickman, Mendel, 90
Goethe, Johann, Wolfgang von, 53–54, 100
Goff, Bruce Alonzo, *35*; academic credentials issue, 90; aesthetic values, evolution of, 87; birth of and early years, 3, 4; Chicago Academy of Fine Arts, 49; death of, 269; education of, 3; first architecture experiences, 9; grave, *270*, 271; on his works of art, 27; military career, 73–74; personality and character, 105; statue of at OU, 271. *See also* paintings/art of Goff; University of Oklahoma (OU) School of Architecture
Golden, Jack, 91, *153*, 269
Golden Mean, 122
Golden Pagoda of Burma, 117
Gothic style, 43, 117
Graves (B. L.) House, 37–38
Great Depression, 48–49
Greek architecture, 107
Greene, Herb, *114*, 160, 178, 208
Greenough, Horatio, 55
Gresham, James A., 98, *116*
grid-based design, 13, 14
Griffith, Brandon, 91
Gropius Walter, 24, 86, 90, 94, 96
growth. *See* evolution
Gryder (W. C. and Elaine) House, 222–23, 224–25, *224–25*
Gustafson, Grant, 271
Gutman (Emil) House, 205–8

Hanna House (Wright), 115
Harbison, Robert, 51
Harder (Glen and Luetta) House, 239, 242–44, *245*
Harder (Jacob and Anna) House, 239, 244, 246–49
Harper's Bazaar, 25
Harris, Douglas, 208
Harris, Harwell Hamilton, 90
Haskell, Douglas, 93
Hasui Kawase, 28
Henri, Pierre, 26
Herder, Johann Gottfried von, 54
Herring Coe, Matchett, 74
heterogeneity, 12, 56
hexagonal elements/spaces: bathtub, *78*; design themes, 62; shingles, 136; signage, 74, *75*; windows, 44. *See also* Price (Joe) House
Hiller, Kurt, 23
hipped roofs, 187, 202, 205, 208, 214, 234, 238, 243
Hiroshige, Utagawa, 28
historicism in architecture, 10, 24, 94. *See also* traditional design, disdain for
Hodges, Jerri, 91
Hoffmann, Josef, 24, 98, 113
Hokusai, Katsushika, 28
Hollyhock House (Wright), 80
homosexuality, Goff's, 278n30
Honegger, Arthur, 26
Hopewell Baptist Church, 136–42
Horace (Q. Horatius Flaccus), 80
Hoskins, D. B., 136
household objects in design. *See* common objects in design
Hrdy, Olinka, 46, *49*
"human-divinity" concept, 52, 53
Hundertwasser, Friedensreich, 24
Hurtig, John C., *111*
Hyde (Lawrence) House, 232, 234–38

Iannelli, Alphonso, 39–40, 46, 49, 74, 89, 91
Imel, Blaine, 96, *97*
imitation *vs.* influence/inspiration, 92. *See also* traditional design, disdain for
Improvisation for Thirteen Percussion Players (Varèse), 108
incident, design principle, 115–17, *118*, 252
India, architecture of, 121
individuality in architecture, 15, 16
informal balance, 113
inorganic design, 106

integration of elements, 10, 81, 87
intellectualism *vs.* feelings, 23
International Style, disdain for, 4, 70, 92, 95, 98
"In the Cause of Architecture" (Wright), 9, 11
intuition, 18, 23
inward-looking design, 59
Irma Bartman House, 62–63, *64–65*
irregular rhythm, 107–8
Itō Jakuchū, 27
Ives, Charles, 137

Jakuchū, Itō, 27
Japanese architecture, 118–19, 122
Japanese art: influence of, 27–28, 71, 82–83, 99; Joe Price's collection, 78, 181, 185, 187, 190, 260, 262; music, influence of, 26
Japanese Pavilion, L.A. County Art Museum, 70, 181, 259, 262–67
Javanese influence, 26, 222
Johnson, Philip, 96
Johnson Wax Building (Wright), 108, 115
Jones, E. Fay, 91
Jones family of Oklahoma City, 158–59
Jones (Howard) House, 208, 214–15, *216–17*

Kahn, Louis, 96
Kamphoefner, Henry, 2, 89, 90, 130
Kansas City, Missouri years, 179–80, 223, 226–49
Kant, Immanuel, 53, 54
Kasamatsu Shirō, 28
Katsura Palace, 119
Katsushika Hokusai, 28
Kerr, Harrison, 165
Klimt, Gustav, 24, *25*
knowledge *vs.* experience, 23
Kohara, Arthur, 91
Kōrin, Ogata, 28
Kuhlman, Richard, 90

Las Brea Tar Pits, 263, 266
La Mer (Debussy): composition of, 3; Goff's interpretive painting of, 30, 249–50, *251*; in Goff's teaching, 107, 116; as inspiration to Goff, 21, 56
Land, The (Zola), 80
Lang, Fritz, 104
Langhorst, Fred, 89
Lautner, John, 90
Le Corbusier, 87, 92, 98, 110, 113, 122
Ledbetter (H. E.) House, 71, *72*, 81, 130–36
Ledoux, C. N., 86
Leidig (Don) House, 84–86, 96, 130, 160, 163
"less is more," 106
Libby-Owens-Ford Glass Company, 49, 74–75
Lieneweber, John, 91
LIFE (magazine), 136, 148, 165–66
light, natural, 75, 80, 81–83, 130, 152, 200, 205, 223, 253. *See also* opacity effects; skylights; translucency effects; transparency effects; windows
"Lily Pad" House, 84
Los Angeles County Art Museum, 70, 181, 259, 262–67
Luckhardt, Hans and Wassili, 24

McGregor (Wallace) House, 38, *39*
Mackintosh, Charles Rennie, 122
Mallarmé, Stephane, 18, 19
Man Ray, 73, 103
Maruyama Ôkyo, 28
masts as structural elements, 143, *148*, *149*, 159, 164, *167*, *225*
materials: orchestration of, 119–21, *123*; selection of, overviews, 72–75, 214, 226. *See also* common objects in design; natural elements
Matta, Roberto, 24
Mayan architecture, 13
Mendelsohn, Erich, 74, 91, 97, 99
Messaien, Olivier, 25
metaphors, 18–19, 137, 223
Midway Gardens (Chicago), 40
"Miesburgers," 92
Mies van der Rohe, Ludwig: academic credentials, lack of, 90; asymmetry example, 113; Goff's admiration of, 92; Goff's criticism of, 117; and inorganic design, 106; ornament techniques, 122; style philosophy of, 4, 86, 92
Milhaud, Darius, 25
mirror tile, 74, 209, 238, *248*, 249
MIT Chapel (Saarinen, Eero), 110
Mock, Elizabeth, 90–91
modernism, 98
modular design: Ford House, *145*, *147*; Pollock House, 202; Price House, 180; Wilson House, 152–53, *154–55*, 202
modulation, *112*; design principles of, 110; examples of, 66, 158, 193, 232; hierarchical, 66; horizontal projection, 71; and terminal concept, 115
Modulor pr portional system (Le Corbusier), 122
"Monsieur Croche, the Dilettante Hater" (Debussy), 105
Monument to the Third International (Tatlin), 163
Moser, Koloman, 24
Mostenbocker (J. O.) House, 199, 201–2
motifs and repetition, 113–15
murals: and Goff's affinity for mirror tile, 74; Harder House(s), 244, *248*, 249; Hyde House, 235; Price House, 78, *79*, 185, *188*, 191–92, 193, *195*, 197; Riverside Studio, 46, *49*
music: and affinity with architecture, 25, 47, 71, 99–100; Goff's composition of, 26; in Goff's teaching, 107–8, 114, 115, 123–24, 127; influence on Goff, 25–27; as inspiration, 4. *See also* Debussy, Claude
Mussorgsky, Modest, 26
mystery: in design, philosophy of, 19, 20–21, 22; and development concept, 115; and

mystery (*continued*)
Goff's architectural design, 73, 171, 223; in Goff's artwork, 28; Japanese culture, influence of, 83

National Architectural Accrediting Board (NAAB), 94
National Historic Landmarks, 44
National Register of Historic Places, 39, 136, 137, 166, 174
natural elements: coal elements, 81, 143, *146*, 184, 187; rope, 143, 146–47; stone, native, 81, 110, 130–31, 159–60, 230, 232, 243–44; trees/branches, 59, 193. *See also* water features
Naturalism: examples/expression of, 131, 135, 147–48, 159–60, 164–66, 239, 263, 266; philosophy of, 12–13, 23–25, 28, 80–86, 230. *See also* natural elements; organic architecture
natural light. *See* light, natural
natural selection, 12, 55–56
Navy, United States, 73
Neo-Gothic style, 41
Neutra, Richard, 91
"new eclecticism," 92
New World Architecture, The (Cheney), 44
Nicol (James) House, 87, 238–39, *240–42*
Nielsen, Kay, 27
"Notes on Architecture," 81

Oak Park (Chicago suburb), 13
octagonal elements/spaces, 214, 234, 238–39
Odes (Horace), 80
Ogata Kōrin, 28
Oglesby, William, 91
oil industry, 38
Oka, Shizuo, 91
Olbrich, Joseph Maria, 24
opacity effects: Bartlesville Redeemer Lutheran Church, 215; Dace House, 226; design principles of, 108–9, *111*, 169, 205; Struckus House, 259
open plan design: Frank House, 174; Garvey House, 68; Ledbetter House, 134; Leidig House, 86; Pollock House, 202; Unseth House, 63
orchestration of materials, 119–21, *123*. *See also* materials
order in composition, 57, 94
organic architecture: organic *vs.* inorganic design, 106–7; overview and characterization, 5, 52–56; Wright's and Sullivan's philosophies, 12–17. *See also* Naturalism
originality: of Debussy's music, 9; and "discipline in freedom," 58, 94; Goff on, 21–22, 57–58; importance of, 10. *See also* traditional design, disdain for
ornament in architecture: design principles of, 121–22; Duncan House, 232; Durst House, 209; and geometry, 25; Price House, 78, 192–93
Overstreet, Robert, 101, 142, 143, 147, 156

Page Warehouse, 45, *46*
"Painter of Modern Life, The" (Baudelaire), 23
paintings/art of Goff: "compositions," 27–28, *29*, 30, *31–34*, *35*, 100–101, *102*, 253, *258*; *La Mer* interpretation, 30, 249–50, *251*; Struckus commission, 253, *258*
Palace of the Soviets (Le Corbusier), 113
Palais Stoclet (Brussels), 24
Pan-American Congress of Architects, 95–96
Parr and Aderhold, 158
Parrish, Maxfield, 27
Partch, Harry, 26
patterns in design: acoustic and visual, correlation between, 26–27; ashlar, 130; brickwork, 246; interwoven, 45; "textile blocks," 13. *See also* geometric techniques, examples of; rhythm/rhythmic elements
Paul Colmorgan House, 59, *60–61*
pavilion-based designs, 84–85, 86
Perret, Auguste, 108
Persian architecture, 109
Phantastische Schule, 24
Phi beta Delta fraternity house, 47–48, 50
Philosophy (Klimt), *25*
Plunkett, Bruce, 249–50
Plunkett (Bruce) House, 250, *254–55*
Poelzig, Fritz, 24
poetry/poets, influence of, 18–19, 21, 27, 55, 56, 73, 80, 99
Pollock (Donald) House, 202–5
Popular Science, 148
Prairie School, 13, 38
Prelude to the Afternoon of a Faun (Debussy), 18, 19, 119
Price, Etsuko, 191, 198
Price, H. C., 180
Price, Joe, 78, 180–81, 239
Price (Joe) House: museum addition, 78, 185–93, 259; studio and house, 78–80, 81, 83, 87, 180–85, *196*, 197–98; tower addition, 193–95
Price Tower (Wright), 115, 180
Prince, Bart, 263
principles of design. *See* Architecture 273 studio
privacy, design strategies: accordion screens/walls, 63, 202, 226, 242, 246; and exterior views, 82, 259; hierarchical modulation, 66; translucent glass, 75
progress, concepts of, 12, 55. *See also* change, concepts of
Prokofiev, Sergei, 26, 114
proportion, 55, 92, 122. *See also* scale

Quonset hut construction, 74

Rackham, Arthur, 27
radial geometry, examples of, 63, 159, 168, 171, 209, 246, 249
"ranchburgers," 93

Ravel, Maurice, 17–18, 25, 116
Ray, Man, 73, 103
rectilinear geometry, examples of, 59, 82, 148–49, 152
Redon, Odilon, 99
reflective materials in design, 49; crushed glass, 205; glass and water, 83–84; metallic tiles, 78; mirrors, 78; mirror tiles, 74, 209, 238, *248*, 249; and mitigation of mass, 108–9
regular rhythm, 107–8
Renaissance design ideals, 16
repetition, 71, 113–14, 131, 159, 168, 202, 205, 228–29, 250, 259
re-purposed objects in design: aircraft parts, 163, 164; barrel hoops, 232; boiler parts, 69, 171, 238–39; glass ashtrays, 71, 131, 234, 238; glass cullets, 165, 184, 187, 215, 271; insemination tubes, 78, 80; oilfield materials, 136, 164; rebar, 209. *See also* common objects in design
research methodology, 3–5
revival styles, 54–55
rhythm/rhythmic elements: counterpoint concept, 71, 84, 107, 108, 124, 215; design principle, 25, 107–8, *109*; in Goff's art, 28; interwoven designs, 45; in music, 25, 26, 107–8; repetition, 71, 113–14, 131, 159, 168, 202, 205, 228–29, 250, 259. *See also* patterns in design; scale
Richter, Hans, 103–4
Rimbaud, Arthur, 18, 27
Rimsky-Korsakov, Nikolai, 26
risk and creation of form, 19–20
Rite of Spring (Stravinsky), 107
Riverside Studio, 45–46, *47*, *48*, *49*
Robie House (Wright), 119
Robinson, Adah, 40, 44–45
Robinson, Sidney K., 26
Romanticism, 12, 18, 53–54, 56
Rooster and Hen with Hydrangeas (Jakuchū), *27*
rope elements, 143, 146–47
Rush, Endacott & Rush, 4, 37, 38, 44, 48–49
Ryoan-ji (Zen garden), 83

Saarinen, Eero, 96–97, 110
Saarinen, Eliel, 39
salvaged materials. *See* re-purposed objects in design
Sam's Tower (Rodia), 122
Satie, Erik, 25
scale: design principles of, 122–24; gradation of, 147–48; and ornament, 121; variation and hierarchy in, 28, 71, 131, 219. *See also* rhythm/rhythmic elements
Scharoun, Hans, 24
Scheerbert, Paul, 274n46
Schegel, Friedrich von, 54
Schelling, Friedrich Wilhelm Joseph von, 54, 100
Schiele, Egon, 24
Schindler, R. M., 90
Schoenberg, Arnold, 26, 108
scholarship on architecture 1940s and '50s, 98–99
Schultz, John J., 98
science and philosophy of design, 12
scuppers, 59, *61*, 71, 215
Seabees, 73
self-expression, freedom of, 15, 91–95, 178
self-reliance and American West ethos, 4. *See also* cultural identity/spirit in design
Serenade (Schoenberg), 108
Sessions, Roger, 26
Shehada, Sohail, 271
Shellabarger, Fred, 91
shingles as design element: Plunkett House, 250, *255*; Durst House, 209, *213*; Ford House, 146; Harder House(s), 243, *245*, 246, *247*, 249; Hopewell Baptist Church, 136, *139–40*; Hyde House, 232, *236*; Jones House, 214–15; Lawrence House, 238; Nicol House, 238, *241*, *242*
Shriner, Patti Adams, 45
Siamese architecture, 109, 121
sight/sound continuum, 26–27
site-centric design, *120*; Barby House, 252; Dace House, 229; design principle of, 117–19; Duncan House, 230; Glen Harder House, 243; Goff's adoption of, 37; importance of, 4, 16–17; irregular-shaped lots, 41; and scale, 122–23. *See also* environment-based design
skylights: Duncan House, 230; Ford House, 146; Gutman House, 208; Hopewell Baptist Church, 137; Ledbetter House, 135; and natural light, 81–83; Nicol House, 238, *242*; Struckus House, 253; Unseth House, 63, *68*, *69*
Slack, Rex, 153
Smay, Joseph, 90
Soleri, Paolo, 178
Sooner Magazine, 158
Space, Time and Architecture (Giedion), 98–99
spatial/functional definition, 13, 38, 58, 66, 68–69. *See also* zoning (functional) strategies
Spencer, Herbert, 55–56
spiral imagery/design, 23, 159–66
square geometry, examples of, 28, 38, 110, 202, 215, 234, 246
"squircles," 168
Starview Farm, 180, 181, 259
Stein, Gertrude, 21–22, 105, 165
Stevens, Wallace, 57–58
Stockhausen, Karlheinz, 26
Stoclet Mansion (Hoffmann), 113
stone, native, 81, 110, 130–31, 159–60, 230, 232, 243–44

Stravinsky, Igor, 26, 107
strings/strips as design element: aluminum, 184; copper, 62, 238; plastic, 83, 185, *186*, *189*, 235, *237*, 238; white string, 73–74, 104, 235
Struckus, (Al) House, 252–53, *260–61*
structural determinism, 45
structural functionalism, 12, 14, 53, 55
subconscious inspiration, 18
Sub-Saharan music, 26
Sullivan, Louis, *11*; influences on, 55–56; modulation example, 110; and ornament techniques, 122; philosophy and influence of, 11–17, 41, 52, 78, 107, 230
surplus materials in design. *See* re-purposed objects in design
Surrealism, influence of, 24, 27, 73
"suspended" elements, 70. *See also* floating design elements
Symbolist movement, 18–19, 21, 27, 30, 56, 73
symmetry: axial, 13; and balance, 113; Dace House, 226; Duncan House, 230; Sullivan's use of, 11. *See also* asymmetry
"Symphony of the Arts" (Hrdy), 46
synthetic (inorganic) design, 106

Taliesin West (Wright): as environment-based design, 14–15; Goff on, 21; light, strategies and techniques, 108; native stone techniques, 110; and ornament techniques, 122; site-centric design of, 119
Tatlin, Vladimir, 163
Taut, Bruno, 24, 83, 192, 274n46
Taut, Max, 24
terminal, design principle, 115–17, *118*, 252
"textile blocks," 13
texture, ornament as, 121–22
Thai architecture, 109, 121
theme, design principle, 113–15, *116*, 158, 193, 246
Thomas, Gail, 91
Thomas, J. L., 136
tile work, examples of: Frank House, 171, *176–77*; mirror tile, 74, 209, 238, *248*, 249; Price House, 78, 187, 192
TIME (magazine), 142
"Tipi Church," 136
tokonomas, 187, 253, 263, *266*
Toller, Ernst, 23
Tosi, Don A., 143
tract housing, 92–93
traditional design, disdain for, 16, 19, 87, 92, 94–95. *See also* classicism in architecture; historicism in architecture; progress, concepts of; self-expression, freedom of
Transformation (Toller), 23
transitions. *See* modulation
translucency effects: Comer House, 200; design principles of, 108–9, *111*, 169, 205; "Flutex" glass, 75; Japanese Pavilion, 262
transparency effects: Cox House, 152; design principles of, 108–9, *111*, 169, 205; Struckus House, 259
trees/branches as design elements, 59, 193
"Triaero," 62
triangular elements/spaces: Bartman House, 62; Gutman House, 205–8; Nicol House, *241*; Price House, 62, 181, *183*, 184, 185, 187; Unseth House, 63
Tulsa, Oklahoma: Goff designs in, 38, 39–48; Rush, Endacott & Rush apprenticeship/employment, 4, 37
Tulsa Building, 39
Twenty-Five Year Award AIA, 166
Tyler, Texas years, 179, 180, 249
ukiyo-e (Japanese woodblock prints), 28
uniqueness, expression of, 15, 20. *See also* originality; traditional design, disdain for
unity in Goff's work, 87. *See also* integration of elements
Unity Temple (Wrights), 119
University of Oklahoma (OU) School of Architecture: detractors of Goff and OU, 96–98; Distinguished Visiting Professorship, 269; exhibits of student work, 95–98; faculty highlights, 90–91; faculty position accepted, 89–90; and freedom of self-expression, 91–95; Goff's teaching style, overviews, 95, 99–100, 101, 103–5, 124, 127, 178 (*See also* Architecture 273); physical environment, 104; resignation from, 178; statue of Goff, 271
Unseth (Helen) House, 63, 66, *67–68*, *69*
Usonian architecture, 13–14, 152

Varèse, Edgar, 26, 108, 250
variation, design principle, 113–15, *116*, 123, 193, 246
Verlaine, Paul, 18
Vienna Secession, 24
Villa-Lobos, Heitor, 26–27
Villa Savoy (Le Corbusier), 110
visual termination design principle, 43, 252
Vitrolite (glass), 49
vocalizations and sounds, 26
Vogue (magazine), 253

Wagner, Richard, 124
Wallace McGregor House, 38, *39*
Warriner, Joe and Laura, 202
water features: aquaria, 191–92, 279n22; Bruno Taut's, 83–84; elemental force symbology, 152–53, 239, 252; fountains, 46, 134–35, 184, 249; Leidig (Don) House, 84, 86; lily/fish pools, 59, 84, 160, 184,

214, 218, 222; live water, use of, 159; "rain" pool, 238–39; reflecting pools, 62, 74, 83–84, 152, 156, 171; and reflectivity effects, 109, 168; scuppers, 59, *61*, 71, 215
Welch, Philip B., 91, 96
White and Red Plum Trees (Ogata Kōrin), 28
Whitman, Walt, 53, 55
Willow Tearooms, The (Mackintosh), 122
Wilson, William H., 91
Wilson (J. D.) House, 69–70, 152–53, *154–55*
windows: angular, 63, *67*, 71, 226, *241*; cat-eye, 223, *225*; circular/domed, 208–9, *211*, 230, 253, 259, *261*; music-inspired, 46. *See also* clerestories; glass, techniques in; light, natural; skylights
World War II, 73
Wright, Frank Lloyd, *10*; asymmetry example, 113; criticism of Goff, 180; friendship with Goff, 9; incident, terminal, and climax techniques, 117; influences on, 54, 55–56; and Naturalism, 80; on organic expression-53, 52; and ornament techniques, 122; on OU School of Architecture, 96; OU speaking engagements, 91; philosophy and influence of, 11–17, 78, 92; recommendation of Goff to OU, 90; on rejection of Goff's Crystal Chapel design, 158; site-centric design techniques, 119; and translucency effects, 108; Usonian houses, 13–14, 149. *See also* Taliesin West
Wurster, William, 158
Wythe, Joseph, 91

Yeh, W. H. Raymone, 269
Yoshida, Akihiko, 28

Zola, Emile, 80
zoning (functional) strategies, 66, 130, 134, 143, 200, 218, 223, 228, 246. See also spatial/functional definition

Colophon

Art credits:

Frontispiece, Bruce Goff, ca. 1952. OU College of Architecture, Design and Research Center. Courtesy College of Architecture, University of Oklahoma.

Page vi, Skylight in James Nicol House, Kansas City, Missouri. Photograph by author.

Page viii, Detail of clerestory in Joe Price House, Bartlesville, Oklahoma. Photograph by George W. Lewis.

Copyedited by Bonnie Lovell
Indexed by Susan M. Gaines
Design and composition by Anthony Roberts
Set in Scala Pro and ITC Avant Garde
Jacket design by Anthony Roberts
Image prepress by University of Oklahoma Printing Services
Text printed and bound by Tien Wah Press, Malaysia